Gena Casy

Thanks for taking on This
leadership role.

Best of luck during your
presidential year.

Dan B Worth

5/5/08

HEROES OF PHARMACY
PROFESSIONAL LEADERSHIP IN TIMES OF CHANGE

HEROES OF PHARMACY
PROFESSIONAL LEADERSHIP IN TIMES OF CHANGE

DENNIS B. WORTHEN, PhD

LLOYD SCHOLAR

LLOYD LIBRARY AND MUSEUM

CINCINNATI, OHIO

WASHINGTON, D.C.

Managing Editor: Julian I. Graubart
Acquiring Editor: Sandra J. Cannon
Layout and Graphics: Scott Neitzke, APhA Creative Services
Cover Design: Richard Muringer, APhA Creative Services
Indexing: Mary Coe, Potomac Indexing
Proofreading: Kathleen Kelly and Donna Weiss, Publications Professionals LLC
File Conversion: Ashley Young, Publications Professionals LLC

©2008 by the American Pharmacists Association
APhA was founded in 1852 as the American Pharmaceutical Association

Published by the American Pharmacists Association
1100 15th Street, NW, Suite 400
Washington, DC 20005-1707

To comment on this book via e-mail, send your message to the publisher at *aphabooks@ aphanet.org*

Library of Congress Cataloging-in-Publication Data

Worthen, Dennis B.
  Heroes of pharmacy : professional leadership in times of change / Dennis B. Worthen.
     p. ; cm.
  A collection of 28 articles previously published in Journal of the American Pharmacists Association plus 2 new articles.
  Includes bibliographical references and index.
  ISBN 978-1-58212-111-6
  1. Pharmacists--United States--Biography. 2. Pharmacy--United States--History. I. American Pharmaceutical Association. II. Journal of the American Pharmacists Association. III. Title.
  [DNLM: 1. Pharmacists--United States--Biography. 2. Pharmacists--United States--Collected Works. 3. Pharmacy--history--United States--Biography. 4. Pharmacy--history--United States--Collected Works. 5. History, 19th Century--United States. 6. History, 20th Century--United States. WZ 112.5.P4 W932h 2008]

  RS71.W67 2008
  615'.10922--dc22
  [B]
                                                    2007039879

How to Order This Book

Online: www.pharmacist.com
By phone: 800-878-0729 (770-280-0085 from outside the United States)
VISA®, MasterCard®, and American Express® cards accepted

*For David Cowen, George Griffenhagen, and
Glenn Sonnedecker with thanks for their mentorship,
encouragement, and friendship.*

Contents

Foreword

So often we trivialize the term *hero*. In a culture where, in Andy Warhol's words, "Everyone will be world-famous for 15 minutes," we even bestow the term on those who make a touchdown or get a song on the charts. In spite of our often indiscriminant use of the term *hero,* there is still a great need and desire for true heroes and a great value in studying their lives and actions—not only the greater-than-life figures, or great soldiers, but the ordinary people who have made big differences in the way we live. In many cases we recognize their accomplishments, but we do not know the people behind the accomplishments.

It is important for pharmacists to understand who the people described in *Heroes of Pharmacy* are and why they were able to have such a great influence on the evolving role of pharmacy in health care. The heroes of this book, and pharmacists throughout our history, have been adept at creatively adapting to the evolution of our health care system. This evolution is, in large part, driven by society's desire to improve the access to quality health care for our citizens. Many changes are fueled by the belief in a "right" to health care and as a consequence the responsibility of health professionals to provide their services as a part of this "right" of citizenship. Other changes initiated by these heroes have resulted from seizing the business opportunity to fill a societal need. And other changes strengthened the profession and enhanced pharmacists' ability to take care of those who look to them for help.

This book presents the highlights of the professional lives of 28 American pharmacists (and the 20 founders of the American Pharmaceutical Association) who helped change the way we use medicines, not only in the United States, but worldwide. They also changed the profession of pharmacy.

Through the lives of these professionals we witness the personal commitments that changed pharmacy education from an informal apprenticeship to that of a Doctor of Pharmacy degree. We learn of the lives of college founders and college presidents.

We see the personal response to the need for quality standards that transformed the production of medicines from the extemporaneous mixtures of mostly botanicals, alcohol, and flavorings to the pharmaceutical industry of today, whose products are pure, uniform, safe, and effective. We read stories of pharmacists who discovered important medicines and pharmacists who founded manufacturers of medicines, some still existing today.

It is important to read these as stories of leadership as well as heroism. In a period in which we crave leaders as well as heroes, these are important case studies of how people see a need and use their personal skills to answer that need.

It is difficult to define leadership other than through example. These examples of leadership will benefit any reader interested in how ordinary Americans with a variety of backgrounds and heritages used their leadership skills to improve their society and become heroes.

As in our society in general, leadership development in pharmacy is an important challenge for the profession. The pharmacy profession and its professional societies suffer from a lack of widespread and sustained leadership. As a result, many of the "remedies" being advanced for the American health care system do not consider the sophisticated clinical skills that pharmacists can bring to the management and therapeutic application of medicines. To help build the leadership that is needed, these stories should be a primer for all students of pharmacy. They can also revitalize the thinking of pharmacists who have been in practice for awhile.

This is a history. It is often said that history is the stories of a bunch of dead white guys. Dead? Yes. White? Not all. Guys? Mostly. But those were the times. This book brings to life our heroes. It does so in such a way that the reader can connect the events of the heroes' lives to the way we experience health care and medication usage in the 21st century. Even more, it shows us that rather than accepting the status quo, we can lead change and make a difference.

Lowell J. Anderson, RPh, DSc, FAPhA
2004 Remington Honor Medalist

Preface

In an address to the APhA annual meeting last year, Barbara Jordan, member of the U.S. House of Representatives, confessed to having had an early interest in becoming a pharmacist but decided against that idea because she had "never heard of an outstanding pharmacist." This member of Congress finally decided on a career in law and has become a successful politician.[1]

Barbara Jordan was the first African American woman elected to the U.S. Congress in Texas, serving from 1972 until 1978, when she retired for health reasons. Raised in Houston, her first successful political campaign was for a seat in the Texas Senate in 1966. Barbara Jordan's observation about unknown pharmacists was not an isolated situation. Unlike medicine, chemistry, and other disciplines, pharmacy does not celebrate its heroes. Pharmacy does not have a tradition of recognition through the use of eponyms, such as anatomy's Islets of Langerhans and biochemistry's Krebs cycle, although there are a few examples such as Lloyd's Reagent, a form of hydrous aluminum silicate named after its inventor John Uri Lloyd.

HEROES OF PHARMACY: THE SERIES
During the APhA sesquicentennial the *Journal of the American Pharmacists* (then *Pharmaceutical) Association* committed to 18 articles covering six topics over a three year cycle.[2] While working on the articles on the pharmaceutical industry, I had the opportunity to ask many pharmacists who their heroes were—who the significant professional role models were. The normal response was one of surprise at why the question was even posed, followed by a halting list of a few names, seldom more than two or three, such as Remington, Tice, and Whitney. When the responders were probed

on the significance of the individuals named, the answer frequently included, "I don't know what they did; I only know the name," or "He has an award named after him." Few seemed to know why these persons had awards named in their honor. There was little comprehension that the profession of the 21st century was hard won by these and others who had risked much to turn the pharmacist from an apprentice-trained shopkeeper to a highly educated health professional.

The series, Heroes of Pharmacy, was first proposed to explore the question of who the heroes of pharmacy were and what they had done to deserve such acclamation. By such an exploration pharmacy may at last probe its collective memory and recover from its historical amnesia. A wealth of benefits would ensue, not the least of which is demonstrating the professional maturity of understanding *and* appreciating pharmacy's role in and contributions to society.

Who Is a Professional Hero?

Webster's Ninth New Collegiate Dictionary provides multiple definitions of *hero,* ranging from a "mythological or legendary figure" to "illustrious warrior" and "one that shows great courage." Other definitions more suited to our purpose are "one admired for his achievements and noble qualities" and "the central figure in an event, period, or movement."[3]

Our culture quickly links heroism with feats of bravery, courage, and selflessness. The immediate reaction is to think of someone who sacrifices his or her life as a hero. There have been pharmacists who were such heroes, persons such as Paul Stanley Frament,[4] who served as a Navy corpsman during World War II and was killed in the Guadalcanal campaign, and Joseph J. Lynch,[5] who died trying to diffuse a bomb planted at the New York World's Fair in 1940.

However, physical heroism is not the theme of this work. Rather, the focus is the hero who sacrifices his or her self-interests to make the profession more than it had been. It is the person who is willing to champion change and advancement in both the clash of opposition and the yawn of disinterest who is a professional hero.

A professional hero is a positive role model. Heroes stick to principles in spite of the pressure to be expedient. Heroes have a vision of what the profession needs to be and the courage and conviction to make it be; the vision to see new possibilities and the conviction to make it work even in the face of opposition or indifference. Heroes accept the consequences of being a leader, a leader who can take on the hard task of breaking with the past to build the future.

Criteria for Inclusion

The initial challenge for the heroes series was to identify the persons to be included. The first requirement was that the person had to be dead.

Perspective and objectivity require the distance of time and place that death affords. It is a hard but honest fact that influence must extend beyond life to lodge itself in the collective history of a profession.

To be considered a hero, the person had to be involved in significant issues of practice, industry, governance, and education; however, not all persons involved in momentous issues were heroes. All of the heroes were well known, highly recognized members of the profession, but not all famous figures were necessarily professional heroes. Celebrity and notoriety are not synonymous with heroism. The heroes selected have a common characteristic: their focus was the betterment of the profession. The battles that they fought seldom resulted in personal financial gain. Quite to the contrary, there were times when the desired objective (such as raising educational requirements) put them at a disadvantage. Nonetheless, they persevered in their drive for change.

There are many obvious characteristics shared by those who might be considered professional heroes. Certainly leadership is an essential attribute. However, leadership alone is not enough. While every hero was a leader, not every leader was a hero. Each hero shared a number of characteristics: they were visionary, passionate, driven, self-starting, iconoclastic. In short, the hero recognized significant issues that needed to be addressed and then did so, understanding that there could be negative personal consequences. Heroes were outspoken—outspoken for change, outspoken for increased professionalism, outspoken about the profession's obligation to serve, not to be served. By and large they did not benefit from the changes that they espoused; others did. They were, in short, altruists.

In no sense are the individual articles in the series complete biographies. Beyond the bare essentials of parents, birth, spouse, and death there is no attempt to provide in-depth biographical details. While many of the persons in the series merit a full biography, that is a task best left to another time and another author. The focus of each hero article is to recount the person's challenges and accomplishments in the profession. Heroic efforts in the professional arena are just that; there is no attempt or intent to idealize or elevate the persons to sainthood. In short, these sketches are not hagiographic. None of the heroes were saints; none were without flaw or error. Indeed, that is what makes their accomplishments worth celebrating. All stand before us as mere mortals, but in various measures mortals triumphant.

THE ROLE OF PROFESSIONAL HEROES

Malcolm Gladwell's book, *The Tipping Point: How Little Things Can Make a Big Difference*, is a recent attempt to explain how something moves from being a fad to being a norm.[6] Similar explanations were offered earlier such as contagion models, which describe how a few "infectives" eventually start a widespread epidemic[7] or the domino effect, which asserts that a few falling dominoes set up a chain reaction with significant consequences.[8] Each of these theories postulates how something enters into the realm of the common, the norm, or the majority. Each seeks to explain how an isolated event or person can trigger the move that frequently defied earlier attempts. Succinctly put, the tipping point is that point in time when a movement or fad moves beyond a self-selected few to become a commonly held practice or perspective.

There are multiple tipping points as pharmacy moved from the apprentice-trained, small shopkeeper model to become a highly educated health care profession. The stories of the tipping points in education, governance, industry, and practice and the men and women who were responsible for them provide insights into today's challenges and opportunities in continuing to progress from a distribution- to a service-oriented profession primarily focused on patients and their outcomes rather than on the product.

Pharmacy's professional heroes were change agents in some area of particular importance. They were responsible for a singular event or were in the right place at the right time when the event took place. William Procter, Jr. was an early visionary who saw the need for an organization to help set standards and help pharmacists provide unadulterated products. He was the driving force in the formation of the American Pharmaceutical (now Pharmacists) Association. Carl Durham gained congressional action authorizing the formation of the Pharmacy Corps in the United States Army despite the opposition of 10 Army surgeons general over 49 years. Today, pharmacists are commissioned officers in the armed services of the United States due in large part to Durham. Donald Brodie articulated the need to move pharmacy from product to patient focus with his concept of drug use control and pharmaceutical care.

The heroes in pharmacy are change agents who helped bring about progress over the past 200 plus years. One example is heroes' continuing efforts to better educational standards. First came a struggle to establish the early colleges of pharmacy because a simple apprenticeship was insufficient for the increasing needs of the public. Then came the requirement of a high school diploma for admission to a college of pharmacy, followed by the requirement of graduation from a college of pharmacy as a prerequisite for taking the state board examination. The progression from a two-year PhG to a three-year PhC degree set the stage for a four-year and then the five-year BS and today's professional entry-level PharmD degree.

The heroes were dissatisfied with the status quo, and they had a vision of a better future and the leadership to effect changes in practice, education, or governance.

WHY HEROES ARE RELEVANT TODAY

Who are the persons who identified, articulated, and led American pharmacy through the challenges of change for the past two centuries? One explanation for the lack of recognition of professional heroes is the absence of a required history course in the pharmacy curriculum. For decades the history of the profession was a required course in all colleges of pharmacy. As the curriculum changed to accommodate more clinical and kinetic programs, the history of the profession course was pushed out. Once a course of its own, it was incorporated into various course offerings that, while well intentioned, obscured historical structure and coherence.

Some people do not recognize the advances that American pharmacy has made over the past two centuries, believing that the profession of today is the way it has always been. This belief is unfortunate since it not only fails to introduce pharmacists to their past, it also fails to provide insights into their future. These observations led to the task of identifying pharmacy's heroes and why they were professional leaders and ultimately to the series in the *Journal of the American Pharmacists Association.*

The recognition of professional heroes has gained relevance due in part to the new accreditation standards effective July 2007. The new Accreditation Council for Pharmacy Education criteria for the Doctor of Pharmacy degree required in the social/behavioral/administrative pharmacy sciences section include the history of pharmacy, as follows:

- Overview of the evolution of pharmacy as a distinct profession
- Movement from focus on the drug to focus on the patient and the drug, including clinical pharmaceutical care and other aspects of patient-provided pharmacist care
- Major milestones and contributors in the evolution of pharmacy.[9]

In 1800 pharmacy was disorganized, its practitioners small shopkeepers. A person became a pharmacist through an apprenticeship of varying length that did little more than pass the skills of the master—no matter how inadequate or incomplete—to the learner. Adulterated and substandard medicines were not rare, and the common therapy was frequently a nostrum composed largely of alcohol (or worse, debilitating mercury and strong opiates) and flavoring. The materia medica of the day was largely an empirical use of botanicals and minerals, but even these were frequently unstandardized and the knowledge of the active principles incomplete.

Compare this with today's profession. Today the pharmacist has at least six years of specialized scientific and clinical training as a prerequisite for licensure. Many have other degrees prior to entering pharmacy school, and many go on to complete residencies before entering practice. Medicines must be proven safe and effective before they are allowed on the market. Empiric experience has succumbed to scientific evidence. Standards for purity and strength are established by bodies such as the United States Pharmacopoeia and enforced by the Food and Drug Administration. The materia medica, the therapeutic armamentarium, has become more specific and effective. Many communicable diseases are curable and chronic conditions, such as diabetes, controllable. The victories have been long fought and hard won.

The heroes series from 2002–2006 included articles on 28 individual professional heroes and the 20 founders of the American Pharmaceutical Association (2 of whom were the subject of full articles in the series). These 46 men and women were the architects of today's profession. They led the way in establishing practice, education, and product standards. They did not do so alone, but their leadership and achievements distinguished them.

This book tells the story of the persons who risked much to gain much, who moved the profession from what it was to what it could be, and who prepared it to continue to change and grow successfully into the future.

Heroes have a distinct importance for today's readers. They display attributes that are important in the progress of the profession. The stories of the challenges that these leaders faced and overcame are inspiring for others who, in their turn, will face challenges they need to overcome. That is, pharmacists can learn from the past what the issues were, how they were addressed, which actions succeeded or failed, and, hopefully, how to effect future successes.

Bearing all this in mind, I invite you to the call issued by Scottish poet and dramatist James Thomson (1700-1748) some two and a half centuries ago:

There studious let me sit,
And hold high converse with the mighty dead.

REFERENCES

1. Fischelis RP. Hubert H. Humphrey: The lesson for pharmacists. *Am Druggist* 1978;177(March):53-5.

2. The six topics were practice, science, education, industry, governance, and associations. The time periods were 1852–1902, 1902–1952, and 1952–2002. The 18 essays were later compiled and published under the title *American Pharmacy: A Collection of Historical Essays* by the American Institute of the History of Pharmacy.

3. *Webster's Ninth New Collegiate Dictionary.* Springfield, Mass: Merriam-Webster, Inc.; 1989:566. *Hero* is used as a gender-neutral noun, and gender-specific pronouns have been removed from the definition.

4. Paul Stanley Frament was a 1939 graduate of the Albany College of Pharmacy. He died November 19, 1942, as a result of battle wounds. The U.S. Navy named a destroyer escort in his honor. This is the only warship named in memory of an American pharmacist.

5. Joseph J. Lynch was a Fordham College of Pharmacy graduate. He joined the New York Police Department and was assigned to the bomb squad. He and his partner were killed on July 4, 1940, while trying to defuse a bomb left at the British Pavilion in the New York World's Fair.

6. Gladwell M. *The Tipping Point: How Little Things Can Make a Big Difference.* New York: Little Brown; 2000.

7. Worthen DB. The epidemic process and the contagion model. *J Am Soc Inf Sci.* 1973;24(5):343-6.

8. The domino theory was primarily used in foreign policy and popularized under the Eisenhower administration to explain the threat of communist expansion.

9. Accreditation Council for Pharmacy Education. Accreditation Standards and Guidelines for the Professional Program in Pharmacy Leading to the Doctor of Pharmacy Degree. Effective July 1, 2007. Chicago: Accreditation Council for Pharmacy Education; 2006:ix.

Acknowledgments

This work extended over 5 years and included 30 essays. In that period of time 23 persons graciously agreed to review one or more of the essays. I am indebted to each of them:

Lee Anderson
Robert Bachman
Amy Bennett
Richard Bertin
Robert Buerki
John Colaizzi
David L. Cowen
Michael A. Flannery
Robert D. Gibson
George Griffenhagen
William Heller
Metta Lou Henderson

Gregory J. Higby
Hugh Kabat
Robert Lantos
L. Michael Posey
W. Steven Pray
William E. Smith
Glenn Sonnedecker
Clarence Ueda
David R. Work
Robert A. Zebroski
William A. Zellmer

I am especially grateful to L. Michael Posey and Ron Teeter, editors of the *Journal of the American Pharmacists Association*. They initially agreed to publish the column and provided insight and editing pencils that resulted in the final essays.

George Griffenhagen has been a staunch supporter of the series and has contributed much to the final appearance and interest of the biographical sketches. He selected the pictures that accompany each essay from the American Pharmacists Association Foundation archives.

Far too numerous to mention individually are the archivists, librarians, museum curators, and family members who have responded to my requests for information about one or more of the heroes. Their graciousness and willingness to share is deeply appreciated.

The staff and my colleagues at the Lloyd Library and Museum in Cincinnati have continued to support my digging in the stacks and asking for interlibrary loans. Thank you all.

Throughout the past five years, Patti Lynn Worthen has been involved in the project. Her willingness to join me on research trips to help with a myriad of tasks has meant that more could be done and done with more fun. There is not a passage that hasn't benefited from her editorial oversight.

As it should be, the responsibility for accuracy is mine.

Author's Note

The Heroes of Pharmacy series has been a regular feature of the *Journal of the American Pharmacists Association* since 2002. The series comprises 30 articles: 28 focus on individual pharmacy leaders, 1 is on the founders of the American Pharmacists Association, and 1 is an introductory essay.

The articles in this collection are arranged in alphabetical order by name of the hero. Since the articles were not published based on a thematic plan there was little reason to maintain them in publication order.

The reader will note an inconsistency in some stylistic features of the articles. Some use subheadings while others don't. Also the way that the American Pharmaceutical/Pharmacists Association is identified differs. These differences are due to the progression in the series over the first five years. For simplicity purposes, the format of the original article was maintained.

Introduction

Single great individuals can be found, and in fact they emerge,
everywhere. It is the continuity of great men coming from pharmacy
which proves this our profession to be a particularly apt ground
for the development of scientific talent and of the responsibility
toward mankind that marks human greatness.[1]

History can be looked at in many ways. One is to focus on the great events and how they affected the subject studied. Another approach is to look at the people and how they and their actions led to great events that affected history. As Urdang notes (above), pharmacy is blessed with a continuity of men—hence the second approach used in this book.

This book comprises the first 30 essays from the Heroes of Pharmacy series in the *Journal of the American Pharmacists Association*.[2] Twenty-eight of the essays are devoted to a single historical figure of American pharmacy. One of the essays provides information on the 20 founders of the American Pharmaceutical (now Pharmacists) Association (APhA). The very first essay published (January–February 2002) is an introduction to the series.[3]

The persons presented in the essays are predominately white males. Females and minorities did not enter the profession in significant numbers until relatively recently. As late as 1940 only 4 percent of the profession was composed of women.[4] In 1932 there were 330 African American pharmacists registered in the United States.[5] The fact that there are few females and minorities among the heroes does not suggest an absence of professional heroes in any group; many women and minority pharmacists who might be considered heroes are still alive and, hence, not yet eligible for inclusion in the series, given the criterion of death.

One of the earliest decision points was to limit the essays to persons who had died. This decision eliminated pressures and preferences for leaders still alive. More important, it allowed a separation between the time of writing and the activities of those selected, illuminating issues and events that, while important at the time, had limited long-term significance.

The essays on the heroes selected for the series are not intended to be full biographies, nor even comprehensive professional sketches. The constraint on word count required each essay to be focused on the major professional accomplishments and issues. Personal relationships (such as families and friends), nonpharmacy struggles (such as Edward Parrish's clashes at Swarthmore), and passions (such as James Beal's collection of exotic sea shells) must be left for another time and place. The essays provide an overview of pharmacy's development from the small shopkeeper status of the Revolutionary War period to the issues and ambitions of the profession in the 21st century. While some may view the essays as hagiographic, reporting only the positive, the space limitations and purpose of the essays required a focus on professional achievements and contributions.

APhA FOUNDERS

American pharmacy certainly did not begin with the founding of the American Pharmaceutical Association in 1852, any more than it started with the establishment of the Philadelphia College of Pharmacy in 1821 or the publication of the first English-language pharmacy journal, the *American Journal of Pharmacy*, in 1825. The formation of the first national professional association of pharmacy, however, did establish a locus for professional aspirations and opportunities. In time it also functioned as the origin of most other pharmacy organizations. Therefore, it was appropriate to consider the founders of APhA as a whole for the Heroes of Pharmacy series.

Twenty men gathered in Philadelphia in 1852 to establish APhA. Each of the existing colleges of pharmacy—Philadelphia, New York, Maryland, Massachusetts, and Cincinnati—was represented by at least one founder of the college. Persons from Richmond, Connecticut, and California also participated in the deliberations and formation. The founders were trained mostly through apprenticeships; six were graduates of the Philadelphia College of Pharmacy and two were graduates of New York. At least three of the founders were physicians. Although the founders were mostly easterners, Charles Bache, a graduate of the Philadelphia College, was living in California and Charles Augustus Smith was from Cincinnati.

The average age of the founders was the mid-30s. Daniel B. Smith, the oldest at 60, was elected the first president of APhA and Bache, at 24, was the youngest. Some, like William Procter, Jr., and Parrish, were prominent in pharmacy affairs for decades after the formation of APhA. Bache died on the return trip to California and Joseph Laidley died in an explosion in 1861 while manufacturing munitions for the Confederate army.

The group did not represent American pharmacy. Mostly from the east and better educated than most, the group fostered a vision of what the profession might become rather than mirroring what it was. The exhortation for improved standards—educational, product, practice, and service—provided a theme that continues to reverberate in pharmacy in the 21st century.

INDIVIDUAL ESSAYS

TIME PERIODS

The time period covered by those featured in the individual essays stretches from Andrew Craigie, the first Apothecary General of the United States in the Revolutionary War, to the late 20th century. Nine persons—C. Lewis Diehl, Albert Ethelbert Ebert, John Maisch, Parrish, Albert Prescott, Procter, Joseph Remington, Charles Rice, and Edward Squibb—spent the major part of their careers between 1850 and 1900. This period saw the emergence of pharmaceutical manufacturing, the expansion of colleges, and the increasing importance of, and dependence on, the United States Pharmacopoeia for product identification and standardization.

The period between 1900 and 1950 is represented by the careers of 12 persons: Beal, Zada Cooper, H.A.B. Dunning, Carl Durham, Robert Fischelis, Edward Kremers, J. Leon Lascoff, Ernest Little, Rufus Lyman, Edward Spease, Henry Whelpley, and Harvey Whitney. Pharmacy schools expanded in the universities, educational requirements for entering a college of pharmacy were standardized and expanded, and the curriculum expanded to a four-year course of study, making pharmacy education truly collegiate. Professional regulation and governance increased with the emergence of state boards of pharmacy and the passage of federal regulations that mandated the purity and safety of food and drugs. Pharmacy underwent major changes during two world wars, including recognition as a profession by the military during World War II. New professional organizations representing the colleges, state boards, community pharmacists, and hospital pharmacists emerged. The enrollment of women in colleges of pharmacy increased steadily.

The final period of the late 20th century is reflected in the careers of six persons: George Archambault, Donald Brodie, C.I. Cooper, Donald Francke, Irving Rubin, and Linwood Tice. Pharmacists' orientation changed from product to patient, and the profession's responsibility to the public moved to the forefront. Minorities became more involved and diversity was embraced as a goal and expectation of the profession. Students began to take an active role in their future profession.

NATIONALITY

Most of the persons in the heroes series were born in the United States, predominately in the East and Midwest, reflecting the national population distribution in the 19th and early 20th centuries. However, rural areas such as Harmonia, Michigan (Whelpley), Table Rock, Nebraska (Lyman), and Denton, Maryland (Dunning), were as well represented as Philadelphia (Remington and Parrish), Boston (Craigie), and Brooklyn (Rubin). Four persons were born in Germany: Diehl, Ebert, Maisch, and Rice. Lascoff was born in Lithuania. Ebert and Diehl immigrated while still young; the others did not immigrate until early adulthood.

EDUCATION

No information was discovered about the early pharmacy education of Maisch or Rice. Maisch studied chemistry and biology in Hanau, Germany, but no information was found about pharmacy education. Rice's background is largely unknown before his mysterious arrival at Bellevue Hospital in New York. In addition, nothing is known about Craigie's pharmacy background or education before the beginning of the Revolutionary War.

Most of the heroes either apprenticed or worked in a pharmacy prior to attending pharmacy school. Some, like Ebert and Diehl, served a formal apprenticeship. Ebert actually served a second apprenticeship to learn pharmacy in the German tradition. Diehl served his apprenticeship in a doctor's shop. Later, many of the persons, including Archambault and Whitney, worked in community pharmacies during their high school days prior to pharmacy school, but their experience could not be considered an "apprenticeship." Beal and Whelpley also "read medicine," a practical training synonymous with a pharmacy apprenticeship, in addition to their pharmacy experience. However, there is no evidence of prior store experience in the case of Chauncey Cooper, Zada Cooper, or Rubin. If they had such experience, records of it have not been found.

A number of the heroes, although not as many as might be expected, gained some pharmacy or medicine experience with a relative. Brodie worked for his father in Pearson, Iowa. Dunning worked in a community pharmacy with his uncle in Denton, Maryland. Francke worked in his father's pharmacy in Athens, Pennsylvania, and Parrish apprenticed with his brother, Dillwyn, in Philadelphia. Whelpley read medicine in Otsego, Michigan, with his uncle, a Civil War hospital steward and surgeon. Three heroes had no pharmacy experience: Prescott and Lyman were physicians and Little was a chemist.

Formal education of the 28 heroes ranged from none known or apprenticeship through advanced degrees. Two, Archambault and Beal, had JD degrees; four (Lyman, Prescott, Squibb, and Whelpley) earned an MD degree, although only Lyman practiced medicine—as the physician responsible for the student health service at the University of Nebraska. Four earned a PhD degree (Brodie, Ebert, Kremers, and Little), and Beal earned a DSc. Many received at least one honorary doctorate in recognition of career achievements.

MAJOR AREAS OF ACTIVITY

It is difficult to assign a single area of activity for most of the persons in the series; all were multitasking over-achievers. For example, Beal, the dean at Scio, taught there and at the Pittsburgh College of Pharmacy, was an attorney and state legislator, developed a model practice act, and served as APhA general secretary and chair of the USP Board of Trustees, among other activities. Similarly, Fischelis was an editor and author, taught at several colleges of pharmacy, and was dean at New Jersey. He was head of the board of pharmacy in New Jersey before joining the War Production Board as director of the Division of Chemicals, Drugs, and Heath Supplies during World War II. Subsequently he became the executive secretary of APhA and, at the age of 70, once again a dean, this time at Ohio Northern. All areas of pharmacy practice are represented by the 28 persons—education, community and institutional practice, industry, government, publishing, association leadership, and military service.

EDUCATION

Almost all the heroes had experience as an educator, the sole exception being Craigie. Squibb taught for several years at the College of Pharmacy of the City of New York. Ebert's experience was more with the administration of the Chicago College of Pharmacy than in the classroom. Several served as deans when deans focused more on managing the educational endeavor and less on fund-raising, the current model. The deans were Beal at Scio, Chauncey Cooper at Howard, Diehl at Louisville, Fischelis at New Jersey and Ohio Northern, Kremers at Wisconsin, Little at Rutgers, Lyman at Nebraska and later Arizona, Prescott at Michigan, Spease at Western Reserve, and Whelpley at St. Louis. Maisch, Remington, and Tice served as deans at the Philadelphia College of Pharmacy.

Three persons affected education in other ways. Parrish was perhaps the most entrepreneurial, starting his own school in Philadelphia in 1849 to teach physicians the rudiments of pharmacy. He was also among the group who formed Swarthmore College, serving as its first president in 1865. Diehl was a founder of the Louisville College in 1870. Ebert was instrumental in rebuilding the Chicago College of Pharmacy in the wake of the Chicago fire of 1871.

COMMUNITY AND INSTITUTIONAL PRACTICE

Many of the heroes were practitioners in either community or institutional settings. Procter owned his own shop and used it as a source for insights in his teaching and textbook writing. Diehl maintained his own pharmacy while working with the Louisville College of Pharmacy. Dunning was a partner in Hynson, Wescott & Dunning, which maintained a community pharmacy practice as late as 1951. Durham worked in a community pharmacy from 1917 until he was elected to the U.S. Congress in 1938. Lascoff was the quintessential community pharmacist from his location on the corner of 83rd Street and Lexington Avenue in New York City. Lascoff was a role model for a generation of pharmacists, showing pharmacy for the great calling that it could be.

Whereas Lascoff was the model for community pharmacy, Rice was the model for institutional pharmacy. New York's Bellevue Hospital was the largest pharmacy operation in North America, and Rice served as the director for the 20 institutions comprising the Department of Public Charities and Corrections. Whitney and Francke were at the center of modern hospital pharmacy developments. Both affiliated with the University of Michigan, they oversaw hospital pharmacy's progression through formularies, unit dose systems, and drug information centers. Spease at Western Reserve initiated the first university-based program in hospital pharmacy and built a model relationship between the college and the hospital pharmacy that still survives in many universities.

INDUSTRY

Manufacturing was an integral part of pharmacy. This has changed over time as innovations required different skills and resources, but the roots and relationship remain strong. The first large-scale manufacturing effort was started by Craigie in Carlisle, Pennsylvania, to meet the needs of Washington's army during the Revolutionary War. Both Diehl and Ebert were involved in manufacturing enterprises but returned to community pharmacy when these failed.

Squibb began manufacturing products for the military in 1857 because of the problems with adulterated and substandard products. By the time of the Civil War his name was synonymous with standardized medicines, especially ether, which was as important to the Confederacy as it was to the Union. Remington and Maisch trained with Squibb; Maisch went on to become the chief chemist at the Army Medical Laboratory in Philadelphia.

Dunning was responsible for expanding the small manufacturing business of Hynson, Westcott & Dunning into an important national company. The firm discovered mercurochrome, a standard medicine cabinet product for generations, and the sterile shaker packet for sulfa that was an integral part of the GI first-aid kit in World War II.

GOVERNMENT

Being the first Apothecary General, Craigie is qualified to head the list of those who served pharmacy in a governmental capacity. His office disappeared from the military table of organization at the end of the War of 1812 and has never been reactivated. Parrish died at Fort Sill, Indian Territory (now Oklahoma) while serving with other Quakers on a government commission to the Indian tribes.

Durham is the embodiment of a pharmacy career paired with government service. The American military refused to recognize pharmacy as a profession or to grant officer's status to those who practiced pharmacy in the military through a succession of 10 surgeons general. In 1942, Congressman Durham took on the seemingly impossible task and gained legislation creating a pharmacy corps in the U.S. Army. Archambault was a pharmacist at a U.S. marine hospital and subsequently was commissioned by the Public Health Service. Named the first chief of the pharmacy branch of the Public Health Service Division of Hospitals, Archambault was the face of the uniformed Public Health Service pharmacist.

PUBLISHING

Many of the 28 heroes were editors and authors of distinction. The following provides only a few examples of their involvement in book and journal activities. Procter wrote the first American pharmacy text, which was largely based on earlier German and English publications. Parrish wrote the second, which was uniquely American. Remington's *Practice of Pharmacy*, first published in 1885, became a staple of pharmacy education that continues today. The first English language journal, the *American Journal of Pharmacy*, was started at the Philadelphia College of Pharmacy in 1825. Procter was the editor in 1852, when he called for the formation of a national organization of pharmacists. Maisch and Tice also served as editors of the journal.

For most of the years between 1873 and 1913, Diehl wrote the Annual Report on the Progress of Pharmacy. Published in the Proceedings of APhA, the report averaged 418 printed pages annually. In 1937 Lyman founded the *American Journal of Pharmaceutical Education*, the first English language journal devoted to pharmacy education. He served as editor until 1955 and then consulting editor until his death in 1957.

Francke was an early editor of what became the *American Journal of Hospital Pharmacy* (now the *American Journal of Health-System Pharmacy*) and the founding editor of other publications including *American Hospital Formulary Service*, the *Drug Information Bulletin*, and *Drug Intelligence* (now *Annals of Pharmacotherapy*). Whelpley was the editor of *National Druggist* and *Meyer Brothers Druggist* as well as a reporter for other pharmacy publications. Fischelis was the founding editor of both the Pennsylvania and New Jersey state pharmacy journals.

None of the heroes, however, focused their career on pharmacy reporting and editing to the extent Rubin did. Rubin began his reporting career with *American Druggist* in 1938 and ended it with *Pharmacy Times* at his death in 1998. Rubin used his bully pulpit to champion the eight-cent pharmacy commemorative stamp, which was issued during the 1972 APhA annual meeting. He followed with efforts to gain pharmacist oversight for dispensing in the U.S. Congressional Dispensary and the adoption of a single symbol for pharmacy in the United States in 1992.

ASSOCIATION LEADERSHIP

With the exception of Craigie, every one of the heroes was involved in professional association activities at the national level as well as state and local groups. Procter and Parrish were among the founding members of APhA. APhA was the first national professional association, founded in 1852. The National Association of Retail Druggists (later NARD and now the National Community Pharmacists Association) was formed in 1898.[6] The American Association of Colleges of Pharmacy (AACP) was formed in 1900 and the National Association of Boards of Pharmacy (NABP) in 1904.

Prescott was the first president of AACP and Whelpley instigated the formation of NABP. Lascoff led a group of pharmacists to form the American

College of Apothecaries in 1940. Whitney was a leader in the creation of the American Society of Hospital Pharmacists, and Archambault was influential in the formation of the American Society of Consultant Pharmacists, Kremers was the person most responsible for the establishment of the American Institute of the History of Pharmacy (AIHP). Dunning is recognized as the father of the American Pharmacists Association Foundation, and Little initiated the American Foundation for Pharmaceutical Education. Chauncey Cooper led the formation of the National Pharmaceutical Association when the National Medical Association could not meet the needs of its pharmacist members. Tice was the champion of what is now the APhA–Academy of Student Pharmacists, one of the three constituent academies of APhA.

STANDARDS, ETHICS, AND LEGISLATION
The impetus for the formation of APhA in 1852 was the continuing problem with substandard and adulterated products. The United States Pharmacopoeia (USP) was first published in 1820, but it was not until the 1840 revision that pharmacy, in the person of Procter, was fully engaged with its revision. By the mid-1870s Squibb reported on the major deficiencies of the USP and looked for a way to align the publication with practice. It was under Rice's leadership, however, that the USP emerged as the preeminent source of standards. Archambault, Beal, Ebert, Little, Maisch, Procter, Rice, Tice, and Whelpley all served on the Committee on Revision or the Board of Trustees. Others, notably Prescott and Squibb, were behind-the-scenes contributors.

In the late 1880s it was clear that the USP could not provide all of the formulas of interest to prescribing physicians and compounding pharmacists. It was Rice who convinced APhA that it should develop and publish the *National Formulary* as a continuing professional resource. By the early 20th century there was again a need for formulas that was not being met by either of the two compendia. Lascoff was the force behind collecting and publishing, through APhA, the *Pharmaceutical Recipe Book* in 1929.

A code of ethics was developed as part of the formation of APhA in 1852. Parrish argued that the code would have a deleterious effect on pharmacy because it barred from membership pharmacists who were economically dependent on the sale of nonofficial (i.e., proprietary) medicines. He opined that the duties of the pharmacist should focus on public health. Over the years others would pick up on the theme of the role of pharmacy and pharmacists. Zada Cooper was an outspoken proponent of the pharmacist's duty to educate the public about self-medication. It was Brodie who later introduced the term *pharmaceutical care,* defining the role of the pharmacist as the link between patients and the safe use of medicines.

Product purity and labeling have been longstanding issues for pharmacy. In 1879 Squibb led a group to develop legislation that would guarantee the purity of medicines and foods. The bill was enacted by New York and New Jersey in 1881, presaging the passage of the Pure Food and Drug Act of 1906. Beal, likewise involved in pharmaceutical legislation, was responsible for drafting sections of the 1906 Pure Food and Drug Act that incorporated the USP and NF as official compendia. He was also influential in the passage of the Harrison Narcotic Act of 1914. Durham was not the only person fighting for the Pharmacy Corps Act during World War II; however, his leadership while a member of the House Military Affairs Committee was critical to its successful passage. Later he was largely responsible for passage of the Durham-Humphrey Amendment to the Food, Drug, and Cosmetic Act of 1938.

MILITARY SERVICE

Military service has been an important part of many American professions, and pharmacy is no exception. During the Revolutionary War, when Craigie was the first Apothecary General, the separation between medicine and pharmacy was recognized. Squibb served in the navy at the end of the Mexican War. A Mediterranean voyage sensitized him to the fact that substandard medicines were being purchased because price was the sole determinant of acceptability. Prescott and Diehl both served in the Civil War on the Union side. Dunning, as a young man, served in Cuba with the army during the Spanish American War. Durham was a navy veteran, and Fischelis served in the Army Chemical Warfare Department during World War I.

Military service was much broader during World War II. Rubin served in the army in Europe, and Archambault trained merchant marine and coast guard pharmacist mates in pharmaceutical arithmetic and compounding. Tice, as a coast guard reservist, commanded a picket boat on anti-submarine duty in the waters of the Delaware Bay. Fischelis was a director in Donald Nelson's War Production Board. Brodie and Whitney worked on the Manhattan project, Whitney at the Hanford Engineering Works in Richland, Washington.

HONORS

Many of the preeminent awards of pharmacy are named in honor of those featured in the heroes series. Such awards acknowledge the profession's affection for the persons and the recognition for what each has done for individual organizations and the profession at large.

In 1874 Ebert established the first major award in American pharmacy to encourage publication of original research. In 1918 the New York branch of APhA established an award to honor lifelong or special achievement in pharmacy. Named after Remington, the first award was given to Beal in 1919. In 1950 ASHP established its signal honor for career achievement in the name of Whitney and, in 1973, instituted an award for contributions to international hospital pharmacy in the name of Francke.

Significant honors have been named after other heroes in recognition of their service to the profession. In 1959 the Association of Military Surgeons of the United States established the Andrew Craigie Award. Given annually, it is a career achievement award for pharmacists in the federal service.

The American Society of Consultant Pharmacists established the George F. Archambault award as its highest honor in 1972. In 1984 APhA established the H.A.B. Dunning Award to recognize a company for its contributions to the profession. Beal is honored with awards in his name at both the Ohio State Pharmacists Association and the West Virginia Pharmaceutical Association, and the USP established the Beal Award for Public Service in 2000. The National Pharmaceutical Association named its highest award in honor of its founder, Chauncey Cooper.

Kremers' contributions to the history of American pharmacy are celebrated with the Kremers Award by AIHP. In 1943 the American College of Apothecaries named its achievement award in honor of Lascoff. AACP honors Lyman, founding editor of the *American Journal of Pharmaceutical Education*, with an annual award for the best judged paper in the journal. In 1994 the APhA–Academy of Student Pharmacists renamed its highest honor in memory of Tice.

LEGACY

These heroes left no area of pharmacy untouched. Indeed it is difficult to choose just one enduring legacy of each. Early education certainly benefited from Procter, Parrish, Maisch, and Remington, while Lyman, Kremers, and Prescott were architects of university-based education. Lyman, Parrish, Zada Cooper, and Tice pushed to establish student organizations that would add students' voice to the profession. Squibb and Beal influenced the passage of legislation for product purity and labeling. Procter, Remington, Rice, Beal, and Whelpley were among the leaders in gaining compendial standards. Craigie and Durham did much to gain recognition of pharmacy by the military. Today's pharmacists in the federal service owe their professional standing to these pioneers.

Archambault, Francke, Spease, Whelpley, and Whitney saw the need for professional associations to reflect the work of pharmacists and worked to establish appropriate organizations. Both Coopers, Chauncey and Zada, as well as Lyman and Tice were voices of conscience, advocating for inclusion of all qualified people without regard to gender or race in the practice of pharmacy. Procter, Parrish, Rubin, and Brodie, among others, worked to heighten society's expectation that pharmacy was a profession and pharmacists professionals, responsible to the public and patients, not just purveyors of product.

CONCLUSION

The heroes in this series are not representative of pharmacy. They were iconoclasts who had the courage to break with the past to build a new, better profession. It was clear from the very beginning in writing the series that risk-taking was a personal characteristic of the heroes. Each took risks, not for the sake of personal gain but for the advancement of pharmacy and its practitioners.

The heroes in this series are not the only heroes of pharmacy. Many others from time to time were dissatisfied with the status of pharmacy education, practice, legislation, governance and associations. Many others tried to change the status quo for the better. These persons are also heroes whose contributions are waiting to be recognized and whose stories are waiting to be told.

REFERENCES

1. Urdang G. The concept of the history of pharmacy. *Am J Pharm Educ.* 1950;14:134.

2. The journal name changed from *Journal of the American Pharmaceutical Association* to *Journal of the American Pharmacists Association* with the May/June issue, 2003, volume 43.

3. The information on the heroes in this introduction is drawn from the essays in the heroes series. Consequently, I have included no references unless the information is not given elsewhere.

4. Henderson ML. *American Women Pharmacists: Contributions to the Profession.* New York: Pharmaceutical Products Press; 2002:69.

5. Mullowney JJ. What future is there for the Negro pharmacist? *J Am Pharm Assoc.* 1932;21:1185-8. Approximately 10% of the total population was African American.

6. There were other attempts to form national associations, such as the Conference of Teaching Colleges of Pharmacy in 1870 and National Retail Druggists Association in 1883. These organizations did not last long, but the special interests were later taken on by AACP and NARD. Founded in 1876, the Western Wholesale Druggists Association later became the National Wholesale Druggists Association; the focus of the group was on wholesale distribution rather than pharmacy practice.

Who Are *Your* Heroes?

Each fall quarter, on the first morning of the history of pharmacy course I teach at the University of Cincinnati, I challenge my new students to name three individuals in pharmacy whom they consider heroes. Usually, the students' responses are bewilderment: they can't name one, much less three. I then promise them that, before the end of the course, they will be able to identify their pharmacy heroes and explain why they deserve the title.

I believe it is important to have heroes. One of the distinguishing marks of a profession, one way to separate a profession from a trade, is by identifying its heroes. After all, a hero is someone who has a vision for what a profession can be and who has the courage to act on his or her vision. A hero shows us what *good* looks like and how we, ourselves, can get there.

What qualities or actions (or qualities *of* action) make someone a professional hero? Those who stick to their principles despite the pressure to be expedient are heroes. Those who exhibit characteristics and virtues or act in ways others want to emulate are heroes. A hero is a positive role model. It is someone who puts others before him- or herself.

Heroes may be universal or personal. Universal heroes are those who are recognized by many. Most American pharmacists would probably agree that William Procter, Joseph Remington, George Archambault, and Harvey A.K. Whitney are universal heroes of pharmacy. Each of these individuals acted decisively on a vision of how the pharmacy profession should serve society.

Personal heroes are those pharmacists whom we each hold in our own hearts as special; their examples have inspired us in very specific ways. Someone who may have helped us when they did not have to, or someone who went to extraordinary lengths to help us identify and then follow a dream or goal, can be a personal hero, and personal heroes can include friends, teachers, or even relative strangers.

Other heroes, perhaps less well known, deserve the title for their perseverance in the face of significant challenges. Zada Cooper, one of the first women in academic pharmacy, distinguished herself through her service to the American Association of Colleges of Pharmacy and the establishment of Rho Chi. Troy Daniels, the dean of the college of pharmacy at the University of California–San Francisco, worked to find positions for his Nisei (Japanese-Americans born in the United States) alumni and students who were forced into relocation camps during World War II. Aaron Henry, an African-American graduate of Xavier in 1950, owned a successful pharmacy. An influential figure in the Civil Rights Movement, Henry is remembered for his involvement in improving health care for the poor in Mississippi. And, yes, there are pharmacists who gave their lives for their country or for others. Robert Knecht was serving as the pharmacist-in-charge of a hospital on the Anzio beachhead when the hospital was strafed and he was killed. Paul Stanley Fremont was with the Marines on Guadalcanal when he was killed. He received a Silver Star posthumously and the Navy named a ship after him—the only pharmacist so honored.

In an informal e-mail survey, I invited members of *JAPhA*'s Editorial Advisory Board to name their professional heroes. Rebecca Prevost, director of pharmacy at Celebration Health in Florida, mentioned Mary Ann Koda Kimble; a lecture by this accomplished author and pharmacist brought home for Prevost the importance of balancing a vital career with an active family life. Earlene Lipowski, associate professor at the University of Florida College of Pharmacy, named the late Joseph B. Wiederholt as "my mentor, teacher, colleague, and one of my best friends. His greatest contribution may be his teaching us as professionals and individuals about being a patient." Gary Smith, professor and chair of the University of Maryland Department of Pharmacy Practice and Science, found a hero in Donald C. Brodie. "His work on DUR in the 1960s led the way for the clinical pharmacy and pharmaceutical care movements," Smith said. Karim Calis, coordinator of the National Institutes of Health Drug Information Service, holds the late Ralph Shangraw in the highest regard. "He made major contributions to pharmacy practice and education, and he helped me understand the importance of specialization." Bernard Sorofman, associate professor of clinical and administrative pharmacy at the University of Iowa, named Gloria and Don Francke, the only husband and wife team who each won the Remington and Whitney Awards, for their vision and leadership in hospital pharmacy.

This is the first installment of a new *JAPhA* column on Heroes of Pharmacy. Each article will be a short biography of an individual and a brief consideration of how his or her contributions advanced the profession. In the future, subjects may include some more contemporary heroes, but, initially, the columns will have a historical bent. Historical events, after all, are the consequences of decisions and actions by individuals, and I believe it is important to keep reminding pharmacists—particularly the younger readers— why pharmacy's heroes deserve their title.

Founders of the
American Pharmaceutical Association

The second half of the 19th century opened in a tumultuous time. Millard Fillmore was president, having succeeded Zachary Taylor, who died in office. Admiral Perry and his fleet were opening Japan to American trade. The United States was expanding into the southwestern territory acquired after the Mexican War, and the dominant domestic issue was the status of slavery in the new territories. Overall, the time could be characterized as one of great opportunity: Horace Greeley had already advised young men to "Go West," and California was in the midst of the gold rush. It was also a period of few standards and regulations; the rule of commercial intercourse was *buyer beware*.

THE FORMATION MEETINGS

The state of pharmacy in the United States was similar to that of other small businesses and professions. Pharmacy organizations, called colleges, were few in number, and most apothecaries of the day received only apprentice training. Adulteration and lack of standards were problems for many medicines, especially botanicals. In response to the importation of adulterated medicines, pharmacists and physicians supported the passage of the Drug Import Act of 1848.[1] The act, however, failed to meet its desired ends; in 1851 the New York College of Pharmacy invited all of the other organized colleges in Baltimore, Boston, Cincinnati, and Philadelphia to send representatives to discuss possible future actions against drug adulteration. In October, nine representatives from Boston, New York, and Philadelphia met to establish a "set of standard strengths and qualities of drugs and chemicals for the government of the United States Drug Inspectors."[2]

William Procter Jr. and his Philadelphia colleagues arrived at the meeting with a broader agenda in mind. In an editorial in the *American Journal of Pharmacy*, Procter had stated that the meeting would be an opportunity to reach pharmacists throughout the country and institute changes that

Figure 1. Robert Thom's painting The Founding of the American Pharmaceutical Association (1852) depicts the signing of the first Code of Ethics of APhA. The representative group of American pharmacists shown in the painting gathered in Philadelphia in October 1852 and launched the national professional society of pharmacists. See Figure 2 for their names.

would revolutionize pharmacy. At the conclusion of the New York meeting, a resolution was passed calling on all incorporated and unincorporated pharmaceutical societies to meet in Philadelphia in October of the next year with the purpose of organizing a national association. Procter, George Coggeshall of New York, and Samuel Colcord of Boston were appointed to organize the meeting.

In 1852, 20 men responded to the Call for Convention. Who were these men, and what vision guided them to gather in Philadelphia for the October 6–8 meeting? The colleges of Maryland, Massachusetts, Cincinnati, New York, and Philadelphia were represented. There were also representatives from California, Connecticut, and Richmond, Va. Philadelphia had the largest number of representatives, with six. New York sent four; Massachusetts, three. Maryland and Richmond each sent two, while California, Cincinnati, and Connecticut each had one representative at the meeting. One of the outcomes of this meeting was the development and acceptance of a constitution establishing the American Pharmaceutical Association (APhA), which the group envisioned meeting annually to advance knowledge and elevate the professional character of its members.

Figure 2. The following key from Reference 24 identifies the 20 pharmacists, depicted in Figure 1, who took an active part in the founding of the American Pharmaceutical Association:

1. *Daniel B. Smith (first president)*
2. *William Procter Jr. (corresponding secretary)*
3. *George D. Coggeshall (recording secretary)*
4. *John Blair Hodge Campbell*
5. *Samuel Runnels Philbrick*
6. *Samuel M. Colcord (vice president)*
7. *Edward Parrish*
8. *Charles Augustus Smith (vice president)*
9. *John Meakin*
10. *Alexander Duval*
11. *Joseph Burnett*
12. *Llewellyn S. Haskell*
13. *Charles A. Heinitsh*
14. *Charles Ellis*
15. *Henry F. Fish*
16. *Eugene Dupuy*
17. *Alfred Bower Taylor (treasurer)*
18. *David Stewart*
19. *Joseph Laidley*
20. *Charles L. Bache*

Each of the 20 men had learned his profession first through apprenticeship. In addition, at least 12 had attended or graduated from college; 6 of those were from Philadelphia, and 3 were from New York. The Philadelphia College of Pharmacy (PCP) was formed in 1821. The Massachusetts College was established in 1823, New York's in 1829, Maryland's in 1840, and Cincinnati's in 1850. Among the representatives were founders of each of the five colleges. Three of the representatives were also educated as physicians.

The attendees were relatively young in 1852. For the 17 whose birth date is recorded, the average age was 37. The youngest was only 24, the oldest was 60, and the median age for the group was 35. The members of the group had both enough experience to understand the problems of the profession and a vision for what it could become. They also brought the energy of youth to the undertaking at hand.

Five of the men at the Philadelphia convention had been present at the 1851 meeting in New York; they and others became the leaders of the new national association. As such, their record can be followed. Little is recorded of the others, whether because of early death or because they left pharmacy for other endeavors. What is known of the 20 is summarized below. The number preceding the individual's name is keyed to the Robert Thom painting (see Figures 1 and 2) commemorating the founding of APhA. Table 1 lists the individuals' names, the college or area they represented, their formal education, and their age at the time of the formation meeting.

Table 1. Founders of the American Pharmaceutical Association

Bender Key	Name	Represented
1	Daniel B. Smith	PCP
2	William Procter Jr.	PCP
3	George D. Coggeshall	NY
4	John Blair Hodge Campbell	MD
5	Samuel Runnels Philbrick	MCP
6	Samuel M. Colcord	MCP
7	Edward Parrish	PCP
8	Charles Augustus Smith	Cincinnati
9	John Meakim	NY
10	Alexander Duval	Richmond
11	Joseph Burnett	MCP
12	Llewellyn S. Haskell	NY
13	Charles A. Heinitsh	PCP
14	Charles Ellis	PCP
15	Henry F. Fish	Connecticut
16	Eugene Dupuy	NY
17	Alfred Bower Taylor	PCP
18	David Stewart	MD
19	Joseph Laidley	Richmond
20	Charles L. Bache	California

MCP = Massachusetts College of Pharmacy; MD = Maryland College of Pharmacy;
PCP = Philadelphia College of Pharmacy; NY = New York College of Pharmacy.

The Founders

[20] Charles L. Bache graduated from PCP in 1849. Joining the gold rush in 1849, he opened an apothecary in San Francisco in 1850. On a visit east, he was invited to represent the pharmacists of the western frontier. Bache caught yellow fever on the sea voyage home and died on the ship.[3]

[11] Joseph Burnett, a graduate physician, never practiced medicine. He was a pharmacist and owner of a Boston pharmacy. Later, he manufactured flavoring extracts and other chemical specialties. An early supporter of the Massachusetts College of Pharmacy, he was active in pharmacy association work in Boston.[3,4]

[4] John Blair Hodge Campbell served his apprenticeship in West Virginia before purchasing a pharmacy in Maryland. No record has been found of his pharmacy activities after the 1852 convention.[3]

[3] George D. Coggeshall was an 1828 graduate of PCP. He moved to New York City, where he established his own pharmacy. A founder of the New York College of Pharmacy, he was its president from 1851 to 1854.[5] Coggeshall represented the New York College at the 1851 meeting, where he was elected recording secretary.[3]

Note	Birth/Death	Age in 1852
Founder of PCP	July 14, 1792–March 29, 1883	60
Graduate of PCP 1837	1817–February 10, 1874	35
Graduate of PCP 1828, founder of NY	1807–November 5, 1891	45
—	1821–1876	31
Physician	1822–1859(?)	30
Attended NY	May 18, 1817–March 5, 1895	35
Graduate of PCP 1842	May 3, 1822–September 19, 1872	30
Founder of Cincinnati College of Pharmacy	1809(?)–March 19, 1861	43
Graduate of NY 1836	1812–October 17, 1863	40
—	—	
Physician, founder of MCP	November 11, 1819–August 12, 1894	33
—	—	
—	1822–December 29, 1898	30
Founder of PCP	January 31, 1800–May 16, 1874	52
—	October 29, 1813–August 21, 1868	39
Swiss trained, graduate of NY 1839	September 17, 1817–October 20, 1901	35
Graduate of PCP 1844	January 6, 1824–February 28, 1898	28
Physician, founder of MD	February 14, 1813–September 3, 1899	39
Graduate of PCP 1850	(Unknown)–1861	
Graduate of PCP 1849	1828–December 28, 1852	24

[6] Samuel M. Colcord apprenticed in New Hampshire before attending the New York College. He moved to New Orleans, where he learned the wholesale drug business, and eventually moved to Boston. An early supporter of the Massachusetts College of Pharmacy, he served as one of its delegates to the 1851 meeting. Colcord served as president of APhA in 1859–1860. A member of the United States Pharmacopoeia (USP) Committee on Revision in 1860 and 1870, he remained active in pharmacy until his retirement.[3,6]

[16] Eugene Dupuy was born in Switzerland, where he trained as a manufacturing pharmacist. He immigrated to America, graduating from the New York College in 1839. A practicing pharmacist, he became a trustee of the New York College. He remained involved in pharmacy activities, eventually moving to Detroit. He was the last surviving founder of APhA when he died in 1901.[3,7]

[10] Alexander Duval represented Richmond at the convention. Trained by his father, he was a third-generation pharmacist. An early officer of APhA, he was involved in its activities for many years.[3]

[14] Charles Ellis served his apprenticeship in the Marshall Apothecary under Elizabeth Marshall, eventually purchasing the business. One of the founders of PCP, he served in a number of college offices, including president. He was one of the Philadelphia representatives to the 1851 meeting in New York, going on to serve as president of APhA in 1857–1858.[3,8]

[15] Henry F. Fish was born and trained in New York before he moved to Waterbury, Conn., where he managed a pharmacy wholesaler. He was the only man at the convention not representing an organized group of pharmacists. He was active in pharmacy organizations until poor health forced him to retire in 1864.[3,9]

[12] Llewellyn S. Haskell, a member of the New York College of Pharmacy, was one of its representatives to APhA's founding meeting. He left the practice of pharmacy soon after the convention, and little is known about him.[3]

[13] Charles A. Heinitsh was a third-generation pharmacist in Lancaster, Pa. He apprenticed with his father and, in 1848, toured Europe to further his scientific interests. Heinitsh, a representative from PCP at the October 1852 meeting, remained active in pharmacy until his death. He served as president of APhA in 1882–1883 and was one of the founders of the Pennsylvania Pharmaceutical Association in 1878.[3,10,11]

[19] Joseph Laidley apprenticed in Philadelphia and was an 1850 graduate of PCP. He moved to Richmond after graduation and engaged in manufacturing. An early officer of the Association, he had withdrawn from all pharmacy activities by 1856. Laidley, in support of the Confederate cause, served as chemist in the Virginia armory in Richmond. In 1861 he was killed in an explosion as he was manufacturing detonating powder.[3,12]

[9] John Meakim (also spelled Meakin) served his apprenticeship in the apothecary's department at the New York City Dispensary. Graduating from the New York College of Pharmacy in 1836, he became one of its staunchest supporters and served as its president from 1854 to 1861. He represented

the college at the 1852 meeting. Meakim served as president of APhA in 1855–1856. He was a practicing pharmacist all his life, and he was filling a prescription at the moment of his death.[3,13]

[7] Edward Parrish apprenticed in Philadelphia and graduated from PCP in 1842. In 1849 he established a school of practical pharmacy for medical students at the University of Pennsylvania. This experience led to the publication of his book *Introduction to Practical Pharmacy* in 1855. He assumed a professorship at PCP in 1864 and served in many offices at the college. A Quaker, he was involved in the establishment of Swarthmore College and served as its first president. Parrish, president of APhA in 1868–1869, was credited with being instrumental in the development of the first code of ethics for pharmacists. In 1872 he was appointed by the U.S. government to visit the tribes in the Indian Territory. Parrish died of fever at Fort Sill, Choctaw Nation.[3,14]

[5] Samuel Runnels Philbrick graduated from the medical school at the University of Pennsylvania but never practiced medicine. He moved to Boston, where he became an apothecary specializing in the manufacture of coal tar derivatives. A representative of the Boston College at the 1852 meeting, he died only 7 years later.[3]

[2] William Procter Jr. apprenticed in Philadelphia and graduated from PCP in 1837. A practicing apothecary, he became the professor of pharmacy at the college in 1846. He was one of the Philadelphia representatives to the 1851 meeting in New York. Procter was appointed as the secretary of the USP Committee on Revision in 1841 and remained one of its leaders through all revisions until his death. He published the first pharmacy text in the United States, *Practical Pharmacy*, in 1849 and was the editor of the *American Journal of Pharmacy* from 1850 to 1871. Procter was president of APhA in 1862–1863. His contributions were acknowledged after his death with the unofficial title "Father of American Pharmacy."[3,15]

[8] Charles Augustus Smith, one of the founders of the Cincinnati College of Pharmacy, was the only delegate from that college to attend the formation meeting of APhA. He was active in the affairs of the Association until he retired from his retail pharmacy due to poor health. Involved with pharmacy manufacturing, he was also the owner and publisher of *The Druggist*, a professional journal, in Cincinnati until his death.[3,16]

[1] Daniel B. Smith. Having apprenticed in Philadelphia, Smith was engaged in the business of pharmacy there for his entire life. He was a founder, and perhaps the dominating spirit, of PCP, where he served as president for 25 years. He was the only pharmacist who was acknowledged for contributions to the 1833 edition of the *United States Dispensatory*, and was also one of the principal sponsors of the *American Journal of Pharmacy*. Smith was among the Philadelphia contingent at the 1851 meeting in New York. At the formation meeting of APhA, he was elected the Association's first president. Smith was well-read and self-taught. In addition to his pharmacy interests, he taught moral philosophy at Haverford College for 12 years.[3,17,18]

[18] David Stewart studied pharmacy in Baltimore and went on to receive a medical degree from the University of Maryland in 1844. One of the founders of the Maryland College of Pharmacy, in April 1844 he was appointed to the chair of theory and practice of pharmacy. This was the first chair in pharmacy in the United States. Stewart was among the first to advocate the adoption of decimal weights and measures in the USP.[3] From 1850 to 1853 he was the inspector of drugs at the Port of Baltimore and drew on this experience during discussions concerning the importation of adulterated medicines.[19] Stewart was the first to use the official title of the American Pharmaceutical Association in the motion for the group to meet in Boston in 1853.[20]

[17] Alfred Bower Taylor apprenticed in Philadelphia and was an 1844 graduate of PCP. In 1848 he was appointed inspector of drugs at the Port of Philadelphia. A Philadelphia delegate to the 1851 meeting in New York, he was elected secretary of the meeting. He was a valued contributor to the USP Committee on Revision from 1860 through 1890. Taylor was elected president of APhA in 1890–1891.[3,21,22]

For whatever reasons, four additional men, approved representatives to the meeting, were not in attendance at the 1852 meeting. They were George Wansey Andrews (Maryland), William Barker Chapman (Cincinnati), John Purcell (Richmond), and Edward S. Wayne (Cincinnati). Chapman was elected APhA president 1854–1855; Andrews became Association president 1856–1857.[3]

PROFESSIONAL HEROES

Twenty individuals of various backgrounds and talents came together in Philadelphia in fall 1852. They certainly did not represent the average pharmacist of their day; they were better educated than most. They did not represent the profession geographically; they were predominately from the East. In spite of their differences from the average pharmacist, they forged a vision for what the profession could be and had the courage to act on that vision.

In an editorial published in the *American Journal of Pharmacy* 6 months after the 1851 meeting in New York, Procter laid out some of the issues that the 1852 meeting should address. Among these were how practitioners could be induced to improve their education to give better service without negatively affecting their current duties, how to better train apprentices, how the Association could help those in need, and how to deal with nostrums, quackery, and secret formulas. The final question posed continues to reverberate in pharmacy practice 150 years later: How can the Association "hold out inducements sufficient to engage and direct the latent talent of our ranks, to such useful and interesting scientific objects as will redound to the improvement of our profession at home, and its reputation abroad?"[23]

REFERENCES

1. Anderson L, Higby GJ. *The Spirit of Voluntarism: A Legacy of Commitment and Contribution the United States Pharmacopoeia, 1820–1995*. Rockville, Md: United States Pharmacopeial Convention; 1995:70.

2. Pharmaceutical Convention held in New York, October 15th, 1851 [editorial]. *Am J Pharm*. 1852;24:85–6.

3. Founders of the American Pharmaceutical Association. *J Am Pharm Assoc. (Pract Pharm Ed)*. 1952;13:704–8.

4. Joseph Burnett. *Proc Am Pharm Assoc*. 1894;42:26.

5. Wimmer CP. *The College of Pharmacy of the City of New York: A History*. New York, NY; 1929:297.

6. Samuel Marshall Colcord. *Proc Am Pharm Assoc*. 1895;43:41–2.

7. Eugene DuPuy. *Proc Am Pharm Assoc*. 1902;50:66–7.

8. Remington JP. Charles Ellis. *Proc Am Pharm Assoc*. 1907;55:583–8.

9. Henry F. Fish. *Proc Am Pharm Assoc*. 1868;16:22.

10. Charles A. Heinitsh. *Proc Am Pharm Assoc*. 1899;47:42–4.

11. Redsecker JH. Charles Augustus Heinitsh. *Am J Pharm*. 1899;71:78–80.

12. Joseph Laidley. *Am J Pharm*. 1861;33:479–80.

13. John Meakim. *Proc Am Pharm Assoc*. 1864;12:23.

14. Edward Parrish. *Am J Pharm*. 1873;45:225–31.

15. Memoir of Prof. William Procter, Jr. *Am J Pharm*. 1874;46:512–33.

16. Charles Augustus Smith. *Am J Pharm*. 1862;34:192.

17. England JW. *The First Century of the Philadelphia College of Pharmacy 1821–1921*. Philadelphia, Pa: Philadelphia College of Pharmacy; 1922:353–4.

18. Memoir of Daniel B. Smith. *Am J Pharm*. 1883;55:337–46.

19. Osborne GE, David Stewart, MD: first American professor of pharmacy (1813–1899). *Am J Pharm Educ*. 1959;23:219–30.

20. *Proceedings of the National Pharmaceutical Convention Held in Philadelphia October 6, 1852*. 2nd ed. unaltered. Philadelphia, Pa: Merrihew & Son Printers; 1865:20.

21. England JW. *The First Century of the Philadelphia College of Pharmacy 1821–1921*. Philadelphia, Pa: Philadelphia College of Pharmacy; 1922:200–1.

22. Alfred Bower Taylor. *Am J Pharm*. 1898;70:177–82.

23. Convention of 1852. What steps have been taken? [editorial] *Am J Pharm*. 1852;24:186–7.

George Francis Archambault (1909–2001): Pharmacy's Change Agent

For members of the pharmacy profession, George Archambault was a heroic figure, larger than life. On April 22, 1999, on the occasion of Archambault's 90th birthday party, Deputy Surgeon General RADM Kenneth P. Moritsugu presented him with a certificate that proclaimed Archambault a "Living Treasure of the United States Public Health Service Commissioned Corps."

Known always as "Archie," Archambault was given a number of other nicknames by his pharmacist colleagues throughout his life, including "Father of Consultant Pharmacy," "Number 109," and "Coach." He also received numerous professional honors, including the American Society of Health-System Pharmacists' (ASHP) Harvey A.K. Whitney Award (1956), the Association of Military Surgeons' Andrew Craigie Award (1962), the Public Health Service's (PHS) Distinguished Service Medal (1965), and the American Pharmaceutical Association's (APhA) Remington Medal (1969). Little wonder that many consider him the "Pharmacist of the Twentieth Century."[1]

George Francis Archambault was born to George Charles and Catherine V. (Mayette) Archambault on April 29, 1909, in Springfield, Mass. As a teenager, the young Archie worked for Springfield pharmacist Fred Flittner.[2] After graduation from Cathedral High School, he enrolled at the Massachusetts College of Pharmacy (MCP), where he earned his PhG (1931) and PhC (1933).[3] In 1941 Archambault received a JD degree from Northeastern University, and he was admitted to the Massachusetts bar in 1942. MCP gave him an honorary PharmD in 1960; the Philadelphia College of Pharmacy and Science conferred an honorary DSc in 1951, and Temple University granted Archambault an honorary LLD in 1961.

A DISTINGUISHED RECORD IN PUBLIC HEALTH

After graduating from MCP, Archambault took a teaching position at the college as an assistant in commercial pharmacy and remained on the MCP faculty until 1943. He had an early interest in hospital pharmacy and became a charter member of the American Society of Hospital Pharmacists in 1942. Thus, his taking a pharmacist position at the U.S Marine Hospital* at Brighton, Mass., in 1943 was a natural progression. In 1944 one of his duties was teaching pharmaceutical arithmetic and compounding to Merchant Marine and Coast Guard pharmacist mates after they completed their basic training at Sheepshead Bay or Columbia University.

Archambault began his duties at the Marine hospital as a civilian, but he soon applied for a commission. In 1945 he was notified to execute the oath of office and report to active duty in the PHS reserve. In 1947 he was named chief of the newly formed Pharmacy Branch of the PHS Division of Hospitals; he served in this capacity until 1965. From 1959 to 1967 he was the pharmacy liaison officer to the Office of the Surgeon General of the United States.[4] Archambault wore his uniform as a commissioned officer proudly until he retired with the rank of captain in 1967.

In 1932 George Francis Archambault accepted an appointment as assistant in commercial pharmacy at Massachusetts College of Pharmacy. Source: Massachusetts College of Pharmacy Commencement Bulletin. 1932;21(2):24.

The creation of Medicare and Medicaid in the mid-1960s led to major changes in the provision and payment of health care for senior citizens and low-income people. In 1965 Archambault became the Medicare pharmacy planning consultant to the Division of Medical Care Administration of PHS. In this position he had the responsibility for writing the regulations governing pharmacy's role in Medicare and Medicaid.[1] Through his writing and numerous speeches he vigorously informed pharmacists about the obligations and opportunities the new programs created for the profession. In 1966 *American Druggist* named Archambault its Man of the Year for his ongoing efforts in advocating the role of the pharmacist in Medicare and Medicaid, noting that the selection was made by a national panel of pharmacy leaders to "honor the individual who makes the most significant contribution to the welfare of the field in that year."[5]

Archambault's experience with Medicare sparked his interest in pharmacy services in nursing homes.[4] An early discussion between Archambault and Rick Berman eventually led to the formation of the American Society of Consultant Pharmacists (ASCP) in 1970. Berman would become ASCP's founding president. Archambault, a charter member of ASCP, was well known for his early mentoring of the young activists who came together to form a new organization that focused on pharmacy services in nursing homes. As L.M. Posey[2] wrote in a profile in *Consultant Pharmacist*: "Archie became their guru—the one who had the experience to show them the path, even if

---

* The Marine hospitals were part of the Public Health Service and had the mission of serving merchant seamen. The hospitals were closed in the 1980s.

the generation gap kept him from becoming one of them completely." ASCP considers Archambault the father of consultant pharmacy, and in 1972 the society established the George F. Archambault Award as its highest honor, given annually in recognition of "outstanding contributions to consultant or senior care pharmacy."[6]

OFFICER AND EDITOR

A strong believer in the value of professional associations, Archambault served as a leader for several groups. A charter member of ASHP, he was elected its 11th president, serving the 1954–1955 term. One of Archambault's nicknames, "Number 109," arose from his service as the 109th president of APhA during 1962–1963. In his speech as incoming APhA president, titled *"Praesentem in diem incedet futuris…* Into Today Walks Tomorrow,"* Archambault clearly articulated his vision of the pharmacist's role: "It is the pharmacist's professional responsibility to protect the public against iatrogenesis, physician-induced injury or disease in the area of drug prescribing especially as to overdosage, incompatibilities, contraindications and synergistic drug actions." His philosophy was to "return at once to the direct patient–pharmacist contact in the acceptance and dispensing of prescriptions."[7]

Captain George Archambault (USPHS) wore his uniform as a commissioned officer in the Public Health Service with great pride until his retirement. This photograph is from the early 1960s. Photograph supplied by George Griffenhagen.

Archambault also held leadership positions in the American Society for Pharmacy Law (ASPL). He served the *United States Pharmacopoeia* (*USP*) as a member of the Revision Committee from 1950 to 1960 and as a trustee from 1960 to 1975, where he "helped USP begin to include aspects of the clinical movement in its standards-setting activities."[8]

Archambault was sought after as a writer and editor, and his perspectives as a pharmacy leader, attorney, and public servant provided him with a broad brush to analyze and comment on unfolding issues in health care and pharmacy. He served as the editor of *Hospital Formulary* from 1967 until 1979. In 1979 he became the Washington, D.C., editor of *Drug Intelligence and Clinical Pharmacy* (now *Annals of Pharmacotherapy*). His friend and colleague Whitney dubbed Archambault "Coach" for the insider information he provided on legislation that was increasingly affecting pharmacy.[9]

A LIFETIME OF HONORS

In 1956 ASHP awarded Archambault its Whitney Award. In his acceptance address, Archambault spoke about professional ethics and responsibilities, concluding, "What you, and you, and I, as individuals and as a group, think and do … in the years ahead will decide whether hospital pharmacy remains a profession or becomes a mere job of work, a combination of technician–tradesman."[10] Although he was speaking to hospital pharmacists and about hospital pharmacy, Archambault's words were taken as being directed to the profession as a whole.

APhA named Archambault its Remington medalist in 1969. Never one to miss an opportunity to share his vision of pharmacy, he titled his address "Unfinished and New Business."[11] Manpower was his central theme, and he spoke about the potential opportunities for pharmacy technicians to serve as manpower extenders and the career opportunities offered to them through some form of standardized training. He noted that while they "are intended for hospital pharmacy service, it is quite likely that chain and independent pharmacies, in their search for manpower, will also show considerable interest."[11] He added that legal issues regarding technicians taking on duties restricted to pharmacists in some practice acts needed to be resolved. These comments preceded the establishment of the Pharmacy Technician Certification Board by almost three decades.

In 1962 the Association of Military Surgeons presented Archambault with the Craigie Award, which honors individuals for outstanding accomplishments in the advancement of professional pharmacy within the federal government. ASPL presented him with its first President's Award in 1982. Other groups also honored Archambault for his consistent advocacy of the role and responsibilities of the profession.

PERSONAL

George Archambault married Lillian May Herbert in 1934. They had six children, four girls (Joan, Lillian, Patricia, and Frances) and two boys (George Jr. and William). George withdrew from most of his public activities after Lillian's death in 1984. He later suffered a stroke, but his children put him to work gathering his notes and the course materials from the 1944 "Postgraduate Course for Pharmacist Mates of the Coast Guard and Maritime Services." George Francis Archambault died on January 1, 2001.

LEGACY

Progress is made when someone envisions a goal and then works assiduously to achieve it. Never one to reflexively embrace the status quo, Archambault addressed the need for change many times during his career. First, he challenged the lack of professional status for PHS pharmacists and led the move to improve pharmacy services in PHS. His momentum never flagged as he moved forward to call for and help establish standards in hospital pharmacy services and then in clinical pharmacy. A consistent and vocal advocate for expanding the role of pharmacy in health care, he never hesitated to point out when the profession was moving too slowly or not moving at all on a given issue or problem. His philosophy was well articulated during the 25th anniversary meeting of ASHP when he suggested that a more apt title of his address would be "The Courage to Change." In his address, Archie recognized the courage of those who left the status quo behind to seek progress in spite of the obstinacy of those who were hostile to change.[12] Given his vigorous advocacy of progressive change in pharmacy throughout his long career, perhaps another nickname for the "Pharmacist of the 20th Century" might be "Master Change Agent."

REFERENCES

1. Posey LM. George F. Archambault: pharmacist of the 20th century. *Pharmacy Today.* January 2000:9,13.

2. Posey LM. Profile: George F. Archambault. *Consult Pharm.* 1994:9:1302–10.

3. Commencement Bulletin. *Bull Mass Coll Pharm.* 1931;20(4):2.

4. Archambault dies at 91; influenced pharmacy through six decades. *Am J Health Syst Pharm.* 2002;58:278, 281.

5. Archambault named 1966 Man of the Year for his efforts to explain Medicare. *American Druggist.* December 16, 1966:11–12.

6. George F. Archambault Award. American Society of Consultant Pharmacy Web site. Available at: www.ascp.com/public/award/archambault. Accessed March 13, 2003.

7. Archambault GF. *Praesentem in diem incedet futuris …* into today walks tomorrow. *J Am Pharm Assoc.* 1962;NS2:290–2.

8. Anderson L, Penningroth K. *Good Works and True: The United States Pharmacopeial Convention Board of Trustees 1900–2000.* Rockville, Md: United States Pharmacopeial Convention; 2000:87.

9. Whitney H. George F. Archambault, JD, ScD, PharmD, 1909–2001. A salute to my coach. *Ann Pharmacother.* 2001;35:383–4.

10. Archambault GF. Ethical standards: professional conduct and responsibilities. In: *Harvey A.K. Whitney Award Lectures 1950–1997.* Bethesda, Md: American Society of Health-System Pharmacists Research and Education Foundation; 1997:47–61.

11. Archambault GF. Unfinished and new business. In: Griffenhagen G, Blockstein W, Krigstein D, eds. *The Remington Lectures: A Century in American Pharmacy.* Washington, DC: American Pharmaceutical Association; 1974;241–5.

12. Archambault GF. Goals for hospital pharmacy: transforming objectives into reality. *Am J Hosp Pharm.* 1967;24:204–7.

James Hartley Beal (1861-1945): Educator-Statesman

In a memorial of James Hartley Beal, Henry M. Whelpley, American Pharmaceutical (now Pharmacists) Association (APhA) past president and longtime treasurer, noted, "James Hartley Beal has made an impression on his day and generation which will be felt for the benefit of pharmacy and the welfare of humanity for time to come."[1] Whelpley's tribute to his friend, unpublished until Beal's death, provides a contemporary's perspective of the man that Robert Fischelis would recognize as one of "American Pharmacy's most commanding figures."[2]

EARLY YEARS

James Hartley Beal, born on September 23, 1861, in New Philadelphia, Ohio, was the oldest son of Jesse T. and Mary McKnight Beal.[3] James, whose interest in nature had been cultivated by his father, quickly became adept at gathering medicinal plants, including ginseng, in the Tuscarawas River Valley. James' first exposure to pharmacy was selling these products to John Smith, a local apothecary. This in turn led to Beal's reading medicine with George L. Tinker, an eclectic physician, before clerking in the drugstores of J. C. Fraley and W. W. Alexander, first in Uhrichsville, Ohio, and later in Akron.[4]

In Akron, Beal studied with several teachers at Buchtel College (now the University of Akron) while clerking for Warner & Hollinger. He left to enroll in the School of Pharmacy at the University of Michigan where he arranged to work with tutors in other disciplines, including physics and geology. At the end of his first year he had amassed more than 2 years of college credits. He then enrolled at Scio College (Scio, Ohio) where he completed a bachelor of science degree in 1884. He returned to Ann Arbor to attend law school but after a year transferred to the Cincinnati Law School, where he graduated in 1886. In 1887 he joined the faculty at Scio and soon undertook graduate work in toxicology at Mt. Union College, graduating with a doctor of science in 1895.[4]

James Hartley Beal married Fannie Snyder Yong in 1886; the couple had two children, George Denton and Nannie Esther. J. H. Beal died on September 20, 1945, in Fort Walton, Fla.[5]

EDUCATOR

Scio College was a small, thriving Methodist institution in 1887 when James Hartley Beal joined the faculty as an instructor to fill a temporary vacancy. He was soon asked to remain and reorganize the Department of Natural Science into a Department of Pharmacy. In 1889, when Scio changed the department into the College of Pharmacy, Beal was named the chair of pharmacy and chemistry and dean.[6]

Beal also had an association with the Ohio Medical University, which was formed in 1892 and would later become part of the Ohio State University College of Medicine. In the 1892–93 catalog, J. H. Beal is listed as a faculty member in both the medical and dental schools and dean of the department of pharmacy. This relationship may never have been consummated since his name is missing from subsequent catalogs.[7]

In 1895 Beal was invited to help establish the Pittsburgh Dental College and subsequently teach chemistry and metallurgy. This led to an invitation to lecture on applied pharmacy at the Pittsburgh College of Pharmacy. For many years he traveled the 70 miles from Scio to Pittsburgh, working the first part of the week in Scio and the latter in Pittsburgh. This was a period when graduation from a college of pharmacy was not required to take state pharmacy licensing examinations. *Pharmaceutical Era*, a weekly trade publication, offered a home study course in pharmacy, and Beal was named director of the program in 1897. In 1908 the Pittsburgh College of Pharmacy bought the Scio College of Pharmacy. Beal, the dean at Scio, became the vice dean and a faculty member of the Pittsburgh College of Pharmacy.[8] In 1911 he resigned from the college to accept the position of general secretary of APhA.

In 1914, Beal joined the Department of Chemistry at the University of Illinois at Urbana.[9] Beal was subsequently named the director of pharmaceutical research and remained in Urbana until 1920.

ORGANIZATION LEADER AND ACTIVIST

Henry Whelpley commented on James Hartley Beal's involvement with pharmacy associations on all levels, observing that "he had mastered association work in and out."[1] Beal joined the Ohio State Pharmaceutical (now Pharmacists) Association in 1894, served on the Committee of Adulterations and Sophistications in 1895, and was elected its 15th president in 1898.

Beal joined APhA in 1892 and quickly immersed himself in committee work. In 1896 he presented a recommendation calling for the development of a model pharmacy act.[10] As chair of the Section of Education and Legislation in 1898, he turned to the topic of reform, questioning whether pharmacy in its current state had outlived its usefulness and argued that its future depended on reform and the passage of strong legislation. As possible reform measures, he discussed the possibility of limiting the number of pharmacies, creating two classes of pharmacies, and requiring graduation from a college of pharmacy as a prerequisite for licensure. He concluded that "unless the pharmacist can render the public a service which it cannot perform for itself, and perform it better and cheaper than any one else, the public will not avail itself of his services. Unless the pharmacist can make himself useful to the next century, the next century will have no use for him."[11]

At the 1900 APhA annual meeting, Beal produced the long-awaited model pharmacy law and the Association voted to distribute it to the state boards of pharmacy and associations.[12] This was followed in 1903 with Beal's development of a draft anti-narcotic act and its distribution to the states and public press.[13]

In 1898 Beal was elected first vice president of APhA and served as chair

James Hartley Beal was selected as the first editor of JAPhA in 1912 providing guidance under which the APhA journal assumed a unique personality.

of the APhA Council in 1902–08, 1910–11, and 1923–25. In 1904 he was elected APhA president; during his tenure in office he called for the establishment of a monthly publication, the *Bulletin of the American Pharmaceutical Association*.[14] The following year the first issue was published under the editorship of C. S. N. Hallberg of Chicago. The *Bulletin* was published until replaced by the *Journal of the American Pharmaceutical Association (JAPhA)* in 1912.

In 1911 Beal had been elected the general secretary of APhA and moved to the Association offices in Chicago. In 1912 Beal became the first editor of *JAPhA*. He resigned due to poor health in 1914 and took the aforementioned position at the University of Illinois at Urbana.

In 1894 Beal, along with George Kauffman of Ohio State University, invited representatives of colleges of pharmacy to meet during the APhA annual meeting.[15] While this attempt was unsuccessful in establishing a sustainable organization, Beal did not despair. In 1900, he was part of the group that succeeded in establishing the American Conference of Pharmaceutical Faculties (ACPF; now American Association of Colleges of Pharmacy). In 1906 Beal was elected the organization's president.

In 1900 this group established the American Conference of Pharmaceutical Faculties. They are (left to right) George Kauffman, Murray Galt Motter, Julius Koch, and James Beal.

In 1912 James Hartley Beal introduced a resolution to create the APhA House of Delegates. Representatives of various state and national pharmacy organizations attended the annual meeting as a mere formality, with no voice in deliberations. The resolution created a truly representational body with a "stated function to consider and report resolutions to the Council."[16]

In addition to being deeply involved with APhA and ACPF, Beal also had a good working relationship with other pharmacy organizations, believing that each served the needs of its pharmacy constituency. In the debate over federation before 1913, the various organizations were neither willing nor able to be assimilated into the APhA structure. Beal suggested the compromise that established the National Drug Trade Conference. Each organization sent representatives to the Conference to consider matters of common concern without binding the individual organization to any action unless specifically approved by the constituent membership.[17] This organization still functions as the National Conference of Pharmaceutical Organizations.

James Hartley Beal was also one of the founders of the American Druggists Fire Insurance Company in Cincinnati in 1906. Fire was a constant concern in the pharmacies of the day; mutual companies were formed to provide insurance for pharmacies that would otherwise lack or have insufficient insurance.

In 1909, Beal was invited to join the Chicago Veteran Druggists Association. The group was formed in 1898 for fellowship; one of the requirements for membership was being a pharmacist for at least 25 years. Eventually a number of other cities, such as Cincinnati and St. Louis, formed similar groups.

STANDARDS AND THE UNITED STATES PHARMACOPOEIA

James Hartley Beal's active participation in developing standards and regulations began at least as early as 1894 when he presented a paper on poisons at the APhA annual meeting.[3] His presidential address at the 1898 Ohio State Pharmaceutical Association annual meeting covered a broad range of topics including the need for a strong practice act and an admonition to quickly amend the poison act, noting pragmatically that the law didn't have to be perfect since it was not intended for the ideal commonwealth. Part of his objective was to protect public safety, but he also sought to instruct "the public in the fact that only a skilled pharmacist is competent to handle and dispense substances which are inimical to human life."[18]

During the 1898 National Pure Food and Drug Congress, Beal served as the chair of the Committee on Uniformity of Methods of Analysis and Marketing of Food Products. Participants in the Congress included women's groups, such as the Woman's Christian Temperance Union, professional associations, and other voluntary organizations that joined together to lobby for federal food and drug legislation.[19] Beal's involvement in this movement, and his efforts to develop legislation on poison and narcotics, certainly made him influential in the passage of the 1906 Pure Food and Drug Act and the 1914 Harrison Narcotic Act. In 1912 an Ohio delegation urged President Taft to name Beal as the successor to Harvey Wiley at the Bureau of Chemistry (now the Food and Drug Administration).[20]

Beal represented the Scio College of Pharmacy at the 1900 meeting of the United States Pharmacopoeial (USP) Convention. In 1901 he was named to the USP Board of Trustees. Beal was responsible for drafting the sections of the 1906 Pure Food and Drug Act that established the definitions of "drug" and "adulteration" by incorporating the USP and the National Formulary as the official compendia.[21]

Arguably more important, however, was Beal's advocacy of what would become known as the *variation clause*. At the time, some were concerned that the inclusion of the compendia would make the act unconstitutional. Pharmaceutical manufacturers worried they might be compelled to produce only official formulas and thereby be precluded from new dosage forms or even new medicines. The variation clauses allowed products to deviate from official standards provided that any such variations were clearly labeled.[22]

In 1901 Beal was elected to the Ohio state legislature. He later noted that his principal contribution was passage of the Ohio Municipal Local Option Law, which permitted the voters of each municipality to determine the laws pertaining to the sale of intoxicating beverages. This law later became a model in other states.[4]

In 1910 Beal was elected chairman of the USP Board of Trustees and served in that capacity until his retirement in 1940. He led the Convention through difficult times and was a respected voice of moderation, an "eminence grise" of sorts, standing, for example, between feuding physicians and pharmacists and playing an important role in preserving the USP's place in the Food, Drug, and Cosmetics Act.[23]

EDITOR AND AUTHOR

James Hartley Beal was a prolific writer. He recalled that his first paper on the definition of poison had been refused publication in the 1894 *APhA Proceedings*, but following that he consistently authored articles in both APhA and Ohio publications.[4] He served as the editor of the *Midland Druggist and Pharmaceutical Review* in 1908 and was the Ohio correspondent for the *Meyer Brothers Druggist*. In 1912 Beal became the first editor of *JAPhA* and served in that capacity for 2 years. He was the author of a number of pharmaceutical texts, including a five-volume work, *Elementary Principles of the Theory and Practice of Pharmacy* (1910).

OTHER INTERESTS

James Hartley Beal had many interests and activities outside of pharmacy. During his time in Scio and Pittsburgh he met a number of men involved in the oil business and invested in the wildcat ventures in West Virginia—profitably, he later maintained.[4] However, his greatest love was for the outdoors and fishing. During a trip to Florida in 1888 he started to collect seashells and continued to do so, especially after moving to Florida when he retired. In 1940 he donated his collection, which numbered more than 70,000 shells, to Rollins College in Winter Park, Florida.[24]

HONORS

In 1919, James Hartley Beal received the first Remington Honor Medal. In 1902 the University of Pittsburgh awarded him with a doctor of pharmacy degree and the Philadelphia College of Pharmacy bestowed a master of pharmacy degree in 1913. In the mid-1940s the Ohio State Pharmaceutical (now Pharmacists) Association established its Beal Award, using the proceeds of his stock shares in the American Druggists Fire Insurance Company, to recognize a pharmacist for sustained contributions to the profession. In 1947, the West Virginia Pharmaceutical Association established its highest honor for service, naming it in honor of Beal. For a number of years, the American Society of Pharmacy Law gave a Beal Award for the best paper published the previous year. In 2000 the USP established the Beal Award for Public Service in honor of the lifetime services of James Hartley Beal and his son George Denton Beal. This award is given every 5 years at the USP Convention.

LEGACY

James Hartley Beal had many roles in his career—teacher, administrator, politician, editor, and practitioner—just to name a few. However, it was in his role as a diplomat that he was particularly accomplished. He had the ability to look at divergent views and develop a win–win solution that frequently carried the day. Framing standards of practice and product, working with USP to avoid constitutional challenges, and building consensus on acceptable compendia are just a few examples of his statesmanship. Whelpley summarized the loss at his passing: "James Hartley Beal made an impression on his day and generation which will be felt for the benefit of pharmacy and the welfare of humanity for time to come....He was not a 'horn blower' but his whispers carried far. Their echoes will reverberate in the ears of pharmacists for generations to come."[1]

REFERENCES

1. Whelpley HM. James Hartley Beal, 1861–1945. *J Am Pharm Assoc, Prac Pharm Ed.* 1945;6:344–7.

2. Fischelis RP. James Hartley Beal. *Am J Pharm Educ.* 1945;9:592–3.

3. Anonymous. James Hartley Beal. *J Am Pharm Assoc.* 1918;7:115–6.

4. Beal JH. Letter to H. Bodeman with typescript autobiographical sketch entitled partial confession of James Hartley Beal. A2: Beal, James Hartley; Kremers Reference Files, School of Pharmacy, University of Wisconsin–Madison.

5. Beal, James Hartley. *Who Was Who in America* Vol II 1943–45. Chicago: Marquis Who's Who; 1950.

6. Comensky WJ Jr., Hook GB, Beal GD. The life and character of James Hartley Beal [undated manuscript]. A2: Beal, James Hartley; Kremers Reference Files, School of Pharmacy, University of Wisconsin–Madison.

7. Announcement of the Ohio Medical University, Columbus, Ohio Session of 1892–93, Departments of Medicine, Dentistry and Pharmacy.

8. Reif EC, Reif TC. *A Contribution to Western Pennsylvania Pharmacy.* Pittsburgh: University of Pittsburgh Press; 1959:51.

9. Research work in pharmacy. Twenty-seventh report of the board of trustees of the University of Illinois Urbana, Illinois for the two years ending June 30, 1914:765.

10. Beal JH. What is the best method for bringing about greater uniformity in pharmacy legislation in the different states? *Proc Am Pharm Assoc.* 1896;44:345–7.

11. Beal JH. The reform of pharmacy by law. *Proc Am Pharm Assoc.* 1898;46:438–45.

12. Beal JH. A general form of pharmacy law suitable for enactment by the several states of the United States. *Proc Am Pharm Assoc.* 1900;48:309–18.

13. Beal JH. An anti-narcotic law. *Proc Am Pharm Assoc.* 1903;51:478–89.

14. Beal JH. President's address. *Proc Am Pharm Assoc.* 1905;53:5–16.

15. Buerki RA. In search of excellence: the first century of the American Association of Colleges of Pharmacy. *Am J Pharm Educ.* 1999;62(fall suppl):13.

16. Beal JH. Third (called) general session [of the 1912 annual meeting]. *J Am Pharm Assoc.* 1912;1:928–9, 1079–84.

17. Beal JH. The proposed pharmaceutical federation. *Drug Circ.* 1919;63:131–5.

18. Beal JH. Presidential address. *Proc Ohio State Pharm Assoc.* 1898;20:15–25.

19. Anderson L, Higby G. *The Spirit of Volunteerism: a legacy of Commitment and Contribution—the United States Pharmacopoeia 1820–1995.* Rockville, Md.: U.S. Pharmacopoeial Convention; 1995:218.

20. Anonymous. Urged for Dr. Wiley's Place. *New York Times.* April 7, 1912:7.

21. Anderson L, Penningroth K. *Good Works and True: The United States Pharmacopoeial Convention Board of Trustees 1900–2000.* Rockville, Md.: U.S. Pharmacopoeial Convention; 2000:24.

22. Sonnedecker G. Drug standards become official. In: Young JH, ed. *The Early Years of Federal Food and Drug Control.* Madison, Wisc.: American Institute of the History of Pharmacy; 1980:34–6.

23. Anderson L, Higby G. *The Spirit of Volunteerism: a Legacy of Commitment and Contribution—the United States Pharmacopoeia 1820–1995.* Rockville, Md.: U.S. Pharmacopoeial Convention; 1995:317.

24. Beal Maltbie Shell Museum. Rollins College archives. Accessed at http://archives.rollins.edu, June 23, 2005.

Donald Crum Brodie (1908–1994): Pharmacy Theoretician

In his 1973 Rho Chi lecture, Don Brodie posed the critical question of whether pharmaceutical education was prepared to lead the profession. This seemingly simple question was a continuing concern to pharmacy, although not to all pharmacists. In his lecture, Brodie also introduced and defined the term *pharmaceutical care*.[1] Brodie is credited as the theoretician behind the shift of pharmacy's focus from the product to the patient.[2]

PERSONAL AND EDUCATION

Donald Crum Brodie was born in Carroll, Iowa, on March 29, 1908, the only son of James Alexander Brodie and Faith Crum. One of three children, he had two sisters, Ruth and Helen. His father owned a drugstore in Pearson, Iowa, and Don worked there, gaining early experience in small-town pharmacy. In 1926 he began his college education at Morningside College, a small liberal arts college founded by the Methodist Episcopalian Church in Sioux City, Iowa. After 2 years he transferred to the University of Southern California (USC), where he received his baccalaureate in pharmacy in 1934. He received a master of science degree from USC in 1938 while also working as a laboratory assistant in the College of Dentistry. He then moved to Purdue University, where he taught as an instructor of pharmaceutical chemistry in the College of Pharmacy. He completed his doctor of philosophy degree in pharmaceutical chemistry in 1944. Donald Brodie married Francis Schrier on November 18, 1934. They would have no children.

In 1943, Brodie's first publication as a graduate student described a unique course on X-ray technology being taught at the College of Pharmacy at Purdue.[3] While appearing incongruent 60 years later, many colleges during the war years broadened course offerings and forged partnerships with other programs to maintain enrollments and keep the school open. When Brodie completed his doctoral degree, World War II was still in progress. His first position was as a pharmacology assistant at the University of Rochester in

Rochester, New York. At the end of 1942, the University had contracted with the Manhattan Project to study the health effects of the atomic bomb components. The various project sites forwarded data from instrumentation, clinical samples, and physical exams to Rochester for analysis, where the evidence indicates that Brodie was involved in classified work.[4]

ACADEMIC CAREER

After the war Brodie joined the pharmacy faculty of the University of Kansas as an associate professor. He remained there until 1947, when he went to the University of California–San Francisco (UCSF) as an associate professor; he was promoted to full professor in 1953. He also served as a lecturer in pharmacology at the UCSF School of Medicine from 1948 until 1966. In 1974 Brodie retired from UCSF and joined the College of Pharmacy at the University of Southern California as an adjunct professor in the colleges of pharmacy and medicine. In 1988 he joined the College of Pharmacy at the University of Arizona as an adjunct professor and was involved with graduate education in the areas of drug use and policy. He was also an active

> *If the service to pharmacy continues to be dominated by its distributive function of which it has become a captive, it cannot fulfill the needs of a new social order. Only when pharmacy's contribution to society is dominated by the capacity of its practitioners to apply their scientific knowledge to the needs of society and by their concern for public health and safety will the profession be justified in claiming all of the privileges of an essential health service.*
>
> —Don Brodie, 1966

participant in the development of that college's Center for Health Outcomes and Pharmacoeconomic Research.

The beginning of Brodie's academic career coincided with the work of the Pharmaceutical Survey led by Edward C. Elliott and funded by the American Council on Education. Working from 1946 through the General Report in 1950 and the Pharmaceutical Curriculum in 1952, the committee investigated "pharmaceutical education, practices, services and trade" to develop proposals "designed for the progressive betterment of pharmacy as a profession."[5] One component of the Survey was a prescription study that examined what medicaments and products pharmacists were dispensing. The results showed that because only 26% of all prescriptions were compounded, most prescriptions required little more than affixing a label to a container.[6] This finding, along with other data, led to a number of recommendations for curricular changes including preparation for furnishing accurate drug

Don Brodie presents one of his many lectures, this one at the Institute of Hospital Pharmacy in Salt Lake City (circa 1957). Photograph courtesy of William Smith.

information to members of the heath care teams and providing pharmacy services to the public. The committee also called for establishment of a 6-year program leading to a professional degree, the doctor of pharmacy.[7]

CLINICAL PHARMACY AND DRUG-USE CONTROL

Brodie's early papers show his growing interest in teaching and professional issues. In a presentation to the Institute of Hospital Pharmacy in 1953, he explained his support for a 6-year educational program for entry into pharmacy practice. After listing the services of the hospital pharmacist, he emphasized that the basic philosophy of hospital practice was the care and welfare of the patient. After a year's sabbatical at the University of Michigan in 1957, he returned to San Francisco as director of pharmaceutical services at the Moffitt Hospital at the UCSF Medical Center. His publications from this period reflect a waning involvement in chemistry and a growing interest in practice issues, especially in the hospital setting.

UCSF had inaugurated a 6-year PharmD degree in 1955. While the curriculum stressed the role of the pharmacist as a consultant, an experiential element was lacking. In 1965 an experiment to put pharmacists on a surgical floor of the Moffitt Hospital was being planned and would become known as the 9th Floor Pilot Project.[8] In 1966 this experiment opened with a 24-hour pharmacy service providing drug distribution based on unit dose, consulting services, and a drug information center. The project was an identifiable, working model for diffusion of the concept of clinical pharmacy.[9] Among its role-defining innovations were a drug-use history taken by the pharmacist at the time of admission to the floor and a medicine-counseling interview at discharge.[10] Brodie—along with Troy Daniels, Jere Goyan, Eric Owyang, Bill Smith, and others—moved the experiment from plan to performance.

In 1967 Brodie continued to develop his signature concept of *drug-use control* in the first of many publications on this concept. He defined drug-use control as that "system of knowledge, understanding, judgments, procedures, skills, controls and ethics that assures optimal safety in the distribution and use of medication" while adding that it linked the professional responsibility of the pharmacist to patient welfare.[11] Brodie questioned whether pharmacy still had a mainstream of service, or reason for being, or whether it had disappeared as a consequence of new science, technology, and professional neglect. In response to his own question, he argued that drug-use control was the core of pharmaceutical service and that it required a relationship between the pharmacist and the patient.

Also in 1967, Brodie spoke for the pharmacy section at the Pharmacy–Medicine–Nursing Conference on Health Education in Ann Arbor, Mich. Addressing once again the changing patterns in pharmacy practice, Brodie cited the American Pharmaceutical Association's pharmaceutical service center concept, the prototype of which was Eugene White's office-based pharmacy practice in Berryville, Va. Brodie argued for the urgent need to get the pharmacist and pharmacy student involved personally with patients—just as medicine and nursing did.[12]

PHARMACEUTICAL CARE

Don Brodie retired from the University of California as an emeritus professor in 1973. In July of that year, he was invited to present the annual lecture during the meeting of Rho Chi Society in Boston. He used this occasion to recall the failure of education to lead the profession to the professional 6-year degree, reviewed the clinical pharmacy movement, and introduced the term *pharmaceutical care*. His definition, "the care that a given patient requires and receives which assures safe and rational drug usage," provided a clear link between the patient and the safe use of medication.[1] He returned to the definition of the term in 1980 and expanded it as "the determination of the drug needs for a given individual and the provision not only of the drug required but also the necessary services (before, during, and after treatment) to assure optimally safe and effective therapy. It includes a feedback mechanism as a means of facilitating continuity of care by those who provide it."[13] Importantly, he broadened the societal needs to include all patients, whether in an institution or ambulatory environment. In 1997, upon the occasion of receiving their Remington medals, Charles Douglas Hepler and Linda Strand acknowledged the work of Brodie as the basis for their own efforts.[14]

CONSULTANT AND VISIONARY

In 1964 the American Pharmaceutical Association and the American Society of Hospital Pharmacists cosponsored the Commission on Pharmaceutical Services to Ambulant Patients by Hospitals and Related Facilities. Brodie was engaged as a consultant to develop a background paper documenting pharmaceutical services being delivered to private patients and to provide recommendations for meeting changing societal needs. The 10 recommendations ranged from the role of government, outpatient services, and welfare to education.

Arguably, the most important was the recommendation on pharmacy's stewardship in which Brodie articulated pharmacy's contract with society: "If the service to pharmacy continues to be dominated by its distributive function of which it has become a captive, it cannot fulfill the needs of a new social order. Only when pharmacy's contribution to society is dominated by the capacity of its practitioners to apply their scientific knowledge to the needs of society and by their concern for public health and safety will the profession be justified in claiming all of the privileges of an essential health service."[15]

Almost continuously from 1965 until 1973 Brodie was either consulting or working with the Department of Health, Education, and Welfare in Washington. He served as the Director of Drug-Related Studies at the National Center for Health Services Research and Development from 1970 to 1973. During this period he helped publish a number of special reports on pharmacy services, drug information, and clinical pharmacy services, including the 1970 report on drug-use control.

In 1970 Brodie facilitated an invitational conference on pharmacy manpower at the UCSF School of Pharmacy. The stated objectives for the conference were to examine future roles for pharmacists and the requisite education, but most of the papers and panels focused primarily on the emerging role of the clinical movement. The active participation of other health professionals—from medicine, nursing, and dentistry—reflected Brodie's lifelong belief in the need for the pharmacist to function in a patient-focused team. While he was not an official speaker, Brodie's presence and influence was obvious in the printed proceedings by the focus on the "what and how" of manpower capability rather than the quantitative accounting and census.[16]

As a consequence of the pharmacy manpower meeting Brodie convened a task force through the drug-related studies program. One of the mandates of the task force was to develop a definition of clinical pharmacy in terms of function. This taxonomy, or pharmacy practice activity classification, pointed out that a clinical role, while largely confined to the institutional setting, had important applications in the ambulatory environment as well.[17]

In 1972 the American Association of Colleges of Pharmacy commissioned the Study Commission on Pharmacy, chaired by John S. Millis. The modus operandi of the Millis Commission was to meet with a number of presenters and then privately discuss the session. The only time this process was not followed was during the second session, when Brodie sat through the presentations of six practitioners and then met privately with the Commission. Brodie was clearly concerned with the isolation of pharmacists during their training and its continuance in practice; he insisted that the pharmacist must be engaged with and accountable to the health care system.[18]

Brodie also extended his message of professional accountability to patients internationally when consulting with colleges and governments. In 1978 he served as a World Health Organization fellow at the Welsh School of Pharmacy, University of Wales.

HONORS

Donald C. Brodie was well recognized for his contributions to pharmacy. In 1980 he received the Harvey A. K. Whitney Award, the highest honor of the American Society of Hospital [now Health-System] Pharmacists. In his Whitney Lecture, Brodie spoke to the need for pharmacy to develop a theoretical base for practice. He took the position that pharmacy had the choice of fashioning its own future or passively accepting what other parties decided. That same year he was named the honorary president of the American Association of Colleges of Pharmacy. In 1984, Purdue University conferred a doctor of science *honoris causa* on him. In 1987 he served as the honorary president of the American Pharmaceutical [now Pharmacists] Association.

LEGACY

One cannot consider trends and developments in pharmacy education and practice during the period ranging from the Elliott Survey through the articulation of pharmaceutical care as a goal for pharmacy practice without coming upon the work of Donald C. Brodie. As a theoretician he continuously probed to understand the underlying principles of pharmacy. In the process he moved his understanding of the professional paradigm from a product focus,

Upon receiving the 1980 Harvey A.K. Whitney Award, Don Brodie admonished: "Don't go where the path leads, rather go where there is no path and leave a trail." Portrait photo courtesy of Francis Brodie.

through drug-use control and clinical pharmacy, to pharmaceutical care. He articulated the need for accountability to society as a requisite to professional standing. No doubt his questions were unwelcome and caused discomfort since the answers frequently required changes from the known. In his Whitney Lecture he shared the admonition: "Don't go where the path leads, rather go where there is no path and leave a trail."[19] Brodie lived this message until his death in Green Valley, Arizona, on February 17, 1994.

REFERENCES

1. Brodie DC. Is pharmaceutical education prepared to lead its profession? [Ninth Annual Rho Chi Lecture, Boston, Massachusetts, July 23, 1973] Report of Rho Chi. 1973;39 (Nov):6–12.

2. Maine LL, Penna RP. Pharmaceutical care—an overview. In: Knowlton CH, Penna RP, eds. *Pharmaceutical Care*. New York City: Chapman and Hall; 1996:133–54.

3. Brodie DC. A preparatory course in X-ray technic. *Am J Pharm Ed*. 1943;7:375–8.

4. The Manhattan Project: a new and secret world of human experimentation. Accessed at http://tis.eh.doe.gov/ohre/roadmap/achre/intro_3.html, December 6, 2003.

5. Elliott EC. The general report of the pharmaceutical survey, 1946–49. Washington, D.C.: American Council on Education; 1950:3.

6. Ibid., 227.

7. Ibid., 229–30.

8. Day RL, Goyan JE, Herfindal ET, Sorby DL. The origins of the clinical pharmacy program at the University of California, San Francisco. *Ann Pharmacother*. 1991;25:308–14.

9. Smith WE. The future role of the hospital pharmacist in the patient care area. *Am J Hosp Pharm*. 1967;24:228–31.

10. Owyang E, Miller RA, Brodie DC. The pharmacist's new role in institutional patient care. *Am J Hosp Pharm*. 1968;25: 624–30.

11. Brodie DC. Drug-use control: keystone to pharmaceutical service. *Drug Intell*. 1967;1: 63–5.

12. Brodie DC. Emerging patterns of education and practice in the health professions: pharmacy. In: Deno RA, ed. Proceedings: pharmacy–medicine–nursing conference on health education. Ann Arbor, Mich.: 1967:23–38.

13. Brodie DC, Parish PA, Poston JW. Societal needs for drugs and drug-related services. *Am J Pharm Ed*. 1980;44:276–8..

14. Hepler CD. Four virtues for the future. *J Am Pharm Assoc*. 1997;37:470–3.

15. Brodie DC. The challenge to pharmacy in times of change: a report of the Commission on Pharmaceutical Services to Ambulant Patients by Hospitals and Related Facilities. Washington: American Pharmaceutical Association and American Society of Hospital Pharmacists; 1966:4.

16. Graber JB, Brodie DC, eds. Proceedings of an invitational conference on pharmacy manpower. University of California School of Pharmacy and National Center for Health Services Research and Development; September 10–12, 1970. Rockville, Md.: Health Services and Mental Health Administration.

17. Anonymous. Report of the task force on the pharmacist's clinical role. *J Am Pharm Assoc*. 1971; NS11:482–5.

18. Worthen DB. *A Road Map to a Profession's Future: The Millis Study Commission on Pharmacy*. Amsterdam: Gordon & Breach; 1999:72–5.

19. Brodie DC. Need for a theoretical base for pharmacy practice. *Am J Hosp Pharm*. 1981;38:49–54.

Chauncey Ira Cooper (1906–1983): Champion of Minority Pharmacists

In 1963, Chauncey I. Cooper received the University of Minnesota Outstanding Achievement Award. The award, recommended by the College of Pharmacy, cited Cooper, a distinguished educator, for his "energetic pursuit of higher educational standards for Negroes* and greater opportunities for Negroes in pharmacy and for his activities which led to the founding of the National Pharmaceutical Association." The citation succinctly summarized Dean Cooper's passion for better education, higher expectations, and greater opportunity than had been the norm.

Beginnings

Chauncey Ira Cooper, the son of Ira Luther Cooper and Mattie Salina Horton Cooper, was born on May 31, 1906, in St. Louis, Mo. He attended elementary and high schools in St. Louis, graduating in 1923. He enrolled in the College of Pharmacy at the University of Minnesota and graduated with a pharmaceutical chemist (PhC) degree in 1927. He immediately joined the faculty of the Meharry Medical College Department of Pharmacy as an instructor. In 1933 he returned to the University of Minnesota, earning a bachelor of science in pharmacy in 1934 and a master of science in 1935.

In 1937 Chauncey Cooper married Marie T. Hyde and became the stepfather of a son and daughter; the couple subsequently had one son. Chauncey I. Cooper died on September 20, 1983.

Educator

Howard University was chartered by the U.S. Congress on March 2, 1867, for the "education of youth in the liberal arts and sciences."[1] Howard was one of the first institutions established to educate African Americans, both those who had been free before the Civil War and those emancipated; it was also the first such institution to establish a department of pharmacy. Although instruction

---

*The noun "Negro" was standard nomenclature for persons of African descent during the period of Dean Cooper's professional life. The term is used in quoted materials for historical context.

had begun in 1868, enrollment remained small, with one graduate in 1870, one in 1872, and none again until two graduated in 1880.[2] The enrollment remained low through the 1880s.[3] This may have been caused by the difficulty that students had in finding stores that would allow them to complete the required practical experience needed for graduation. In 1926 Howard named its first African American president, Mordecai Johnson. An able administrator, he was a builder of faculties, recruiting for excellence and increasing salaries. Johnson was an "aggressive champion of the pharmacy program, refusing to yield to a move to close the school for low enrollment; he successfully argued for increased funding."[4] In 1934 he addressed the annual convention of the National Association of the Boards of Pharmacy. After describing the status of the African American pharmacists and their challenge in gaining acceptance, he acknowledged the help that some pharmacy leaders gave in increasing educational standards at the Howard pharmacy school.

In 1935 Chauncey Cooper accepted a position at Howard University in Washington, D.C., as an instructor in pharmaceutical chemistry. The total enrollment was 24 students; there were only two full-time faculty, a part-time instructor, the dean, and himself to handle the required 4-year bachelor of science program. An early challenge was to address the failure rate on state board examinations. Many of the graduates of the college took positions with the federal government to avoid the need for state licensure. In 1938, Cooper was promoted to associate professor and named as the acting dean of the institution, thus serving as the first African American appointed as a chief administrator in an American college of pharmacy.[5] In 1941 he was named dean and served in that capacity until his retirement in 1972.

IN MEMORIAM

Chauncey I. Cooper, D.Sc.
1906-1983

Founder of the
National Pharmaceutical Association

Chauncey Cooper (1906–1983) was memorialized on the cover of the November 1983 issue of the National Pharmaceutical Association Journal, which he founded in 1954 and served as editor of until his death.

THE PHARMACEUTICAL SURVEY (ELLIOTT REPORT)

In 1940, Cooper described the state of the African American pharmacist in the United States, noting that the minority community had less interest in the profession of pharmacy. Meharry had discontinued its pharmacy program in 1937, leaving only Xavier of Louisiana and Howard with programs among those institutions listed as "Historically Black Colleges and Universities."

Chauncey Cooper (center) receives the Bowl of Hygeia award in 1966 for outstanding community service. On the left is A.H. Robins' Donald Brooks; on the right is R. David Allen, D.C. Pharmaceutical Association president.

However, the total number of graduates was small and decreasing. From 1932 through 1936, a total of 122 African American students graduated from American colleges of pharmacy, with exactly one-half of them completing studies at Meharry, Howard, and Xavier, and the other half finishing at 35 other pharmacy schools. By 1939, the total number of African American graduates in pharmacy decreased to fewer than 20 a year. While pharmacy graduates overall declined during this period, the decrease in the African American population was much greater than the average. Cooper argued that the community needs for health services included pharmacists' services, and to meet these needs, the best qualified students must be identified and provided with the best possible education.[6]

Edward C. Elliott invited Chauncey Cooper to prepare a section, "The Negro in Pharmacy," for the *General Report of the Pharmaceutical Survey*. In opening the chapter, Cooper noted that in the process of becoming a "successful pharmacist, the Negro has all the problems of his white brother, and, in addition, those peculiar to his race."[4] Of the 65 colleges included in the survey, 40 accepted minority students; all of the schools refusing minority admission were in the South. He took on the issue of admission standards of minority students at all colleges, arguing that the same rigorous standards

National Pharmaceutical Association secretary, Chauncey Cooper, and NPhA president G. F. Waters (center), are shown pharmacy artifacts by Lederle Laboratories representative Arthur Velordi (right) during the NPhA 1959 national convention.

must be applied to all students for the good of the profession. He noted that ill-prepared applicants were unlikely to make good pharmacists and that "those colleges admitting Negro students on what appears to be a purely patronizing basis are rendering a distinct disservice to pharmacy as a whole, and to the Negro in pharmacy in particular."[4] In his summary Cooper again returned to the theme that all pharmacists shared the same problems and all should be held to the same standards of admission and requirements of law.

National Pharmaceutical Association

The National Medical Association (NMA) was formed in 1895 to provide an organizational structure for physicians denied admittance to the American Medical Association. Later dentists and pharmacists formed sections within the group, but by 1939 few pharmacists held membership. In 1939 Cooper wrote of the decreasing numbers of African American drugstores and pharmacists and the need for African American physicians to help both in recruitment and patronage, adding that "the drugstore is recognized as one of the first lines of defense in public health, yet the line is growing weaker and weaker among us."[7]

In 1946 pharmacist members of NMA started to explore the establishment of a separate organization, and 45 pharmacists met on May 30, 1947, at Howard University College of Pharmacy and elected Chauncey Cooper as their president. The plan was for the pharmacists to maintain their relationship with NMA on an equal footing with the physicians. The proposed relationship was not forthcoming and in 1948 Chauncey Cooper became the president of the newly independent National Pharmaceutical Association (NPhA). The objectives of the association included providing an atmosphere in which minority pharmacists could exchange ideas, share continuing education, and build community relationships. In a later, unpublished statement, Cooper recalled that NPhA was established "as an educational vehicle to bring the Negroes into the mainstream of American pharmacy, with the idea from the beginning that it would not become a permanent organization once Negroes gained total acceptance in organized pharmacy."* The NPhA Constitution also reflected Cooper's orientation to professional integration with a requirement, later a recommendation, that membership in NPhA would also require membership in an additional recognized national association.[8]

Chauncey Cooper served NPhA as president from 1947 to 1949 and executive secretary from 1954 until 1972. He arranged the annual conventions for a number of years, including engaging speakers and gaining the necessary financial support. In 1954, he became the founding editor of the *Journal of the National Pharmaceutical Association*.

ORGANIZATION ACTIVIST

Chauncey Cooper was an active member of many professional associations, starting with the American Pharmaceutical (now Pharmacists) Association in 1927. Also active in the group's Washington Branch, he was instrumental in the formation of the Washington District of Columbia Pharmaceutical Association and served as its executive director for 11 years.[9]

Cooper was also active in the American Association of Colleges of Pharmacy, having served and chaired a number of committees, including the Committee on Public Health and Civil Defense, 1957–1960. In 1954 he was elected vice president of the Association.

LEGACY

Chauncey Cooper was an active participant and leader in pharmacy. He received many honors in recognition of his accomplishments "to unify, encourage and upgrade black pharmacists in the United States of America."[9] In truth, however, his influence was on the entire profession. He was honored for his accomplishments as a leader and educator by the University of Minnesota, his alma mater. In 1970, the Philadelphia College of Pharmacy

* Much of the biographical information has been drawn from the unpublished recommendation for the University of Minnesota Outstanding Achievement Award by the College of Pharmacy. A résumé with some biographical notes was included as part of the nomination package (February 15, 1963, University of Minnesota College of Pharmacy Deans Office, Minneapolis).

and Science awarded him an honorary doctor of science. Howard University named its pharmacy building Cooper Hall in 1986 in honor of the former dean; the alumni established an endowment fund for scholarships in his name. NPhA recognized his legacy by establishing the distinguished service medal honoring Chauncey Cooper's leadership in establishing and preserving the association. It is given annually to recognize sustained and distinguished service to the profession of pharmacy.

REFERENCES

1. Logan RW. *Howard University: The First Hundred Years, 1867–1967*. New York: New York University Press; 1969:20–1.

2. Dyson W. *Howard University: The Capstone of Negro Education, a History: 1867–1940*. Washington, D.C.: The Graduate School, Howard University; 1941:256.

3. Logan RW. *Howard University: The First Hundred Years, 1867–1967*. New York: New York University Press; 1969:89.

4. Cooper CI. The Negro in pharmacy. In: Elliott EC. *The General Report of the Pharmaceutical Survey 1946–1949*. Washington, D.C.: American Council on Education; 1950:181–7.

5. In memoriam: Dean Chauncey Ira Cooper. *Natl Pharm Assoc J.* 1983;29:7–8.

6. Cooper CI. Present and future prospects of pharmaceutical education. *J Natl Med Assoc.* 1940;32:6–10.

7. Cooper CI. Pharmacists and the National Medical Association. *J Natl Med Assoc.* 1939;31:77–8.

8. Anonymous. Retrospect—and renewal. *J Natl Pharm Assoc.* 1978;24:4–5.

9. Anonymous. Chauncey I. Cooper. *Am J Pharm Educ.* 1984;48:98.

Zada Mary Cooper (1875–1961):
Advocate of Women in Pharmacy

The dreamer dies, but never the dream.

—Zada Mary Cooper[1]

"Her influence and service ... have made her the most widely known and distinguished woman pharmacist in America today."[2] With these words R.A. Kuever, dean emeritus of the University of Iowa College of Pharmacy, acknowledged Zada Mary Cooper's contributions to the development of American pharmacy education and practice. She was a pharmacist when there were few women pharmacists, and, more significantly, she was an educator when there were few women educators in pharmacy schools.

Cooper was born in Quasqueton, Iowa, on January 31, 1875. Her parents were James Neil Cooper and Janetta McCaughey; she had two brothers. Zada Cooper graduated as the valedictorian of her high school class in 1895 and enrolled in the College of Pharmacy at the University of Iowa. She graduated from the 2-year program in 1897 with a PhG. Cooper immediately joined the faculty, progressing through the academic ranks while continuing to take liberal arts courses to satisfy her own interests; she retired, as an associate professor of pharmacy, in 1942.

TEACHER AND ADVOCATE

Cooper, who taught pharmaceutical arithmetic and pharmaceutical laboratory courses, was considered a master teacher. She knew her subjects well and was able to communicate the difficult lessons of weights, measures, and concentrations to her students.[3] She encouraged students by offering prizes of membership, first, in the Iowa Pharmaceutical Association and, later, the American Pharmaceutical Association (APhA).[4] Long after her retirement from active teaching, she was remembered as an inspiration to students for maintaining an open door and a ready ear.[2] Cooper was an ardent advocate for women in pharmacy, encouraging young women to enroll in pharmacy schools and become active in the profession. The *Proceedings of the Iowa Pharmaceutical Association* and the *Druggists Circular,* a national journal, published a number of her articles encouraging young women to become pharmacists and arguing that the profession would be well served by the addition of these new practitioners. In 1912 she wrote that women should have the opportunity to be educated as pharmacists and become successful.[4,5]

Cooper was an outspoken proponent of the responsibilities of pharmacists to their patients. As early as 1914 she was advocating the pharmacist's duty to proactively educate the public about self-medication.[6] She remained firm in her support of educational standards and good teaching while opposing the continuation of cram courses. She noted that "the public has these [short course-trained] registered pharmacists thrust upon it and only the recording angel knows how many fatalities are traceable to errors of incompetents."[3]

Zada Mary Cooper in 1912, the year that she was the first woman attendee at the American Conference on Pharmaceutical Faculties (later the American Association of Colleges of Pharmacy) (Druggist Circular. 1912;56:313).

APhA/AACP

In 1912 Cooper became the first woman to attend a meeting of the American Conference on Pharmaceutical Faculties (ACPF) (later the American Association of Colleges of Pharmacy [AACP]).[7] ACPF met concurrently with the Annual Meeting of APhA, and many educators participated in APhA's Section on Education and Legislation. At the 1912 Section meeting, Cooper delivered her first professional paper on the national scene, discussing the teaching of pharmaceutical mathematics.[7] Her experiences at these national meetings led to Cooper's lifelong active participation in both organizations.

Cooper was one of the founding petitioners to form a Women's Section in APhA in 1912. Approved by the APhA Council, the first sessions of the new Section were held during the Annual Meeting in 1913. The membership of the Section was composed of women pharmacists and wives of pharmacists. Cooper served on the Executive Committee of the Section from 1913 through 1916 and was elected Section president in 1917. The Section enjoyed a number of years of activity before disappearing in 1922. In 1937 the group was reformed as the Women's Auxiliary to the APhA.[7]

Zada Mary Cooper (second from left) with a group of Kappa Epsilon women in 1920.

Quickly assigned to committees in ACPF, Cooper served as chair of the committee examining short, or cram, courses in pharmacy and, later, as chair of the Committee on the Relationships of Boards and Colleges. The latter was especially important in establishing standards and agreements on the timing of the state board examinations.[3] For 20 years, from 1922 until 1942, Cooper served as secretary-treasurer of ACPF (AACP after 1925), the one continuing, paid office of the association. She did all of the work from her office in Iowa, receiving an honorarium of $100 a year. In 1937 she also helped launch the association's journal, the *American Journal of Pharmaceutical Education*, and served on the publication's editorial board until her retirement. Speaking of Cooper's contributions to AACP, Kuever[3] noted that it was "safe to say that she contributed immeasurably more than any other single pharmaceutical educator of the entire time that the Association has existed."

Kappa Epsilon

An early project of the APhA Women's Section was promoting the formation of a women's sorority in pharmacy schools. This initiative was joined by the ACPF Committee on Activities of Students and Alumni. Cooper, active in both organizations, enthusiastically supported the idea. By 1919 both parent groups had agreed to the establishment of a sorority, but its actual formation was delayed by World War I and its aftermath.

In 1921, at Cooper's invitation, women students from the Universities of Iowa, Minnesota, and Nebraska sent representatives to meet in Iowa City. On May 31 the group agreed to form a national sorority, assuming the name of the group from the University of Minnesota: Kappa Epsilon. Membership required graduation from high school and a grade average of 80. Cooper took an active role in the growth of the new organization and later served as its president. She also established the sorority magazine, *The Bond of Kappa Epsilon*, and edited it until her retirement.[8]

Rho Chi

Rufus Lyman, dean of the College of Pharmacy at the University of Nebraska, first suggested the establishment of an honor society for pharmacy in 1917 in his presidential address at ACPF's annual meeting. He noted the existence of honor societies in other professions and believed that the formation of a pharmacy society would be of benefit in recognizing superior scholarship.

Despite his advocacy, no agreement could be reached within ACPF to support the formation of such a society. In 1920 Cooper took over the chair of the ACPF Committee on Activities of Students and Alumni and pushed for the establishment of an honor society. Although the deans reached no overall consensus for the establishment of the society, no opposition emerged; ACPF agreed to the establishment of Rho Chi in 1921.[8]

In 1908 a group calling itself the Aristolochite Society had been formed at the University of Michigan. While this society was never able to grow beyond a second chapter at the School of Pharmacy at Oregon Agricultural College in Corvallis, it did form the basis for the new honor society. In 1922, at the suggestion of Harvey A.K. Whitney, Rho Chi was accepted as the name for the National Honor Society of Pharmacy. On May 19 the

Zada Mary Cooper in 1921, at the time she was working for the establishment of a pharmacy honor society, Rho Chi.

society was incorporated by the Michigan secretary of state. From the very beginning, the vision for the honor society was clear; it was to be nonsecret, with scholarship the basis for election. It was to be open to both men and women and have no racial restrictions.[8]

Cooper was the force behind the creation and development of Rho Chi. She worked with the members of the Aristolochite Society to establish and expand the new organization. She was active in the development of the first charter, which was largely the work of the Delta Chapter of the University of Iowa.[8] Cooper served on the executive board and in various offices between 1930 and 1940; she was the only woman to serve as Rho Chi president (1938–1940) until Victoria Roche rose to that position in 1998.[8]

Cooper retired from the College of Pharmacy at Iowa in 1942 and lived with her two brothers in Villisca, Iowa. She was active in genealogic research and the Daughters of the American Revolution, serving as a regent of the Pilgrim Chapter. After she retired from teaching, she prepared a history of the

University of Iowa College of Pharmacy. Although never widely distributed, it provided a significant record of the growth of professional standards and education. When students would visit, she could recall their names and amusing incidents from college days.[2] Cooper died on May 6, 1961, in Omaha, Neb.

LEGACY

The dreams of Zada Mary Cooper live on in the aspirations of thousands of students and pharmacists. As the mother of both Kappa Epsilon and Rho Chi, she was a major influence on the lives of numerous pharmacy students, both male and female, since the 1920s. She was also an ardent champion of opportunities for women in pharmacy, believing in their ability to contribute both to the public good and the profession. Cooper was an advocate for improving the standards of education and worked tirelessly within ACPF and, later, AACP to articulate and improve those standards. Importantly, she was a leading proponent of the position that pharmacy exists to serve the public health.

REFERENCES

1. Jones JW, Wiese GA. Memorials: Zada Mary Cooper. *Am J Pharm Educ.* 1961;25:477–8.

2. Coghill MM. Zada Mary Cooper. *The Bond of Kappa Epsilon.* 1965;45(fall):3–4.

3. Kuever RA. Professor Emeritus Zada Mary Cooper. *Am J Pharm Educ.* 1961;25:1–6.

4. Henderson ML. Zada Mary Cooper: the grand and glorious lady of pharmacy. *Pharm Hist.* 1998;40:77–84.

5. Cooper ZM. A sane view on women in pharmacy. *Drugs Circ.* 1912;56:313–4.

6. Cooper ZM. Some phases of a pharmacist's duty to the public. *J Am Pharm Assoc.* 1914;3:672–5.

7. Henderson ML. *American Women Pharmacists: Contributions to the Profession.* Binghamton, NY: Haworth Press; 2002.

8. Bower RA, Cowen DL. The Rho Chi Society. *Am J Pharm Educ.* 1955;19:244–84.

Andrew Craigie (1754-1819):
America's First Apothecary General

"Without such a one I know not how you could either procure sufficient Medicine for your Department or dispense them when got."[1] With this statement Director-General and Chief Physician John Morgan emphasized the importance of Andrew Craigie's appointment as apothecary general of the Continental Army in 1776.

Andrew Craigie was born in Boston on February 22, 1754, the fourth child and second son of Capt. Andrew Craigie and Elizabeth Gardner Craigie. The senior Craigie is believed to have been a native of the Orkney Islands who had been shipwrecked at Nantucket. In any event, that island was where he married Elizabeth Gardner in 1737, before moving to Boston.[2] The Gardners had been among the earlier settlers of the Cape Ann and Nantucket areas.

In 1763 the younger Craigie was enrolled in the Boston Latin School. Founded in 1635, a year before the founding of Harvard, the Boston Latin School had a long history of teaching Latin, Greek, and the humanities. A number of individuals involved in the fight for independence attended the school during the same period as Craigie, so it is not unlikely that he formed links with those who would later take an active role in the Revolutionary War. No information on any further education or training in pharmacy or medicine has been found for Craigie.

On April 8, 1775, the Congress of Massachusetts approved the establishment of an army to protect the colony, and on April 30 the Committee on Safety appointed Craigie "to take care of the medical stores, and to deliver them out as ordered by this committee."[3] Craigie treated the wounded at the Battle of Bunker Hill on June 17.

On July 4, 1775, he was appointed medical commissary and apothecary of the Massachusetts army.[4] As far as historians know, this was the first time that the role of the apothecary was recognized in an American military institution. In 1777, as part of the reorganization of the medical department of the Colonial Army, the role of the apothecary general was clearly stated: "That there be one apothecary general for each district, whose duty it shall be to receive, prepare and deliver medicines, and other articles of his department to the hospitals and army."[5] As pointed out by Cowen,[6] the interpretation of the terms "receive," "prepare," and "deliver" was that the apothecary was to procure, manufacture or compound, and distribute the necessary medicines and medicine chests. This was considered to be the "first time in American history of pharmacy that the professional duties of the apothecary were clearly defined."[1] The country was divided into four districts, and Craigie was appointed the apothecary general of the Northern Department.

On May 1, 1778, Craigie recommended the establishment of a principal store in Carlisle, Pa., "where all the medicines shall be prepared and the chests completed. ... I would have an issuing store at a convenient distance from the army, from which the hospital and regimental chests might occasionally be replenished."[7] This recommendation was put into operation with the establishment of the "Elaboratory and Stores for the reception of medicines &c. belonging to the military hospitals" at Carlisle. The recommendation included the proposals that an apothecary be assigned to each completed chest and that the surgeon and physician general of the army also be attended by an apothecary with a chest.

Revolutionary Army medicine chest from the collection of the Medical and Chirurgical Faculty of Baltimore. The containers were variously filled with calomel, Epsom salts, opium, Peruvian bark, and tartar emetic. A mortar and pestle and a pewter syringe can be seen in the center compartment. For a complete list of medicine chest contents provided by Andrew Craigie at Fort George in 1778, see Drug Supplies in the American Revolution by George Griffenhagen, Smithsonian Institution, Washington, D.C., 1961.

Medical supplies grew scarce during the early phase of the Revolution, when items could no longer be obtained from England. Initially, the Continental Army obtained its supplies from colonial apothecaries and druggists. During the first half of 1776, for example, the Marshall brothers of Philadelphia provided 20 medicine chests to troops from Pennsylvania, New Jersey, Virginia, and North Carolina.[8] The medications of the day were predominately botanical, and the therapies largely consisted of cathartics and emetics. Peruvian or Jesuits' bark (i.e., cinchona bark) was used for all fevers, malarial and other, and was among the most essential medications. The typical medicine chest contained a supply of bulk botanicals and chemicals; simple preparations such as spirits, ointments, and plasters; the pharmaceutical equipment required for compounding and vessels in which to place the medicines; and surgical instruments and dressings.

In 1778 the first American formulary, the Lititz Pharmacopoeia, was developed in an effort to standardize the medications available in military hospitals. The original Latin title of the formulary translates as the *Formulary of simple and yet efficacious remedies for use of the military hospital, belonging to the army of the Federated States of America. Especially adapted to our present poverty and straitened circumstances, caused by the ferocious inhumanity of the enemy, and the cruel war unexpectedly brought upon our fatherland.* Dr. William Brown, who was appointed physician general of the Middle Department in the same year that the pharmacopoeia appeared (1778), is recognized as the author. The pharmacopoeia contained 84 formulas for internal use and 16 for external use. While there is no direct evidence, the formulary most likely had an influence on Craigie and his Elaboratory in Carlisle, 50 miles distant from Lititz, Pa., where Brown was serving.[9] Brown and Craigie were well acquainted, as shown by a series of letters from Brown inviting Craigie to become a partner in a wholesale drug business in Alexandria, Va.[10]

Although Andrew Craigie was still involved in the army's pharmaceutical matters as late as August 1785, he had been officially mustered out of the army in November 1783. His friendships with the leaders of the revolutionary period persisted. When Alexander Hamilton succeeded in establishing the first Bank of the United States, Craigie was named director. When Henry Knox formed the Order of Cincinnati for officers who served for the duration of the war, Craigie joined, as did many others, including Presidents George Washington and James Monroe, nine signers of the Declaration of Independence, and many who served in Congress and held other early government positions.

Craigie took up trade as a wholesale apothecary in New York after the war, but he gave the practice up by 1789 because of mounting financial losses. He continued to be heavily involved in land and money speculation. He participated in the failed and questionable Scioto Affair with William Duer, an assistant to Alexander Hamilton, and others. The participants in this venture bought up warrants to 5 million acres in Ohio, planning to sell them to French immigrants.[11]

In 1791 Craigie purchased the Vassal Mansion in Cambridge, Mass., which had been Washington's headquarters during the siege of Boston. He was active in Boston society, and in January 1793 he married the much younger Elizabeth Shaw. The two soon became estranged, and there were no children. At the end of his life, Craigie had lost his wealth and lived as a virtual hermit in his mansion, avoiding creditors and venturing forth only on Sundays for worship services at Christ Church.[12] Craigie died of a stroke in his home on September 19, 1819, and was buried in the Vassal family crypt in Cambridge.

Green glass, free-blown "phials" used during the American Revolutionary War were identified by affixing a label around the neck with a string. National Park Service, Jamestown, Va.

In 1959 the Association of Military Surgeons of the United States established the Andrew Craigie Award to honor the legacy of the first apothecary general of the United States. The Craigie Award is given annually to a pharmacist in recognition of career accomplishments in service of the advancement of pharmacy within the federal government.[13]

Craigie took center stage in the significant developments in American pharmacy that were concomitant with the political and social upheavals of the American Revolution. First there was the recognition of the separation of pharmacy from medicine. It was Craigie, not a physician, who undertook the responsibility to "receive, prepare, and deliver medicines" in Massachusetts. It was Craigie who successfully carried out the role of apothecary general, the establishment of that office being a recognition that pharmacy had a special role in military medicine. Second, it was under Craigie that the laboratory was established at Carlisle and the large-scale manufacture and distribution of pharmaceuticals was proven to be feasible and effective.

The Revolutionary War saw two other landmark developments in pharmacy. One was the spelling out of the duties of the hospital pharmacist in a "Plan of a General Hospital," but this was for the Southern Department, which was not under Craigie's jurisdiction. His role in the development of the plan can only be conjectured. Then there was the Lititz Pharmacopoeia, the first indigenous American formulary, prepared to meet the needs of the army. Its author was Dr. William Brown, and although there is nothing to demonstrate Craigie's direct involvement in its preparation, he and Brown were in communication and on friendly terms.

Andrew Craigie, responsible and efficient, brought recognition to the special and basic role of pharmacy in the health professions. He was a true Hero of Pharmacy.

REFERENCES

1. Kremers E, Urdang G. *History of Pharmacy.* 4th ed. Sonnedecker GA, rev. Madison, Wis: American Institute of the History of Pharmacy; 1976:164.

2. Pratt FH. *The Craigies.* Cambridge, Mass: Cambridge Historical Society; 1942:4.

3. Committee of Safety, Massachusetts Provincial Congress. April 30, 1775. *The Journals of each Provincial Congress of Massachusetts in 1774 and 1775, and of the Committee of safety, with an Appendix, containing the Proceedings of the County Conventions—Narratives of the Events of the Nineteenth of April, 1775—Papers Relating to Ticonderoga and Crown Point, and Other Documents, Illustrative of the Early History of the American Revolution.* Boston, Mass: Dutton & Wentworth; 1838:530.

4. Massachusetts Provincial Congress. Third Provincial Congress. July 4, 1775. *The Journals of each Provincial Congress of Massachusetts in 1774 and 1775, and of the Committee of safety, with an Appendix, containing the Proceedings of the County Conventions—Narratives of the Events of the Nineteenth of April, 1775—Papers Relating to Ticonderoga and Crown Point, and Other Documents, Illustrative of the Early History of the American Revolution.* Boston, Mass: Dutton & Wentworth; 1838:448.

5. Duncan LC. *Medical Men in the American Revolution, 1775–1783.* Carlisle Barracks, Pa: Medical Field Service School; 1931:194.

6. Cowen DL. *The Colonial and Revolutionary Heritage of Pharmacy in America.* Madison, Wis: New Jersey Pharmaceutical Association and American Institute of the History of Pharmacy; 1976:14.

7. Gibson JE. *Dr. Bodo Otto and the Medical Background of the American Revolution.* Springfield, Ill: Charles C. Thomas; 1937:155–6.

8. Griffenhagen GB. *Drug Supplies in the American Revolution.* Washington, DC: Smithsonian Institution; 1961:112. United States National Museum Bulletin 225.

9. Kremers E, Urdang G. *History of Pharmacy.* 4th ed. Sonnedecker GA, rev. Madison, Wis: American Institute of the History of Pharmacy; 1976:169–70.

10. Cowen DL. The letters of Dr. William Brown to Andrew Craigie. *Pharm Hist.* 1997; 39(4):140–7.

11. Cowen DL. Craigie, Andrew. In: Garraty JA, Carnes MC, eds. *American National Biography.* Vol. 5. New York, NY: Oxford University Press; 1999:657–8.

12. Kebler LF. Andrew Craigie, the first apothecary general of the United States. *J Am Pharm Assoc.* 1928;17:63–74, 167–78.

13. Ginn RVN. *The History of the U.S. Army Medical Service Corps.* Rockville, Md: Office of the Surgeon General and Center of Military History; 1997:4.

Conrad Lewis Diehl (1840-1917):
APhA's Reporter on the Progress of Pharmacy

Some 17 years after the death of C. Lewis Diehl, John E. Kramer, the registrar of the Philadelphia College of Pharmacy, wrote, "The name Diehl is synonymous with pharmacy, pioneer, and progress."[1] A giant in his own time, this educator, researcher, reporter, and association leader and his contributions were gradually forgotten as his contemporaries and students died. However, Diehl left a significant legacy to pharmacy at both the state and national levels, one that is increasingly recognized as historians assess and analyze American pharmacy's roots.[2]

EARLY LIFE

Conrad Lewis Diehl was born on August 3, 1840, in Neustadt, Bavaria, Germany, the eldest son of Conrad Lewis Diehl and Therese Philippine Rossi. He termed his parentage "cosmopolitan" since his father's family originally emigrated from Germany and his mother's family had come from France and Italy. His father was involved with the revolutionary movement to unify Germany in the 1830s and participated in the Hambacher Fest. Even though this negatively affected the senior Diehl's career as a government notary, he involved himself again, this time in the failed 1848 revolution. He managed to escape to France, but while there he was tried in absentia in Germany and sentenced to death. He made his way to America and settled near other German revolutionary refugees in the St. Louis area; his wife and six children joined him in 1851.[3]

Once in America, the younger C. Lewis Diehl attended Oakfield Academy, west of St. Louis, until 1854. Since he had been well tutored in Europe, most of his efforts went into mastering English. His father moved to Philadelphia after the death of his wife, and the young Diehl joined him there, securing a job with a perfumer, R. & G.A. Wright Company. His father relocated to Chicago to find a position, but his son joined him there only for a short period before returning to Philadelphia and apprenticing himself to a physician, John

This portrait photograph of Conrad Lewis Diehl was taken in 1874 during his term of office as APhA president and shortly after he had commenced his service as author of the Report on the Progress of Pharmacy.

R. Angney, who maintained a drugstore. This afforded young Diehl not only food and shelter but also admission to the Philadelphia College of Pharmacy. He graduated from the college in 1862 with the "earnest wish that I might have the opportunity to engage in the practical production of pharmaceuticals and chemicals in a manufacturing scale."[4] He immediately secured a position with the firm of John Wyeth & Brother and was put in charge of its laboratory, which was under contract to produce medicines for the Union Army.[5]

Diehl recounted that he was jolted by the "reverses to our Army, by the invasion of Maryland, by the disaster at Antietam," and he enlisted in the 15th (Anderson) Calvary, which was assigned to the Army of the Cumberland.[4] During the action leading up to the Battle of Murfreesboro (called the Battle of Stone's River in the Confederacy), Diehl was badly wounded. After discharge, he joined his father in Chicago before returning to Philadelphia, where he joined John M. Maisch at the U.S. Army Medical Laboratory. Maisch put him in charge of the *Fire-Room* and the *Ether-Room*, where from April 1863 until January 1865 he "manufactured large quantities of heavy oil of Wine, hundreds of pounds of Nitrate of Silver, Citrate of Iron and Quinine, Acetate, Carbonate and Citrate of Potassium, Corrosive Sublimate, Permanganate of Potassium, Gun Cotton, Red Oxide of Mercury, Phosphoric Acid, and numerous other chemicals."[3] Diehl noted that the experience provided a practical schooling in the manufacture of both pharmaceuticals and chemicals. At the conclusion of the war he again moved to Chicago but remained only a short time before accepting an offer to manage the defunct Louisville [Kentucky] Chemical Works. Diehl married Catherine Zimmerman of Louisville. They were to have five children; three of his daughters survived him.[6]

In 1866 the Louisville owners decided to sell their business, leaving Diehl in a personal quandary as to whether to seek another manufacturing position away from Louisville or stay and start a pharmacy in the hometown of his new wife. He chose the latter course.[3] In 1869 he purchased a pharmacy in Louisville, one he maintained for more than 30 years. By the time he sold his store and left community pharmacy in 1903, at least partly due to changes "which by the force of modern methods had become an untenable burden,"[7] he had built not only a track record in practice but also a foundation for both Kentucky and American pharmacy.

ESTABLISHING PHARMACY IN KENTUCKY

In 1869 Louisville druggists were concerned with the education afforded to aspirant pharmacists. While the apprenticeship system was still common, the need for more formal training was recognized. The Louisville College of Pharmacy opened the next year with bylaws patterned on those of the Philadelphia College of Pharmacy, and C. Lewis Diehl, one of the founders, was named the first professor of pharmacy.

Diehl's initial course in the new pharmacy school covered "weights, measures, apparatus, classification, and included what lay closest to his own heart and probably that of most other earnest pharmacists of the century:

the manual manufacture of pharmaceuticals."[7] Diehl was elected the first president of the college and served in that capacity until 1881, when poor health required him to vacate the position. However, he continued teaching for 31 more years.

In 1851 Louisville had passed an ordinance establishing a board to regulate the businesses that made up prescriptions or sold poisonous substances. While never enforced, it signaled the attention that pharmacy was beginning to gain in the Appalachian West. Diehl and others in the Louisville College saw the need for pharmacy regulation on the state level, not only to protect the public from dishonest dealings but to protect the honest apothecary from dishonest competition. Primarily because of their efforts, Kentucky passed its first pharmacy practice act in 1874, which made it illegal for anyone other than a registered pharmacist or registered apprentice to "retail, compound, or dispense medicines or poisons."[7] Diehl was named the first president of the Kentucky Board of Pharmacy, a position which he filled three times during a 33-year tenure on the Board.

The Kentucky Pharmaceutical Association was organized in 1877 and Diehl was again at the forefront. He was elected corresponding secretary during the first annual meeting in 1878 and served in numerous other offices, including president. His presidential address in 1901 was a sweeping discourse on American pharmacy "from trade relations and ethics to the *United States Pharmacopoeia and National Formulary*."[2]

Serving Pharmacy Nationally

The objective of disseminating new ideas and information through publications dated from the 1852 formation meeting of the American Pharmaceutical Association (APhA) and was an article in the original *Code of Ethics*.[8] In 1856, APhA established a standing Committee on the Progress of Pharmacy "to report annually to the Association on the improvements in chemistry, practical pharmacy, and the collateral branches, on any new works bearing on these subjects, published in this country or in Europe, and on the condition of the drug market and the quality of drugs and manufactured articles, whether of foreign or domestic production, found in commerce."[9] The first report, provided by William Procter, Jr., on behalf of the committee, covered 29 pages of short abstracts from the literature.[10] While the reports continued, they were frequently issued late and their quality was inconsistent. In 1866, Enno Sander, the committee chair, urged the Association to appoint a single *reporter* and change the process for receiving materials for abstracting.

Diehl had joined the APhA in 1863. His first paper, reporting on the manufacture of Oleum Aethereum at the U.S. Army Medical Laboratory in Philadelphia, was published in the 1864 APhA *Proceedings*, even though Diehl was not present to deliver it.[11] Diehl recalled that at the 1866 meeting the term *pharmacist* was determined to be more appropriate than *apothecary* or *pharmaceutist*. Perhaps more important to the profession at large at that time was the announcement of Diehl's appointment as the Chair of the Committee

During his retirement, Conrad Lewis Diehl spent much time with his family, as evidenced by this photograph with his grandson that was taken on August 12, 1912.

on the Progress of Pharmacy.[12] However, the process was not changed, with the effort remaining that of a committee.

Dissatisfaction with the committee process finally peaked during the 1873 annual meeting when a recommendation was made to alter the Association constitution and a "new officer, to be called the Reporter on the Progress of Pharmacy," was established.[13] The proposal was approved, and Diehl was named the first to hold the office. Diehl set to work; his first report represented a thorough examination of 32 international journals, 16 published in German, 4 in French, and the remainder in English. Of the English titles

8 were published in America, 3 in England, and 1 in Canada. Abstracts were prepared for each original article and classified as pharmacy, materia medica, inorganic chemistry, necrology, or bibliography. The 1872–73 report took a total of 269 pages in the 1873 *Proceedings*.[14] Obviously this undertaking was one of considerable effort. The reporter had to have a considerable grasp of the sciences that made up the many branches pharmacy, be a linguist of skill and breadth, and be capable of a extraordinary amount of work in what largely amounted to a volunteer activity.

Diehl served as the reporter from 1873 until 1891, when he resigned for health reasons. However, he returned to the post in 1896 and served until 1913. His efforts as the reporter were prodigious; he provided APhA members with a total of "15,451 pages, an annual production equivalent to a 418 page text."[2] Looking back at his first stint as the reporter, Diehl noted that a systematic reporting of progress in the sciences first connected with pharmacy started in Germany in 1840, but this was a new undertaking in the English language.[15] Thus, the efforts of the Association and its reporter provided a significant service to American and international pharmacists alike.

Diehl's contributions to the Association went far beyond his work on the annual *Report on the Progress of Pharmacy*. In 1871–72 he served as first vice president of the Association and then as president in 1874–75.

ESTABLISHING NATIONAL STANDARDS

C. Lewis Diehl had an abiding interest in standards and the correct identification of medicines. This interest, perhaps a result of his love of manufacturing and certainly an outgrowth of his activities with APhA, led to his appointment in 1888 as the chair of the Committee on the *National Formulary* (*NF*). APhA's original objective of the *NF* was to provide uniform formulas to pharmacists to encourage physicians to prescribe them rather than mass-manufactured products. Diehl maintained this objective during his term as chairman of the revision committee from the second through the fourth editions of the *NF*. However, the scope of the work changed especially after the *National Formulary* was recognized as an official standard, on a par with the *United States Pharmacopoeia* (*USP*), in the 1906 Pure Food and Drug Act.[16]

Charles Rice was instrumental in establishing the principles for the APhA involvement in the revision of the *USP*. In the work for the 1880 revision, Rice established one-person subcommittees to work through various issues; Diehl took on fluidextracts, an increasingly important and even contentious form of pharmaceutical preparation. Diehl explored the literature to identify 140 formulas, each of which he proceeded to make, and then reported his recommendations for which processes to adopt.[17]

REMEMBERING DIEHL'S LEGACY

Although not always recognized, Diehl's legacy continues in many venues to this day. For a period of 35 years, Diehl worked to communicate professional advances and new knowledge to the growing number of American pharmacists, an objective established at the time of the first annual meeting of the APhA. Modern abstracting and indexing services that cover the pharmaceutical sciences and practice owe their heritage to the work that Diehl carried out, virtually single-handedly for many years. His work as the Reporter on the Progress of Pharmacy and activities with both the *NF* and the *USP* served to disseminate the changes and progress that pharmacy was making. Today one great state university's college of pharmacy (in 1947 the Louisville College of Pharmacy merged with the University of Kentucky, and in 1957 the move to Lexington was completed), the state pharmacy association, as well as the state board of pharmacy owe much of their history to a single individual who had a simple belief that continued learning and sharing provided the best route for the progress of the profession. Kramer had his characterization of Diehl's legacy correct—pharmacy, pioneer, and progress.[1] When Diehl died on March 25, 1917, in Louisville, Kentucky, many of his contemporaries eulogized him with terms of respect and affection such as *soul of honor, loyal patriot, life-long learner, kind, gentle,* and *forebearing.*[18] It was clear that they recognized and appreciated the personal and professional contributions of the Reporter on the Progress of Pharmacy.

REFERENCES

1. Kramer JE. C. Lewis Diehl. *J Am Pharm Assoc.* 1934;23:244–5.

2. Flannery MA. C. Lewis Diehl: Kentucky's most notable pharmacist. *Pharm Hist.* 1997;39:101–12.

3. Personal sketches. Prof. C. Lewis Diehl. *Midland Druggist Pharm Rev.* 1910;44:499–503.

4. Diehl CL. United States Army Laboratory. *Am J Pharm.* 1906;78:559–74.

5. C. Lewis Diehl. Alumni Report (Philadelphia College of Pharmacy). 1898(Oct);34:201–5.

6. Curry GL. Conrad Lewis Diehl, Ph.M. Biographical sketch. *Proc Am Pharm Assoc.* 1917;40:90–5.

7. Wrobel S. *The First Hundred Years of the University of Kentucky College of Pharmacy 1870–1970.* Lexington, Ky.: University of Kentucky; 1972:15.

8. Code of ethics of the American Pharmaceutical Association. *Proc Am Pharm Assoc.* 1852. Philadelphia, Pa.: Merrihew & Sons Printers; 1865:24–6.

9. Constitution of the American Pharmaceutical Association, Article IV, Section 3. *Proc Am Pharm Assoc.* 1857;6:165.

10. Procter W. Report on the progress of pharmacy. *Proc Am Pharm Assoc.* 1857;6:50–79.

11. Diehl CL. Practical observations on the manufacture of Oleum Aethereum. *Proc Am Pharm Assoc.* 1864;12:309–16.

12. Diehl CL. Personal expressions. *Meyer Brothers Druggist.* 1917;38:152.

13. Procter W. Report of the committee on the editorship of the report on the progress of pharmacy. *Proc Am Pharm Assoc.* 1873;21:35–8.

14. Diehl CL. Report on the progress of pharmacy for the year 1872–73. *Proc Am Pharm Assoc.* 1873;21:151–420.

15. Diehl CL. Report on the progress of pharmacy. *Proc Am Pharm Assoc.* 1891;39:257–60.

16. Sonnedecker, G The changing character of the National Formulary (1890–1970) In: Higby GJ. *One Hundred Years of the National Formulary: A Symposium*. Madison, Wisc.: American Institute of the History of Pharmacy; 1989:21–42.

17. Anderson L, Higby GJ. *The Spirit of Volunteerism: A Legacy of Commitment and Contribution: The United States Pharmacopoeia 1820–1995*. Rockville, Md.: United States Pharmacopoeia; 1995:116,125.

18. Obituary. Conrad Lewis Diehl. *J Am Pharm Assoc*. 1917;6:423–27.

Henry Armitt Brown Dunning (1877-1962): Pharmacy Philanthropist and Father of the APhA Foundation

enry Armitt Brown Dunning (frequently referred to as H.A.B.) was the consummate activist and philanthropist. He built upon a successful retail pharmacy practice to develop a pharmaceutical manufacturing company. He led the drive to build the American Institute of Pharmacy, as the American Pharmacists Association (APhA; formerly American Pharmaceutical Association) headquarters building is known. In 1924 APhA secretary Evander Francis Kelly wrote that "if Dr. Dunning should do no more for the American Pharmaceutical Association than he has accomplished as chairman of the Headquarters Building Campaign, he has earned a place among her leaders; if he does no more for organized pharmacy than he has as leader in the first national movement in which pharmacists of every class have joined their efforts, he will deserve the gratitude of every pharmacist."[1] However, Dunning was just beginning his work as fund raiser, philanthropist, and visionary for pharmacy education, and creator of the APhA Foundation.

EARLY YEARS

Dunning was born in Denton, Maryland, on October 24, 1877, of Charles Alexander Dunning and Ella M. Redden.[2] Henry Armitt Brown was named after the noted Philadelphia lawyer and orator, a friend of the father. H.A.B. received his early education in Denton and worked in his uncle J.H. Redden's pharmacy, before moving to Baltimore where he attended the Maryland College of Pharmacy, graduating with a graduate in pharmacy (PhG) in 1897.[1] The 1897 college catalog noted that his preceptor was the firm of Hynson, Westcott & Co.[3] Dunning was undoubtedly influenced by Henry P. Hynson, who also was the professor of commercial pharmacy and dispensing at the Maryland College of Pharmacy and the 1895-96 president of the Maryland Pharmaceutical Association.

This portrait photograph of H.A.B. Dunning was taken in 1902, the year he joined APhA and the year after he had purchased a partnership in Hynson & Wescott in Baltimore.

After graduation Dunning enlisted in the U.S. Army and served in Cuba with the 4th U.S. Volunteers during the Spanish American War; upon discharge he returned to Hynson, Westcott & Co. in Baltimore as head prescriptionist.[4] He also did postgraduate work in chemistry at Johns Hopkins and in 1908 received the doctor of pharmacy degree from the Maryland College of Pharmacy. From 1902 through 1915 he taught chemistry at the Maryland College of Pharmacy.[5]

In 1901 H.A.B. Dunning married Beatrice Fitzgerald; they had two children, James H. Fitzgerald and Catherine Ellen. Beatrice died in 1906. In 1908 Dunning married Ethel Adams; they also had two children, Henry Armitt Brown and Charles Alexander. H.A.B. Dunning died in Baltimore on July 26, 1962.[2]

ASSOCIATION LEADER

Dunning joined APhA in 1902. At the 1902 Philadelphia meeting he presented three papers. In one he championed chemical analysis carried on in the drugstore as an excellent advertisement of the pharmacist's professional capabilities to physicians while adding profit. Dunning served as the secretary of the Section on Practical Pharmacy and Dispensing in 1905–06 and as chairman in 1906–07.[5]

Dunning served as the Association's president in 1929–30; the theme for his presidential address was the need of all pharmacists to be active in, and supportive of, their professional organizations. Addressing the professionalism of pharmacy, he expressed his concern over the public's negative perception of pharmacy because professional services were visibly secondary to nonhealth merchandise in many drugstores.[6] In 1940 APhA decided to split the *Journal of the American Pharmaceutical Association* into two separate publications; one was to focus on the scientific papers while the other was devoted to topics of particular interest to practicing pharmacists in the retail and hospital setting. The start-up costs of the publication change were underwritten by Dunning and Gustavus A. Pfeiffer, president of the William R. Warner Company.[7]

Dunning served as the president of the Maryland Pharmacists Association and later led the campaign to build the headquarters building for the Association on the University of Maryland at Baltimore campus. The building was named the Kelly Memorial Building in honor of his long-time friend and former APhA chief executive officer, Evander F. Kelly.[8]

RETAIL AND MANUFACTURING PHARMACIST

In 1901 Dunning purchased a partnership interest in Hynson & Westcott and the name was changed to Hynson, Westcott & Dunning. The partnership was a thriving professional pharmacy with more than 40 employees in 1900; it was still in operation as late as 1951.[9]

In 1910 Dunning was approached by area physicians to undertake the development and distribution of a phenolsulfonephthalein test solution for the determination of kidney function.[10] This development work led to mercurochrome, the iconic antiseptic product in America's medicine cabinets for the next four decades.[11] Blood coagulation research with heparin was being carried on at Johns Hopkins University as early as 1916; however, it would not enter routine medical practice until after World War II. Hynson, Westcott & Dunning developed a gauze bandage coated with the procoagulant for experimental use. In 1940 the company developed another iconic product, a sterile dispenser pack of sulfa that was carried by allied troops in World War II as apart of trauma first aid on the battlefield.

AMERICAN INSTITUTE OF PHARMACY

In 1912, James Hartley Beal's editorial in the *Journal of the American*

Pharmaceutical Association addressed the practice of moving the Association headquarters to the residence of the general secretary and the resulting scattered records and publications. He advocated the development of a permanent headquarters to allow for the unification of association operations and for the establishment of a testing laboratory called for in the *National Formulary*.[12] The suggestion was repeated almost annually, and in 1921 a committee was formed with Beal as the chair to solicit funds for the establishment of the APhA headquarters building.[13]

The headquarters building was a topic of intense discussion at the 1923 APhA annual meeting in Asheville, N.C. In an interview with the *American Druggist* following the meeting, H.A.B. Dunning provided his perspective. He observed that while everyone wanted a headquarters building, no one seemed to know how to go about getting it. Only $21,000 had been collected in 4 years, far less than the estimated need of $250,000. Noting that success is "merely a question of proper organization, thorough cooperation, enthusiasm, and quick action," Dunning laid out a campaign plan that he was sure would raise the necessary funding.[14]

In an announcement in the April 1924 issue of *JAPhA*, Dunning reported that he had been given "the privilege of organizing a committee of five to show what could be done with my plan." The committee of five included E.F. Kelly, Edwin Leigh Newcomb of the National Wholesale Druggists Association (NWDA), and past presidents Samuel Lewis Hilton and Waldemar Bruce Philip. An advisory committee of 350 representatives of state and city pharmacy associations as well as national organizations such as the National Association of Retail Druggists (now the National Community Pharmacists Association) and the NWDA was established. It was clear that Dunning's grand campaign was one of inclusion of all facets of pharmacy—education, practice, manufacturing, and distribution. He noted that "we require a million dollars to properly endow this great enterprise and we plan to get it."[15]

A decision on the location for the headquarters building was delayed until sufficient funds were raised to assure construction. During the May 1924 APhA Council meeting Dunning noted that aggregate subscriptions exceeded a half million dollars. A resolution was passed to establish the process to choose the location.[16] At the end of the process, Washington, D.C., was the clear preference of the membership.

In 1928 Dunning purchased the land for the new headquarters building on what he considered to be the finest site in the country. A dialogue was begun with the Washington Fine Arts Commission, a partnership that would prove to be pivotal in the final plans and construction of the building.[17] John Russell Pope was selected as the architect, and the relationship with the Washington Fine Arts Commission became increasingly important.

In January 1929 the commission suggested purchasing more land; they desired a magnificent edifice that would be worthy of the location across from the Lincoln Memorial. Dunning personally undertook a special subscription from manufacturers, which raised an additional sum of more than $108,000

H.A.B. Dunning donated the Flag Pole Memorial that stands in front of APhA headquarters honoring all pharmacists who served in the wars of our country. Here he presents the first flag flown on the flag pole to APhA Secretary Robert P. Fischelis (left) at the May 7, 1948, dedication.

for purchase of the additional land. While there were hopes that construction could begin in 1929, Dunning stated that fund raising was far from over. He reported that at least an additional million dollars would be needed to fully meet the objective of providing operating funds.[18]

The question of tax exemption had been raised in 1928 and Dunning came back to the subject in his 1930 APhA presidential address.[6] In 1932 the Commissioners of the District of Columbia questioned whether APhA was a commercial organization. Once assured that the Association was a service organization, approval was given, the final property lines were drawn, and construction begun.[19]

During the annual APhA meeting in Washington in 1934, the American Institute of Pharmacy was dedicated.[20] The occasion was full of grandeur and speeches as was appropriate. True to his nature, Dunning almost immediately called for another campaign to raise an endowment for the operation and maintenance of the building.

Dunning remained involved with the APhA headquarters building for the rest of his life. In 1948 he provided the funds for the erection of a flagpole to honor all of the pharmacists who served in America's wars. By 1956 the original headquarters structure was in need of more space; Dunning was again involved in the fund raising efforts for the addition of an annex, which was formally dedicated in 1960.[21]

APhA FOUNDATION

During the fund raising activities for the construction of the headquarters building Dunning faced the issue of taxation on two levels. The first was the tax-exempt status of APhA. The second, and more pressing, was the ability of donors to make contributions for charitable purposes and receive an income tax credit. In 1951 Dunning questioned how APhA might qualify as a tax-exempt body; the resulting recommendation was to develop a new organization that would be separate from APhA. APhA authorized the formation of the APhA Foundation in 1953. However, the announcement was premature; the Internal Revenue Service (IRS) refused to recognize the Foundation as a 501(c)(3) organization until there was evidence of sustained operations. Dunning's attorney advised him to suspend any further contributions until the situation could be resolved.

Despite the temporary setback the Foundation made its first educational grant to the American Society of Hospital Pharmacists Research Fund in 1958. However, it was the new APhA secretary, William Shoulden Apple, who initiated the transfer of the APhA Library, Museum, Archives, and Drug Standards Laboratory to the Foundation. These actions provided the evidence of operation required by the IRS, allowing exemption from taxation for the Foundation as well as providing tax deductions for donors in 1961. H.A.B. Dunning served as the first Foundation president in 1953–58 and again for the period of 1959–61.[22]

PHILANTHROPIST

H.A.B. Dunning was a major philanthropist for APhA, but his interests and generosity were far broader. He was a major contributor to Johns Hopkins University. He provided the needed financial support for the separation of uranium into isotopes, an essential process for the development of the atomic bomb at the Manhattan Project.[23] In 1932 he established a fellowship in chemical research; his generosity was memorialized by naming the chemistry building on the Homewood campus Dunning Hall. He was also a major donor to Washington College in Chestertown, Md., where he provided the funds for the science building.

AMERICAN FOUNDATION FOR PHARMACEUTICAL EDUCATION

The American Foundation for Pharmaceutical Education (AFPE) was formed in 1942 by nine organizations representing manufacturers, educators, and pharmacy. The initial objective was to provide funding for colleges struggling with wartime enrollment decreases. Dunning was elected to the board of the AFPE in 1945. This was not his first involvement with financial support for pharmacy education; he had established a research fellowship at the University of Maryland College of Pharmacy in 1930. It was Dunning who offered the resolution for AFPE to support the Elliott Commission Pharmaceutical Survey. William Paul Briggs, executive director of AFPE recalled Dunning's influence and active participation through many years on the board and executive committee and as president in 1952. In 1957 AFPE established the H.A.B. Dunning Memorial Fellowship.[24]

Honors

In 1926 Dunning received the Remington Medal, pharmacy's highest award, for his efforts in securing funding for the American Institute of Pharmacy. In 1942 Johns Hopkins presented Dunning with an honorary doctor of laws (LLD) degree. In 1950 the University of Maryland named him the recipient of the first alumni award as the college of pharmacy's outstanding graduate.[25] In 1953 the University of Maryland College of Pharmacy named its new building Dunning Hall. In 1982 APhA established the H.A.B. Dunning Award given annually to recognize exemplary contributions to the practice of pharmacy by a pharmaceutical manufacturer or provider of support services or products.

Legacy

Briggs summarized Dunning's career "from errand boy in a drug store in Denton, Maryland, to Top Sergeant Rough Rider with Teddy Roosevelt in Cuba, to researcher in the laboratories of Johns Hopkins University, to practitioner of pharmacy in Baltimore, to president of his own important pharmaceutical manufacturing company, to leadership in the American Pharmaceutical Association," to which must be added father of the APhA Foundation.[24] In his Remington address Dunning professed the need to "recognize our own obligation to give something of ourselves to the service of our calling, so that it will fulfill its proper mission."[26] Henry Armitt Brown Dunning was deeply committed to pharmacy causes; his leadership and participation were given unstintingly. He was also generous with his personal wealth and used it to support causes that he was passionate about. He was an active participant and leader in the establishment of the American Institute of Pharmacy. He was also a working participant in the creation of the APhA Foundation and AFPE. Henry Armitt Brown Dunning's legacy remains evident in his giving of himself to build the physical capital of the pharmacy edifices and to support the intellectual capital of future pharmacists.

References

1. Kelly EF. H.A.B. Dunning. *J Am Pharm Assoc.* 1924;13:593–4.
2. *Who's Who in the USA*. Chicago, Ill.: Marquis; 1960–61;31:824.
3. *1897–98 Annual Catalog of the Maryland College of Pharmacy*. Baltimore, Md.: Maryland College of Pharmacy; 1897.
4. Alumni news-letter Maryland College of Pharmacy. 1899(Dec):10.
5. Two prominent APhA members. *Druggists Circ.* 1908;52:45.

6. Dunning HAB. Address of the president of the American Pharmaceutical Association. *J Am Pharm Assoc*. 1930;19:487–98.

7. The Journal and its origins. *J Am Pharm Assoc (Practical Pharm Ed)*. 1957;18:25.

8. In memoriam: Dr. H.A.B. Dunning. *Md Pharm*. 1962,37.016,848.

9. Kremers E, Urdang G. *History of Pharmacy: A Guide and a Survey*, 2nd ed. Philadelphia, Pa.: J.B. Lippincott; 1951:434.

10. DuMez AG. Development of pharmaceutical chemistry in Maryland. *J Chem Educ*. 1931;8:471–84.

11. Dunning F. Some interesting facts about Mercurochrome. *J Am Pharm Assoc*. 1927;16:329–31.

12. Beal JH. The need of an association home. *J Am Pharm Assoc*. 1912;1:1189–90.

13. Beal JH. Committee on A.Ph.A. Headquarters Rpt. 1922;11:726–8.

14. HAB Dunning, Baltimore, MD. *Am Druggist*. 1923(Oct);71: 48,50,52.

15. Dunning HAB. Announcement of the chairman of pharmacy headquarters campaign committee. *J Am Pharm Assoc*. 1924;13:286–7.

16. Dunning HAB. Progress toward realization of the A.Ph.A. Headquarters. *J Am Pharm Assoc*. 1926;15:725.

17. Dunning HAB. Chairman Dunning's report. *J Am Pharm Assoc*. 1928;17:1021–3.

18. Dunning HAB. Headquarters building campaign committee and headquarters plan committee reports. *J Am Pharm Assoc*. 1929;18:1060–7.

19. Dunning HAB. Committees on the headquarters building. *J Am Pharm Assoc*. 1932;21:1242–4.

20. Griffenhagen GB. History of the American Institute of the History of Pharmacy. *Pharm Hist*. 2002;44:47–63.

21. Fischelis RB. An urgent appeal to A.Ph.A. members. *J Am Pharm Assoc (Practical Pharm Ed)*. 1955;16:734.

22. Griffenhagen GB, Ellis W, Kalman S, Schwartz M. *History of the APhA Foundation: Celebrating the 50th Anniversary*. Washington, D.C.: American Pharmaceutical Association Foundation; 2003.

23. Dr. H.A.B. Dunning contributed to the development of the atomic bomb. *J Am Pharm Assoc (Practical Pharm Ed)*. 1946;7:29–30.

24. Briggs WP. Birthday greetings. *The Eightieth Birthday Celebration Honoring Dr. Henry Armitt Brown Dunning* [booklet]. Baltimore, Md,: privately printed; 1957:2.

25. Dr Dunning dies at age 84 [obituary]. *Baltimore Sun*. July 7, 1962.

26. Dunning HAB. Pharmacy headquarters building assured. In: Griffenhagen GB, Bowles GC, Penna RP, Worthen DB. *Reflections of Pharmacy by the Remington Medalists 1919-2003*. Washington, D.C.: American Pharmacists Association; 2004:42.

Carl Thomas Durham (1892–1974):
Pharmacy's Representative

In a 1957 cover article, *Drug Topics* noted the service of Congressman Carl T. Durham (D–N.C.), stating that if pharmacy had an award for the pharmacist who had made the greatest contribution to his country's welfare it would have to go to this North Carolina legislator.[1] Described as soft-spoken, stubborn, and prepared, the 11-term congressman played a major role in national legislation affecting pharmacists.

In his 1963 revision of *Kremer and Urdang's History of Pharmacy*, Sonnedecker wrote about pharmacists in public service: "Any review of recent progress of pharmacy in government service would be incomplete without mentioning the effective support given by the pharmacist Carl T. Durham, former representative in Congress for North Carolina."[2]

BEGINNINGS

Carl Thomas Durham was born in White Cross—in rural Orange County, North Carolina—on August 28, 1892. The son of Claude Peter Durham and Delia Anne Lloyd, he was one of eight children.[3] Carl Durham attended public schools in White Cross and graduated from the Manndale Academy in Saxapahaw, N.C. Though he spent his early years on the farm, he expressed an early interest in pharmacy.[4] In 1912 he went to work at the Eubanks Drug Store in Chapel Hill while he attended the University of North Carolina School of Pharmacy. Durham graduated from the university and passed the North Carolina board examination in 1917.[5] He immediately enlisted in the U.S. Navy, serving as a pharmacist's mate. At the end of World War I he returned to Chapel Hill and resumed his service at the Eubanks Drug Store, now as a pharmacist.

In 1919 Durham married Margaret Joe Whitsett. The couple had five children—four daughters and a son.

Durham noted that he became interested in politics at an early age, even before he was old enough to vote. He was appointed to fill a vacancy on the Board of Education for a minority school established under a Rockefeller grant in 1917, before he entered the Navy. In 1922 he was appointed to the Board of Education for the Chapel Hill schools. In the same year he was appointed to fill a vacancy as an alderman. Along the way he served behind the political scenes managing various campaigns at the county level. He noted the importance of being associated with Mr. Eubanks, a "good business druggist."[6] In 1937 the Legislature elected Durham to the University of North Carolina board of trustees.[7]

In 1938 the congressman from the Sixth North Carolina District retired and the Democratic Party selected a candidate to run for the vacancy. However, the candidate died only 10 days before the election. The district Democratic Committee selected Carl T. Durham to run in his stead. He was unopposed; in less than 2 weeks Durham was the new Democratic Congressman from North Carolina for the 76th Congress starting in 1939. His congressional district (including the cities of High Point, Greensboro, Chapel Hill, and Durham) was the largest and most heavily industrialized in North Carolina and included the University of North Carolina and Duke University.

In describing Durham in 1938, the editor of the *Chapel Hill Weekly* noted, "Carl Durham will give no demonstrations of silver-tongued oratory in Congress. For this his constituents may well be thankful rather than regretful. They know that he will bring good hard sense to bear on the problems that confront him and that he will always be faithful to his trust."[8]

The Honorable Carl Thomas Durham was honored as "Man of the Year in North Carolina," as featured on the cover of the January 1939 issue of the Carolina Journal of Pharmacy.

The *Carolina Journal of Pharmacy* inserted an addendum upon learning of Durham's selection. J. G. Beard, the editor and dean of the college of pharmacy, provided perspective, noting that "the development promises much for Pharmacy in America, not merely pharmacy in North Carolina. But this is not to be understood that Durham is a pharmacist only. He is a well rounded, serious thinking student of public affairs who leads himself to his own decision of good policy."[9] The January issue of the *Journal* carried Durham's picture; in the fashion of *Time* magazine, he was identified as the "Man of the Year in North Carolina Pharmacy."[10]

Durham's initial committee assignment in Congress was to the Post Office and Post Roads Committee. The jurisdiction of the committee included all materials dealing with the U.S. Postal System including postage rates, routes and buildings, and postal money orders. In 1941, with the commencement of the 77th Congress and the beginning of Durham's second term, he was assigned to the House Military Affairs Committee. This committee was responsible for affairs relating to the draft and funding and arming of the Army.

THE PHARMACY CORPS

On July 23, 1942, Carl Durham introduced H.R. 7432, *To Create a Pharmacy Corps in the United States Army.* Since 1894, pharmacists had been trying to gain Army commissions for pharmacists serving as pharmacists; 10 consecutive Surgeon Generals refused to recognize pharmacy as a profession.[11] In 1942 four pharmacy groups (American Association of Colleges of Pharmacy, American Pharmaceutical Association [APhA; now American Pharmacists Association], National Association of Retail Druggists [NARD; now the National Community Pharmacists Association], and National Association of Boards of Pharmacy) formed a committee to coordinate the individual groups' initiatives to gain recognition of pharmacy and the organization of pharmaceutical services in the Army. When Surgeon General James C. Magee refused to support the initiative, the group enlisted the assistance of Carl Durham—pharmacist, military veteran, and a majority member of the House Military Affairs Committee. The legislation had only four provisions, one of which was to increase the authorized number of commissioned pharmacists from 12 to 72. The most important part of the bill was its objective: "to centralize the purchase, shipment, storage and standardization of medical supplies under those best equipped by education and training to perform the duties, pharmacists."[12] Durham enlisted the aid of North Carolina Senator Robert Rice Reynolds, ranking majority member on the Senate Military Affairs Committee, to introduce a companion bill, S. 2690.

The Army remained intransigent in its opposition to the formation of a Pharmacy Corps during House hearings, stating that "the safeguarding of and compounding of prescriptions, is now provided in our hospitals and our field installations, and that the technical services rendered by registered pharmacists does not demand or merit a commission."[13] During Senate hearings, Durham emphasized pharmacy's position that the legislation had but two purposes: "to give the men and women in the armed forces the same protection in the use of medicines enjoyed by civilians and ... to place all procurement and distribution of medicines under the control of the corps of pharmacy officers."[14]

The Army Surgeon General, now Norman T. Kirk, underestimated the support for the Pharmacy Corps. At least 20 states had passed legislation supporting pharmacy, and the American Legion was also in favor of the bill. On July 12, 1943, President Franklin D. Roosevelt signed the legislation establishing the Pharmacy Corps. However, the Army moved very slowly, too slowly for organized pharmacy's expectation. Surgeon General Kirk remained convinced that the Army did not need pharmacists since only medicines on the official supply table were available and any trained enlisted soldier could dispense them without being a registered pharmacist.[15] Carl Durham and the APhA committee met with the Surgeon General's staff to develop a process to implement the legislation.

DURHAM–HUMPHREY AMENDMENT

The 1938 Food, Drug, and Cosmetic Act (FDCA) had established that medicines available only by a physician's prescription were exempt from labeling instructions that were understandable by consumers. It also mandated that patients needed prescriptions for products that previously could be purchased without them.[16] For nonnarcotic products, the manufacturer was solely responsible for deciding which products to label for use only by direction of a physician and which were appropriate for self-medication—and different manufacturers could and did label the same medicine differently. The 1938 law failed to define just what constituted a prescription-only medication.

In 1948 the U.S. Supreme Court reversed a lower court decision that inappropriate dispensing could only be prosecuted under state regulations. Subsequently, Congress passed an amendment to FDCA providing federal jurisdiction for distribution of medicines "at all stages of shipment, storage and transfer until the goods reached the hands of the ultimate consumer."[17] There was considerable confusion and disagreement between pharmacy and the Food and Drug Administration (FDA) over pharmacists' authority to refill prescriptions and the legality of telephoned prescriptions. Finally pharmacists, especially NARD members, and FDA sought legislative clarification; Congressman Durham was enlisted to introduce legislation that would clarify the situation for practitioners, manufacturers, and regulators.

Durham took the lead in the House by offering an amendment to the FDCA in the 80th Congress and, when it failed, again in the 81st. At the beginning of the 82nd Congress in 1951 he again introduced an amendment (H.R. 3298) to amend the FDCA, and 2 days later Senator Hubert Humphrey (D-MN) introduced S. 1186, a companion bill. Serious debate ensued, with the manufacturers, pharmacists and their associations, and the FDA staking out positions on issues ranging from labeling and the ability of grocery and candy stores to sell proprietary medicines, to the question of what products were safe for self-medication. As the debate raged in the House and Senate the lay press paid little or no attention.[18] After numerous revisions and compromises, the Durham–Humphrey Bill was sent to President Truman for his signature in October 1951, with implementation set for April 1952. This landmark amendment and its resultant regulations established labeling requirements for manufacturers, defined the division between prescription and nonprescription products, and clearly allowed for both appropriate refill and telephone prescriptions.

Speaking about the legislation in 1964, Durham noted, "It is a good law; I do not believe that it is a perfect law. Furthermore, if I were in Congress today, and in a position to introduce this kind of legislation for the first

Congressman Durham awaits his address at the 1950 APhA annual meeting on his efforts to enact the Durham–Humphrey Amendment to the Food, Drug and Cosmetic Act.

time, I would introduce a more extensive bill. In other words, the Durham–Humphrey amendment was good as far as it went. In 1964 we can see that it didn't go far enough."[19]

Legislator

As Dean Beard had predicted in 1939, when Durham first went to Congress, his influence went far beyond that of pharmacy. He was appointed a member of the Joint Committee on Atomic Energy when it was formed in 1946. While he was an outspoken advocate for the development of atomic weapons, he also led the effort to develop peacetime uses of atomic energy. In 1957 Durham threw the switch to open the Atomic Energy Commission's Argonne National Laboratory boiling water reactor—the first in America. Always the pharmacist, Durham shared that the scientific training in pharmacy school prepared him for studying nuclear energy and predicted that it "will have a greater effect on drugs and medicines than any other development in history."[1]

In 1957, the *New York Times* described Durham as working mostly behind the scenes, infrequently taking the floor in the House and then speaking "with a drawl combined with clipped words that leave Yankee reporters unsure of their notes."[20] Again echoing Beard's prediction, the *Times* article added that he gained recognition for being independent, stubborn, or both.

THE PHARMACIST

Durham identified himself first and always as a pharmacist. Speaking at the North Carolina Pharmaceutical Association annual meeting in 1941, he began, "I am very proud of my profession as a druggist and I want you to know that I am first a druggist."[21] He repeated this sentiment years later in the *New York Times* when describing the prescription counter as a neighborhood gathering space where "folks bring their joys and their troubles. An eighteen-hour day becomes routine, plus calls in the night from mothers with ailing babies requiring syrups for coughs and croup."[20]

In 1943, APhA named Congressman Carl Durham an Honorary Member in appreciation for his leadership in passing the Pharmacy Corps Bill. In 1959, after enactment of the Durham–Humphrey Amendment, APhA cited him for distinguished service. In 1963, after he retired from Congress, Durham accepted an appointment to work with APhA as a special consultant on legislative matters. The following year he was elected APhA Honorary President. In his comments at the annual meeting he complimented the increased focus on pharmaceutical service and the role of the pharmacist as a member of the public health system. He added that increased authority results in increased responsibility and that pharmacists must prove their competency to both the Congress and the public. He concluded, "The best representative for pharmacy remains, as always, the practitioner back home who keeps himself informed about his profession….An informed, alert, articulate community pharmacist is the best representative our profession could ever have."[19]

LEGACY

Carl T. Durham died in Durham, N.C., on April 29, 1974. While not the first pharmacist in the national legislature, Carl Durham was the architect of two landmark pieces of twentieth century legislation of great importance for pharmacy—the Pharmacy Corps Bill and the Durham–Humphrey Amendment. While many individuals were part of the battle to gain military's recognition of the professional status of pharmacy and the benefits of pharmaceutical service, undoubtedly this North Carolina pharmacist and representative was the driving force who guided the bill through the legislature and gained presidential approval despite the military's objections. Today, pharmacists providing pharmaceutical services in the military are commissioned officers, recognized as professionals, largely because of the efforts of Durham.

FDA historian John Swann noted that the Durham–Humphrey Amendment "effected fundamental changes in the practice of pharmacy and in the self-medication habits of every American."[22] The bill clearly defined which medicines required prescriptions and which were safe for self-treatment. It also clarified everyday practice issues such as the ability to refill prescriptions and the ability to accept telephoned prescriptions.

The legacy of Representative Carl Durham continues to affect practice positively. His example of a pharmacist involved in public service fits well with the admonition of W. Paul Briggs, executive director of the American Foundation for Pharmaceutical Education: "The future place of pharmacy will certainly be a reflection of its value and integrity as a profession, but its comparative status will be determined by its effectiveness on the political stage."[23]

REFERENCES

1.   Pharmacist is Atomic Energy Committee head. *Drug Topics*. 1957;101(14):1.

2.   Sonnedecker G. *Kremers and Urdang's History of Pharmacy*. 3rd ed. Philadelphia: J.B. Lippincott; 1963:306.

3.   Candee MJ, ed. Durham, Carl Thomas. *Current Biography Yearbook*. New York: H.W. Wilson; 1957:162–4.

4.   Durham CT biographical information. Unpublished biographical Information for historical reference collection. American Institute for the History of Pharmacy Kremers Files A2; 1960.

5.   Report of F.W. Hancock, Board of Pharmacy. *Proc NC Pharm Assoc*. 1918(June): 115–7.

6.   Janssen W. From drug clerk to congress: the story of Carl T. Durham. *Am Druggist*. 1944;109:141–2,146–7,152.

7.   Graves L. Carl Thomas Durham. *Carolina J Pharm*. 1937;18:218.

8.   Graves L. Carl Durham. *Carolina J Pharm*. 1938;19:214b.

9.   Beard JG. Carl Durham to go to congress. *Carolina J Pharm*. 1938;19:214a–214b.

10. Beard JG. Man of the year. *Carolina J Pharm*. 1939;20:cover, 2.

11. Worthen DB. *Pharmacy in World War II*. Binghamton, N.Y.: Haworth Press; 2004:191.

12. Kendig EH. Report of the committee on the status of pharmacists in the government service. *J Am Pharm Assoc, Sci Ed*. 1942;31:393–9.

13. A bill to amend the National Defense Act by providing for a Pharmacy Corps in the Medical Department, United States Army: Hearings on HR 7432 before the Committee on Military Affairs, 77th Cong., second sess. (1942).

14. A bill to amend certain Provisions of the National Defense Act of June 3, 1916, as Amended, Relating to the Medical Department of the Regular Army. Hearings on HR 997 before the Committee on Military Affairs, 78th Cong., first sess. (1943).

15. Einbeck AH. Report of the Committee on the Status of Pharmacists in the Government Services. *J Am Pharm Assoc, Sci Ed*. 1945;34:382.

16. Temin P. *Taking Your Medicine: Drug Regulation in the United States*. Cambridge, Mass: Harvard University Press; 1980:47.

17. *Scope of FDCA Congress and the Nation 1945–1964: A Review of Government and Politics in the Postwar Years*. Washington, D.C.: Congressional Quarterly Service; 1965(1):1170.

18. Pray S. *A History of Nonprescription Product Regulation*. Binghamton, N.Y.: Haworth Press; 2003:141.

19. Durham CT. An appropriate time for legislative review. *J Am Pharm Assoc*. 1964;NS4:534–6.

20. Nuclear pharmacist: Carl Thomas Durham. *New York Times*. February 20, 1957:19.

21. Durham CT. Proceedings of the sixty-second annual meeting. *Carolina J Pharm*. 1941;22:186–7.

22. Swann JP. FDA and the practice of pharmacy: prescription drug regulation before the Durham–Humphrey Amendment of 1951. *Pharm Hist*. 1994;36:55–70.

23. Briggs WP. Pharmacy must train men in the science of politics. *Am Professional Pharm.* 1962;28:53–8.

Albert Ethelbert Ebert (1840-1906):
Founder of American Pharmacy's Oldest Award

In a memorial booklet published after Albert Ethelbert Ebert's death in 1906, pharmacy colleagues shared memories of the man who was variously called the "Nestor of American Pharmacy" and the "Plumed Knight of American Pharmacy."[1] Statements from colleagues in retail practice, educators, editors, and others reiterated the theme that Ebert had been a force to be reckoned with. The man was an outspoken and relentless champion of the professional aspects of pharmacy and decried what he thought was the increased commercialism of pharmacy and the extremes in educational requirements.

BEGINNINGS

Albert Ethelbert Ebert was born in Bavaria, Germany, on December 23, 1840. His parents emigrated to the United States in 1841 and settled in Chicago, where his father worked as a horticulturist and gardener. Ebert attended schools in Chicago until 1853, when he began an apprenticeship with F. Scammon & Co. After 4 years he began a second apprenticeship with Henry Bronold to learn pharmacy in the German tradition, which focused more on compounding than on selling ready-made remedies. After 2 years he returned to his first shop, now called Sargent and Ilsey, and managed the retail department until 1861. From 1861 to 1863 he was employed in the shop of F. Mahla.

When the Chicago College of Pharmacy opened in 1859, Ebert enrolled and attended lectures until the college suspended operations in 1861 due to the outbreak of the Civil War. In 1863 he left Chicago for Philadelphia, where he enrolled in the Philadelphia College of Pharmacy. During his sojourn in Philadelphia he worked with Edward Parrish, who was providing classes in pharmacy to medical students from the University of Pennsylvania. Ebert graduated from the college at the head of his class in 1864 and returned to Chicago to manage Sargent's shop. Deeply dissatisfied with his education,

Ebert enrolled at the University of Munich in 1867, studying chemistry under the tutelage of Professor Justus von Liebig, a chemist of international renown, and earned a PhD. Ebert made much of his opportunities to travel while abroad; he accompanied William Procter, Jr., to the International Pharmaceutical Congress in Paris in 1867 and the two continued their journey by visiting Switzerland, Germany, and other parts of France. Ebert also represented the American Pharmaceutical Association (APhA; now American Pharmacists Association) at the British Pharmaceutical Conference in Scotland and was made an honorary member of the Conference.[2] During these travels Ebert met and became friends with many of the leading pharmacists of the day, including John Attfield, professor of practical chemistry with the British Pharmaceutical Society. When Ebert returned to Chicago to open his own drugstore, he was more highly educated than most of his peers.

In 1871, Ebert married May L. Whiteley. Obituary materials are inconsistent with regard to the number of children the couple had. One reference notes that there was only one child, who had died before the deaths of each parent.[3] Another reference notes that a foster daughter survived her father.[4]

CHICAGO COLLEGE OF PHARMACY

On his return from Europe, Albert Ebert quickly renewed his relationship with the Chicago College of Pharmacy. From 1869 until 1876 he was a co-editor and frequent contributor to *The Pharmacist*, the college's publication. On October 8, 1871, the college was destroyed during the Great Chicago Fire. Ebert immediately contacted his European friends, including John Attfield, asking for help in rebuilding the college. In September 1872, the college reopened with 34 students.[5]

The college faced increasing economic pressures in the decades after the fire; by the 1890s its ability to survive was in doubt. Early efforts to affiliate with a state institution had been unsuccessful; Ebert and others were opposed to establishing a proprietary school. Finally, in 1896, Ebert was actively engaged in the transfer of the Chicago College of Pharmacy to the University of Illinois.[6] He remained involved with the college in an advisory capacity for the rest of his life.

WORK

Ebert opened his first drugstore when he returned from Europe in 1868, operating it until 1877 when he retired after making a "fortune."[7] He turned his attention to the manufacture of grape sugar and glucose, using a process that he invented. He opened plants in several cities and was very successful until the bottom fell out of the market.[5] He returned to the practice of retail pharmacy in Chicago in 1883.

Ever the scientist, Ebert approached his practice with an eye for the scientific method. In 1885 he undertook a prescription survey to determine what items were prescribed by physicians in Illinois. One third of the more than 15,000 prescriptions analyzed were from his store. This work was the

This portrait photograph of Albert Ethelbert Ebert was taken in 1872 during his term of office as APhA president, shortly after he had returned from Europe and opened his own pharmacy in Chicago.

first of a number of prescription ingredient surveys that were used in the revisions of the *United States Pharmacopeia (USP)*.[8] In 1896, Ebert, with A. Emil Hiss, a fellow Chicago pharmacist and member of the Chicago College of Pharmacy faculty, published *The Standard Formulary: a collection of over four thousand formulas for pharmaceutical preparations, family remedies, toilet articles, veterinary remedies, soda fountain requisites, and miscellaneous preparations, especially adapted to the requirements of retail druggists.* While long, the subtitle provides an excellent description of Ebert's application of the science and art of chemistry and pharmacy to the drugstore setting. By the time of Ebert's death the book had gone through 16 editions and been expanded to nearly 5,000 formulas.

ASSOCIATIONS

Albert Ebert joined the American Pharmaceutical Association in 1864 and presented his first scientific paper at the 1865 meeting. Always candid, he was engaged in the work of the Association as noted in a report that he delivered at the 1870 annual meeting: "There is a committee on Unofficial Formulas [those approved by USP or the Committee on Revision and therefore expected to be stocked in fully equipped pharmacies], consisting of Mr. Markoe, Moore, and myself. The Committee has failed to make any report for two years. I do not wish to be on a committee that is not going to do any work. If the Chairman of that Committee cannot do the work that is assigned to him, he had better resign. We come here every year without a report, and it is the fault of the chairman of the Committee."[9]

Ebert was elected vice president of APhA in 1868 and was president in 1872–73. During his presidential address he noted that European organizations presented awards for work of special merit and suggested the establishment of a suitable prize for the best pharmacy essay. In an 1873 letter addressed to the Association, Ebert provided a check for $500 with the stipulation that it be used "for conferring a suitable prize for the best essay or written contribution, containing an original investigation of a medicinal substance, determining new properties or containing other meritorious contributions to knowledge, or for improved methods of determined merit for the preparation of chemical or pharmacal products."[10]

Ebert had a very clear vision of his ideals for APhA: the organization existed to hold an annual meeting. As a consequence of this belief, he was opposed to APhA's taking on sponsorship of the *National Formulary* (*NF*) since it meant that the association would have to incorporate so that it could obtain a copyright. Subsequently Ebert reconsidered and offered the motion that opened the process for APhA's sponsorship of the *NF*.[11] Ebert served on many standing and special committees for APhA after his presidency. His scientific expertise and experience made him the ideal representative to see to pharmacy's interests in the nation's capital.

The Illinois Pharmaceutical Association, formed in 1880, elected Ebert an honorary member in 1883. He became an active leader, frequently representing the needs of the profession in Springfield. In reviewing Ebert's activities of the period, pharmacy historians Weinstein and Mrtek report Ebert's continuing efforts to practice retail pharmacy ethically and to eschew internecine bickering. His position was clear: pharmacists must solve pharmacy's problems.[5] In 1885 Ebert was appointed to a 5-year term on the Illinois State Board of Pharmacy.

In 1870, shortly after his return from Europe as a new PhD, Ebert was selected to join the USP Committee on Revision. Still largely under the control of physicians, the 1870 convention established an important precedent "to investigate any new medicine that may be brought forward, and to devise formulas for the appropriate preparations of it, and to publish such formulas, and that the formulas shall thenceforward be considered officinal."[12] He served

In 1873 Ebert made a grant to APhA to establish a prize for the "best essay on a medicinal substance." This medal depicting Ebert has since been awarded to more than 200 pharmaceutical scientists from 1874 to 2004.

as the fourth vice president of the convention in 1890. The USP underwent a major reorganization in 1900 with the establishment of a Board of Trustees whose first task was to incorporate the convention. Albert Ebert was elected as one of the first trustees. The regard of the Board of Trustees after his death was demonstrated by a gift of a large framed portrait of Ebert to all of the member colleges of the American Conference of Pharmaceutical Faculties (now the American Association of Colleges of Pharmacy).[13]

Historian

In the late 1890s the Chicago Historical Society arranged for Ebert to collect the history of pharmacy in Chicago as part of a project to document the professions and trades of the city. This project led to the formation of the Chicago Veteran Druggists' Association (CVDA) in 1898.[14] The original members of CVDA were those individuals who were in business before the 1871 fire. An objective that Ebert shared with Edward Kremers of the University of Wisconsin was "recording the history of the drug trade and profession of early Chicago."[15]

Enthused by his work on Chicago pharmacy, Ebert determined that an account of the profession should be prepared for the entire country. To that end he recruited Kremers and John Uri Lloyd of Cincinnati to develop a proposal, to be presented at the 1902 annual meeting, for the establishment of a committee on history as part of the official APhA structure. The original purpose was to hold an annual meeting of the section in conjunction with the APhA annual meeting.[16]

Ebert pushed to have Kremers appointed as the historian of the new section when APhA established it in 1905.[17] Ebert also was instrumental in the development of what became the Kremers Reference Files at the University of Wisconsin by contributing much of his own collection of letters and other papers. It was Kremers who would later team up with the German historian George Urdang to author *History of Pharmacy*, and the Reference Files was an important data source for the book.[18] In 1941 the American Institute of the History of Pharmacy was formed, eventually absorbing the Section on Historical Pharmacy.

THE MAN AND HIS LEGACY

Joseph Remington described Ebert in his student days at the Philadelphia College of Pharmacy as a "short, rosy-cheeked young man, with an interesting face, bright, intelligent eyes and a budding mustache and beard....as brave as a lion and as tender hearted as a loving woman."[19] In a different forum Remington reminisced that Ebert was "frank, almost to brusqueness, picturesque in appearance, earnest in debate, strong in his convictions, he was a power that had to be reckoned with."[20] Others remembered him for his "absolute sincerity and helpful disposition," as a "champion of true pharmacy," "idealistic," an "indefatigable worker for the betterment of pharmacy."[21] Henry Whelpley, a past president of APhA, noted that Ebert was a force behind the scenes, generating great influence on the selection of Association officers while always focusing on what he believed to be in the best interest of pharmacy. Ebert can be easily identified in pictures of the period by his ever-lengthening, ever-bushy beard.

Albert Ethelbert Ebert died on November 20, 1906, in Chicago. His reported last words were "The American Pharmaceutical Association, it was my life; it gave me a profession."[22] His wife preceded him in death; he bequeathed most of his assets to the Association.

Ebert's sense of history, science, and practice continue to be part of his legacy. In writing about his old friend, Edward Kremers identified one of the great legacies of Albert Ebert as his being "the only man connected with American pharmacy who has shown enough love for his profession to endow a fund for the stimulation of scientific research."[23] The Ebert Prize continues as the longest presented award of APhA. Ebert's legacy also lives in the Kremers Reference Files of the American Institute of the History of Pharmacy and in the Institute itself.

REFERENCES

1. *In Memoriam Albert Ethelbert Ebert*. Washington, D.C.: American Pharmaceutical Association; 1907.

2. Albert E. Ebert. Chicago Veterans Druggists Association 5th Anniversary. 1904;5:41–7.

3. Albert E. Ebert Funeral. *Meyer Brothers Druggist*. 1906;27:392.

4. Lewis ER. *Prairie State Pharmacy*. Chicago: Illinois Pharmacists Association; 1980:123.

5. Weinstein MM, Mrtek RG. Albert Ebert speaks today. *J Am Pharm Assoc*. 1971;NS11:664–9.

6. Mrtek RG, King CD. *One Hundred and Twenty-Five Years of Pharmaceutical Education*. Chicago, Ill.: University of Illinois at Chicago; 1984.

7. Biographical Sketch. *In Memoriam Albert Ethelbert Ebert*. Washington, D.C.: American Pharmaceutical Association; 1907:11.

8. Gathercoal EN, ed. *The Prescription Ingredient Survey*. Washington, D.C.: American Pharmaceutical Association; 1933.

9. Ebert AE. Minutes of the 18th Annual Meeting. *Proc Am Pharm Assoc*. 1870;18:63.

10. Ebert AE. To the American Pharmaceutical Association [letter]. *Proc Am Pharm Assoc*. 1873;21:58–9.

11. Anderson L, Higby GJ. *The Spirit of Voluntarism: A Legacy of Commitment and Contribution —the United States Pharmacopoeia 1820–1995*. Rockville, Md.: United States Pharmacoepeial Convention; 1995:152–3.

12. As quoted in: Anderson L, Higby GJ. *The Spirit of Voluntarism: A Legacy of Commitment and Contribution —the United States Pharmacopoeia 1820–1995*. Rockville, Md.: United States Pharmacopeial Convention; 1995:101.

13. Jamieson TN. Address at Ebert memorial dedication. *Am Pharm Assoc Bull*. 1909:4:167–9.

14. Mr. Albert E. Ebert. *Bull Pharm*. 1906;20:514–6.

15. As quoted in: Weinstein MM, Mrtek RG. My dear professor Kremers: the Ebert letters. *Pharm Hist*. 1971;13:77–88.

16. Fourth session of the council September 9, 1902. *Proc Am Pharm Assoc*. 1902;50:44–5.

17. Minutes on the section of historical pharmacy. *Proc Am Pharm Assoc*. 1905;53:86–102.

18. Weinstein MM, Mrtek RG. My dear professor Kremers: the Ebert letters. *Pharm Hist*. 1971;13:77–88.

19. Remington JP. The "plumed knight of pharmacy." *In Memoriam Albert Ethelbert Ebert*. Washington, D.C.: American Pharmaceutical Association; 1907:25–6.

20. Remington JP. Albert Ethelbert Ebert. *Meyer Brothers Druggist*. 1906;27:385.

21. Albert Ethelbert Ebert. *Meyer Brothers Druggist*. 1906;27:380–5.

22. Albert Ethelbert Ebert. *J Am Pharm Assoc*. 1918;7:753.

23. Kremers E. Albert E. Ebert. *In Memoriam Albert Ethelbert Ebert*. Washington, D.C.: American Pharmaceutical Association; 1907:59–60.

Robert Phillip Fischelis (1891–1981):
Pharmacy Activist

In a career that spanned seven decades, Robert P. Fischelis was a pharmacist, educator, dean, association executive, and editor. In addition, he served in the military and the U.S. Public Health Service and as an administrator in the War Production Board during World War II. With his array of experiences, Robert Fischelis's broad perspective of the profession led to a clear vision of the responsibilities and potential for a profession undergoing significant change. Many would argue that it was frequently Fischelis himself who was the change agent. In speaking at Fischelis's funeral in 1981, Glenn Sonnedecker, then director of the American Institute of the History of Pharmacy, noted that while Fischelis was an idealist, "his was no ivory-tower dream of a better society or better health system, however, but a goal toward which one worked, and expected others to work, in a dedicated, persistent, and tough-minded way. He was a bold thinker, who knew where he stood, and was ready to fight for what he thought the American pharmacist should represent."[1]

BEGINNINGS

Robert Phillip Fischelis was born in Philadelphia on August 16, 1891; his parents Phillip and Ernestine (Kempt) Fischelis immigrated from Germany. His father was a medical doctor who taught at the Temple University School of Dentistry.[2] Robert received his early education in Lutheran schools and graduated from the Northeast High School in 1908. He immediately went to work for James Huston, a prescription pharmacist in Philadelphia, and entered the Medico-Chirurgical College Department of Pharmacy, graduating first in his class in 1911 with a graduate in pharmacy degree. He continued his courses, subsequently earning a pharmaceutical chemist's degree in 1912 and a doctor of pharmacy degree in 1913. He also took chemistry classes at Temple University and earned a bachelor of science in 1912. In 1913 he received a master of pharmacy from the Philadelphia College of Pharmacy.

In 1919 Robert Fischelis married Juanita Deer of Chicago. The couple had no children. Robert P. Fischelis died on October 14, 1981, in Ada, Ohio.

EDUCATOR

Robert Fischelis started his academic career at the Medico-Chirurgical College Department of Pharmacy in 1912, where he taught pharmacy, pharmaceutical arithmetic, and organic chemistry.[3] Fischelis continued as a full-time lecturer on commercial pharmacy until 1914, when he resigned to join the editorial staff of *Druggists Circular*. He then accepted a part-time lectureship until the department merged with the Philadelphia College of Pharmacy (PCP) in 1916. He continued teaching part-time at PCP until 1921.

In 1921 the New Jersey College of Pharmacy recruited Robert Fischelis as dean. The college, then a proprietary institution, was having difficulties with accreditation. The New Jersey Board of Pharmacy was increasingly reluctant to accredit the college and the New York Board refused to recognize it. Trustees of the college, seeing membership in the American Conference of Pharmaceutical Faculties (ACPF) as the principal way to gain national standing, applied for membership but were rejected. The college needed a "vigorous, competent, knowledgeable, and influential personality" to take on the management of the college if it was to be saved; Robert Fischelis met the search criteria.[4] Fischelis' first objective was to address the shortcomings in the faculty, facilities, and curriculum in order to gain accreditation. He wrote

1929 photograph of Robert P. Fischelis during his term as New Jersey Pharmaceutical Association secretary, 1926–1929 and New Jersey Board of Pharmacy member, 1926–1944.

to Rufus Lyman, dean at the University of Nebraska College of Pharmacy and chair of the ACPF executive committee, dedicating himself to doing anything necessary to gain accreditation. The college immediately hired two full-time faculty, dismissed part-time teachers, and changed the curriculum to comply with the Pharmaceutical Syllabus. In 1923 the college was accepted for membership in ACPF and accredited.[5] Fischelis also led the initiative to affiliate the proprietary college with Rutgers, the State University of New Jersey. While the university was favorable to the transfer, the college's location in Newark and other administrative difficulties were impediments; the affiliation was not successful. Fischelis, leading the drive for the new pharmacy building in Newark, was successful in gaining the trustees' agreement and securing the necessary funding. However, the trustees ignored the space requirements for the enlarged curriculum. In a conflict between the trustees and the faculty, Fischelis resigned in 1925 along with a number of his faculty.[6]

In 1963, at the age of 72, Fischelis was again invited to accept a deanship by a college having accreditation difficulties. He joined the College of Pharmacy at Ohio Northern University in Ada, Ohio. Writing to the alumni in 1964, Fischelis noted that the college had suffered from understaffing and lack of financial resources. He also noted that the university was determined to do what it needed to ensure that the pharmacy program remained a prominent part of the university.[7] The first focus for the Fischelis administration was on revising the curriculum, recruiting qualified faculty, and erecting a new building. In addition, Fischelis articulated the need to provide opportunities for lifelong learning to alumni and championed the establishment of a separate and fully functioning Pharmacy Continuation Study Center. In 1966 he retired as dean but remained an active part of the college until his death in 1981.

EDITOR/AUTHOR

In 1914 Fischelis became the associate editor for *Druggists Circular*, working under Henry V. Arny, who was also the dean of the Columbia College of Pharmacy and chair of the New York Branch of the American Pharmaceutical (now Pharmacists) Association (APhA).[8] *Druggists Circular* was one of only a few national monthly pharmacy publications of the period.[9] In 1916 Fischelis joined the H.K. Mulford Company, a major manufacturer of pharmaceuticals and vaccines, where he wrote and distributed product literature. In 1918 he resigned to enlist in the U.S. Army Chemical Warfare Service.[2]

Largely in response to the negative perception of pharmacy by the military and others, the American Association of Colleges of Pharmacy (AACP) gained financial support from the Commonwealth Fund to perform an in-depth study of pharmacy. W.W. Charters of the University of Pittsburgh, an educational specialist in the area of curricular design, chaired the study. Published in 1927, *Basic Material for a Pharmaceutical Curriculum* (widely known as the Charters Study) concluded that pharmacy was indeed a profession and provided the basis for the 4-year bachelor of science degree requirement.[10] Robert Fischelis served on the staff of the study; his role in the revision of the manuscript and other valuable services was acknowledged.[11]

In 1927 the Committee on the Cost of Medical Care was established to study the impact of sickness and the organizations that manage its treatment; Fischelis was the committee's staff pharmacist. Funded by a number of foundations, a series of studies looked at component parts of the health care system. C. Rufus Rorem, an economist, and Robert Fischelis took on the study of the complex professional and commercial interests involved in the manufacture and distribution of medicines. This was an important public problem, he wrote, "because so many people, prone to self-diagnosis and self-treatment of real or imaginary ills, are easily influenced by the appeal of advertised 'patent' and proprietary medicines."[12] The series of studies became important data elements in the subsequent development of insurance and health care schemes.

Fischelis was a skilled editor and eager communicator. During much of his career he grasped opportunities for part-time editorships and writing assignments. In 1918 Fischelis was the founding editor of *Pennsylvania Pharmacist*, the journal of the Pennsylvania Pharmaceutical Association, as well as the *New Jersey Journal of Pharmacy* in 1928. From 1920 until 1927, Fischelis held editorial positions with the American Chemical Society, first on the *Journal of Industrial and Engineering Chemistry* and later with *Chemical and Engineering News*. In 1936 he assisted H.V. Arny in the revision of the fourth edition of *Principles of Pharmacy*. He also served as the editor of the *Journal of the American Pharmaceutical Association, Practical Pharmacy Edition*, for a number of years and contributed columns designed to put the readers into closer contact with the activities and concerns of the national association. In 1967 he joined Don Francke's new journal, then titled *Drug Intelligence*, and wrote about professional issues. His inaugural essay decried the impersonal delivery of health care and noted that hospital pharmacists were in a unique position to be heard by both patients and decision makers.[13]

GOVERNMENT SERVICE

Through his long career, Fischelis served in a number of governmental and regulatory capacities starting with his service as a sergeant in the U.S. Army Chemical Warfare Service during World War I. In 1926 he accepted the role as secretary and chief chemist of the New Jersey Board of Pharmacy, serving until 1944. In this role, fresh from his experience with the New Jersey College of Pharmacy, he challenged the practice of the boards of pharmacy accepting any college that had membership in AACP. The basis for this position was the lack of any mechanism to ensure that standards were maintained once a college secured membership. He suggested the need for a survey to assess the standards of educational institutions; as a consequence, the National Association of Boards of Pharmacy (NABP) invited Fischelis to prepare a plan for the study that was to become the Charters Study.[14]

It was also during his time at the New Jersey Board that Fischelis was invited to join Donald Nelson's staff at the War Production Board's Office of Civilian Requirements in the early days of World War II, where he assumed the directorship of the Division of Chemicals, Drugs, and Health Supplies. The division was charged with oversight of all medical supplies needed to keep the population healthy, especially the production workers who were vital to the war effort. Fischelis recruited a number of young pharmacists to work with him, including Frederick V. Stock, a Purdue pharmacy graduate on loan from Walgreens, who served as the section head for drugs and cosmetics. Another was John N. McDonnell, a Philadelphia College of Pharmacy graduate who managed the distribution of penicillin to the civilian marketplace.

Long an advocate of the public health role for the pharmacist, Fischelis was commissioned an officer in the U.S. Public Health Service after World

The year after Fischelis became APhA secretary in 1944, he presented the first of his many annual reports at APhA conventions on the status of APhA membership.

War II. He also served as a consultant to the Navy's Bureau of Medicine and Surgery and the Army's Medical Service Corps.

ASSOCIATION EXECUTIVE

Robert Fischelis was a professional association activist, both as an individual member and as a staff person. He joined the Pennsylvania Pharmaceutical Association in 1916 and was immediately elected secretary. He was president in 1919–1920. Upon his move to New Jersey he joined the New Jersey Pharmaceutical Association, serving as its secretary from 1916 to 1929 and as president from 1942 to 1945. As part of his activities in the New Jersey College of Pharmacy and the Board of Pharmacy, he joined and was active both as a member and officer of the national associations AACP and NABP.

Robert Fischelis joined APhA upon his graduation in 1911. He was active in a number of committees and groups, serving as the secretary of the Philadelphia Branch of APhA and president of the New York Branch.[15] He was also elected to the APhA Council, vice president, and finally president in 1934–1935.

As early as 1920, Fischelis was deeply concerned with the issue of the commercialization of pharmacy. He saw the increasing dependence on soda fountains, the sale of alcohol, and merchandizing in lieu of compounding and patient service as threats to the profession. In his presidential address to the Pennsylvania Pharmaceutical Association he issued the call to "adopt all necessary precautions to keep the stigma of the booze traffic forever from the escutcheon of pharmacy."[16] He returned to a similar theme during his address as APhA president-elect in 1934, arguing that the public would pay adequately for pharmacy's service only when it filled a public need, concluding that "pharmacy is not a thing conceived to please pharmacists. It is a thing with which pharmacists must please mankind in general."[17] In the wake of the passage of the Selective Training and Service Act in 1940 there was an outcry about the shortage of pharmacists. Fischelis once again took the opportunity to point out that the real problem was the inappropriate use of pharmacists in stores that were anything but a professional venue for health care. He argued that there may be "fewer so called drug stores but more than enough pharmacies where the men and women…will be given an opportunity to practice the profession for which they were schooled."[18]

In 1945 Robert Fischelis was elected to succeed E.F. Kelly as the secretary and general manager of APhA, a position he held until he retired in 1959. During this period Fischelis was involved in every aspect of pharmacy. He served as a consultant to the Pharmaceutical Survey conducted by Edward C. Elliott, which presaged the transition to the 6-year entry-level professional degree, the PharmD, a half century later. He was also an influential advocate for educational standards as a requisite for recognition of professional status for pharmacists in the Veterans Administration under Civil Service.[19]

Fischelis was also interested in the history of the profession. Just before his death in 1981 he and his wife established a major bequest to the American Institute of the History of Pharmacy to showcase "the accomplishments and issues of American pharmacy." The original gift of $25,000 was followed by a bequest of $900,000 after Mrs. Fischelis' death.[20]

LEGACY

Robert P. Fischelis clearly was capable of multitasking; no facet of pharmacy escaped his touch. He received the honors of his profession, including honorary degrees from the University of Connecticut, Rutgers, Philadelphia College of Pharmacy, and Ohio Northern. He was the recipient of the highest honors of a number of national pharmacy organizations, including the Remington Medal, the Harvey A.K. Whitney Lecture Award of the American Society of Health-System Pharmacists, and the Lascoff Award given by the American College of Apothecaries. He was named the honorary president of NABP. A news item in *Pharmacy in History* noted, "Probably it is the diversity of the Fischelis contribution to pharmacy and medical care that has made his career so remarkable, and the force of his personality that has made his contribution so widely influential."[21]

Throughout his public life, Fischelis returned time and again to the theme of professional standards—whether they be of education, regulation, or practice—and public service. In his 1943 Remington Medal address he noted the need for the profession to be prepared to play a role in the changing environment of health care, adding that the responsibility of pharmacy to serve certainly was as great as that of medicine. He optimistically observed that "the American public may expect from our profession in the future, as in the days of Remington, responsible, enlightened, and effective service in its behalf."[22]

REFERENCES

1. Sonnedecker G, statement at the funeral service for Robert P. Fischelis, Sunday, October 18, 1981 (unpublished manuscript), University Archives, Heterick Memorial Library, Ohio Northern University.

2. Register of Robert P. Fischelis Papers, 1891–1981. Madison, Wisconsin Historical Society. Accessed at http://digicoll. library.wisc.edu/cgi-bin/ead-idx?type=simple;c=shs;view=text;su bview=fulltext;q1=fischelis;rgn1=Collection%20Title;id=uw-whs-mss00619; rgn=item, January 6, 2006.

3. England J. *The First Century of the Philadelphia College of Pharmacy.* Philadelphia: Philadelphia College of Pharmacy and Science; 1921:427–8.

4. Bowers RA, Cowen DL. *The Rutgers University College of Pharmacy: A Centennial History.* New Brunswick, N.J.: Rutgers University Press; 1991:39, 41f.

5. Albert K. Inventory to the records of the New Jersey College of Pharmacy, 1892–1942, Special Collections and University Archives, Rutgers University Libraries, 1994. Accessed at http://www2.scc.rutgers.edu/ead/, January 6, 2006.

6. Bowers RA, Cowen DL. *The Rutgers University College of Pharmacy: A Centennial History.* New Brunswick, N.J.: Rutgers University Press; 1991:39–49.

7. Fischelis R. Report of the dean college of pharmacy Ohio Northern University, 1984, 8 pp. University Archives, Heterick Memorial Library, Ohio Northern University.

8. Wimmer CP. *The College of Pharmacy of the City of New York Included in Columbia University in 1904.* New York: Curt P. Wimmer; 1929:277.

9. The masthead for *Druggists Circular* in 1914 has the tagline "a practical journal of pharmacy and general business organ for druggists."

10. Buerki RA. In search of excellence: the first century of the American Association of Colleges of Pharmacy. *Am J Pharm Educ.* 1999;63(suppl):109.

11. Charters WW, Lemon AB, Monell LM. *Basic Material for a Pharmaceutical Curriculum.* New York: McGraw Hill Book Co.; 1927:xiii.

12. Rorem CR, Fischelis RP. *The Costs of Medicines.* Chicago: University of Chicago Press; 1932: v.

13. Fischelis RP. Sensitivity to the needs of patients. *Drug Intell.* 1967;1:28–9.

14. Buerki RA. In search of excellence: the first century of the American Association of Colleges of Pharmacy. *Am J Pharm Educ.* 1999;63(suppl):57.

15. Anonymous. Robert Philip [sic] Fischelis. *J Am Pharm Assoc.* 1934;23:85–7.

16. Fischelis RP. Presidential address. *Proc Pennsylvania Pharm Assoc.* 1920; 43rd annual meeting:92–102.

17. Fischelis RP. Pharmacy in our changing era. *J Am Pharm Assoc.* 1934;23:274–6.

18. Fischelis RP. The shortage (?) of pharmacists. *New Jersey J Pharm.* 1941;14:6–7.

19. Worthen DB. *Pharmacy in World War II.* Binghamton, N.Y.: Haworth Press; 2004:186–8.

20. Sonnedecker G. Juanita Deer Fischelis, benefactor of AIHP, 1896–1983. *Pharm Hist.* 1983;25:163.

21. Anonymous. New AIHP projects funded on 90th birthday of Robert P. Fischelis. *Pharm Hist.* 1981;23:143–4.

22. Fischelis RP. Higher professional standards. In: Griffenhagen GB, Bowles GC, Penna RP, Worthen DB. *Reflections on Pharmacy by the Remington Medalists 1919–2003.* Washington, D.C.: American Pharmacists Association; 2004:123–7.

Donald Eugene Francke (1910–1978): "Reformer by Nature, Doer by Necessity"

In one of the tributes to Donald Eugene Francke published by the American Society of Hospital Pharmacists (ASHP), Don Brodie wrote, "Don Francke's impact on the lives of others may not have been due to a single strength or combinations of strengths but to the fact that he was an achiever—he made things happen—he was a doer."[1] Brodie, an acknowledged leader in the clinical pharmacy movement, lauded Francke as an early visionary of a more patient-focused profession.*

Francke was a practicing pharmacist, an editor, an educator, an association leader, and an advocate for American participation in international pharmacy. Sonnedecker[2] called Francke a "reformer by nature, a doer by necessity," and Francke's "doing" brought him virtually every honor pharmacy can bestow on one of its own, including the J. Leon Lascoff Memorial Award (1948) from the American College of Apothecaries, the Harvey A.K. Whitney Award (1953) from ASHP, and the Remington Honor Medal (1970) from the American Pharmaceutical Association (APhA). In 1973 ASHP established the Donald E. Francke Medal to honor individuals for significant contributions to international hospital pharmacy.

Donald Francke was born in Athens, Pa., on August 28, 1910, to Edward Owen Francke, a pharmacist, and Margaret Carmalita (Kinney) Francke. The young Francke spent time in his father's pharmacy before leaving for the University of Michigan (UM) in Ann Arbor, from which he graduated with a BS in pharmacy in 1936. He worked at the University Hospital pharmacy under Harvey A.K. Whitney until moving on to graduate school at Purdue University in 1938. Francke earned a master's degree in pharmaceutical chemistry from UM in 1948. In 1951 Purdue conferred an honorary doctorate on Francke; this was followed by a second honorary doctorate from UM in 1967.

---

* Much of the biographical information on Francke was found in a series of tributes by colleagues and family published in the *American Journal of Hospital Pharmacy* 1979;36:459–91.

Donald Francke was elected chairman of the American Society of Hospital Pharmacists in 1944, two years after the society was established. Shown here are (left to right) secretary Thomas Reamer, vice chair Hazel Landeen, Francke, and treasurer Sister Mary John.

Don Francke died on November 6, 1978, in Washington, D.C. He was married first to Maxine Hafey; they had five children—three girls and two boys. He later married Gloria Niemeyer, a pharmacy leader in her own right.

HOSPITAL PHARMACIST

Francke was the director of pharmacy services at the UM Medical Center, where he replaced Whitney, from 1944 until 1963. He served as the secretary of the pharmacy and therapeutics committee during his entire tenure at the hospital and was also responsible for the hospital formulary.

As important as his services were to the university, they were every bit as important to the broader hospital pharmacy community. From 1949 through 1955, while still working at UM, he served as the unpaid director of APhA's Division of Hospital Pharmacy. During this period he headed a study project for the U.S. Public Health Service (PHS) to develop a national audit of pharmacy services in hospitals. This survey elicited information from over 3,600 hospitals, and its results helped PHS examine what pharmacists were doing and how they were doing it. The collection of information on issues such as satisfaction with the current state of pharmacy and pharmacy services and types of services provided led to a series of recommendations that included training and education for hospital pharmacists and the need for pharmacy to fulfill its mission as a public health service. Published as the *Mirror to Hospital Pharmacy* in 1963, the survey results provided a basis for examining what the professional roles for the hospital pharmacist might be in the future.[3]

EDITOR

Francke was one of the most active editors in pharmacy. Although he was involved earlier, his name first appears as an editor of the *Bulletin of the American Society of Hospital Pharmacy* in 1945.[4] In 1958 the publication's title was changed to the *American Journal of Hospital Pharmacy (AJHP)*. Although Francke remained as the editor until 1966, his focus was on more than simply editing a society's journal; he was intent on creating a range of information resources that would support the professional activities of institutional pharmacists.

In the early 1950s Francke conceived of a model hospital formulary and a service to provide access to international pharmacy literature. The first project came to fruition in 1963 as the *American Hospital Formulary Service*. This

Donald Francke (right) was installed as American Pharmaceutical Association president by retiring president Henry H. Gregg at the APhA centennial convention held in Philadelphia, August 1952.

In 1963 Donald Francke and collaborator Gloria Niemeyer Francke proudly displayed a bound copy of Mirror to Hospital Pharmacy, *a survey whose results provided a basis for examining the professional roles of hospital pharmacists.*

was followed a year later by the introduction of *International Pharmacy Abstracts.*[5] Francke served as editor for both of these publications through 1966. In 1966 he became the founding editor of the *Drug Information Bulletin* for the newly formed Drug Information Association.

In 1967 Francke launched a new journal, *Drug Intelligence*, that was international in scope and independent of any specific association. In his opening editorial, he noted that the publication's focus would be on professional problems and "restricted only by the Editor's own conscience and principles. *Drug Intelligence* will strive to produce 'food for professional growth, not weeds for professional narcosis.'"[6] In fact, the focus quickly came to rest on the emerging concept of clinical pharmacy, and in 1969 the journal's title was expanded to *Drug Intelligence and Clinical Pharmacy.*[7] Francke did not just provide a platform for extolling the advancement of the profession; he was a leader in articulating what its future should be.

EDUCATOR

Francke held a faculty appointment at the UM College of Pharmacy from 1948 through 1963, when he left Ann Arbor to join the ASHP staff in Washington,

D.C. In 1967 he returned to academia when the University of Cincinnati College of Pharmacy recruited him to be a professor in and the chairman of the Department of Hospital Pharmacy and the director of pharmacy services at the University of Cincinnati Medical Center. The University of Cincinnati's was the first academic hospital pharmacy department in the United States, and this appointment gave Francke the opportunity to develop his concept of training for institutional practice in both the classroom and hospital. One of the early successes of Francke's vision of combining didactic and practical hospital pharmacy education into a clinical pharmacy program was the establishment of one of the early post-BS PharmD programs in 1968.[8]

INTERNATIONAL PHARMACY
Francke's first involvement with international pharmacy came in 1949, when Gen. Douglas MacArthur invited an APhA team to visit Japan to help with postwar reconstruction. Francke spent 4 weeks visiting pharmacy practice, education, and industry sites.[9]

He continued his efforts with APhA by becoming cochair of the Committee on International Relations. He served as president of the International Pharmaceutical Federation Press and Documentation Section from 1964 to 1978, and became the first American elected an FIP vice president, serving from 1958 to 1966. He was a U.S. delegate to FIP's annual meetings for 25 of the 27 years between 1951 and 1978.

His pursuits and successes led to his receiving honorary membership in a number of national pharmaceutical societies, including the Pharmaceutical Society of Great Britain and the Japanese Pharmaceutical Association. In 1973 ASHP established an award to honor American pharmacists for outstanding international contributions to hospital pharmacy; named in his honor, the first medal was presented to Francke.

ASSOCIATION LEADER
Associations were a crucial part of Francke's professional life. He was an active participant and leader in both APhA and ASHP, serving as president of the fledgling ASHP for three terms, 1943–1946, and as president of APhA during the Association's 1951–1952 centennial year. He strongly advocated that pharmacists have a responsibility to be active participants in their professional associations, a theme he put forward in both his APhA president-elect and presidential addresses. In the latter, he also paid tribute to pharmacy students' support for a strong, united profession and their knowledge that pharmacy was a profession, not just a business.[10]

LEGACY
In a tribute to Francke published in *AJHP* in 1979, Robert P. Fischelis, a former secretary and general manager of APhA, recalled that Francke "visualized the practice of this profession as something of primary essentiality in the healing arts—not a side-line—but an active and continuously developing area of service that must be nurtured in order to fulfill its maximum potential."[11]

At the request of Gen. Douglas MacArthur, Donald Francke joined four other prominent U.S. pharmacists in 1949 to study post-World War II pharmacy in Japan. The study group included (left to right) Troy Daniels, Royce Franzoni, Glenn Jenkins, host Miss Tokulu Hattori of the Japanese Pharmacists Association, Hugh Muldoon, and Donald Francke.

Francke was an outspoken professional advocate who believed that his profession existed to serve the public and that the best way to serve the public was to put the emphasis on the patient. Fortunately for pharmacy, Don Francke was a "doer" who acted on his beliefs.

REFERENCES

1. Brodie DC. In tribute. *Am J Hosp Pharm.* 1979;36:464–5.

2. Sonnedecker G. Remarks at the memorial service. *Am J Hosp Pharm.* 1979;36:459–61.

3. Francke DE, Latiolais CJ, Francke GN, Ho NF. *Mirror to Hospital Pharmacy.* Washington, DC: American Society of Hospital Pharmacists; 1963.

4. Niemeyer G. *The Bulletin of the ASHP.* In: Ten years of the American Society of Hospital Pharmacists. *Bull Am Soc Hosp Pharm.* 1952; 9:347–62.

5. Provost GP. Colleague, mentor and friend. *Am J Hosp Pharm.* 1966;23:233.

6. Francke DE. Drug intelligence—objectives and scope. *Drug Intelligence.* 1967;1:5.

7. Whitney HAK Jr. *Annals of Pharmacotherapy*—more than a face lift. *DICP.* 1989;23:73–87.

8. Flannery MA, Worthen DB. *Pharmaceutical Education in the Queen City: 150 Years of Service, 1850-2000.* Binghamton, NY: Haworth Press; 2001;81–2.

9. APhA mission to Japan. *J Am Pharm Assoc (Pract Pharm Ed)*. 1949;10:496–97, 619.

10. Francke DE. The president's address. *J Am Pharm Assoc*. 1952;13NS:626–8, 630–1, 666–70.

11. Fischelis RP. In tribute. *Am J Hosp Pharm*. 1979;36:473–4.

Edward Kremers (1865–1941):
Pharmaceutical Education Reformer

Writing about his friend and coauthor in 1947, George Urdang characterized Edward Kremers as an important reformer of American pharmaceutical education: "He not only grasped what had to be done but did it without even thinking of compromise at a time when the steps he took required a considerable amount of courage and defiance of what is commonly regarded as collegial courtesy."[1] Kremers, however, was more than just an educational reformer. He spoke out against adulterated drugs as early as 1895, warning Wisconsin pharmacists that their problems would probably be as great as they were in other parts of the country.[2] He later deplored the commercialization of pharmacy, and noted the trend of drugstores being turned into little more than "sandwich and soda establishments."[3] It is little wonder then that Urdang characterized Kremers as a fighter, "one who set an example taking every risk possible."[1]

BEGINNINGS

Edward Kremers was born on February 23, 1865, in Milwaukee, Wisconsin, the son of Gerhard Kremers and Elise Kamper. Gerhard, the secretary of the Milwaukee Gas Light Company, immigrated from Prussia with his parents in 1848. Because the Wisconsin area along Lake Michigan was heavily populated by Germans, most of Edward's elementary school classmates spoke German. He attended a high school, modeled after a German secondary school, which was operated by the German Reformed Church, and graduated in 1882. Kremers then apprenticed with Louis Lotz, who had emigrated to the United States from Kaiserslautern in 1866. Lotz had moved to Milwaukee in 1874, where he established a German-style pharmacy.[4] Having been educated at the University of Munich by some of the leading scientists of the time (including Justus von Liebig), Lotz imbued his apprentice with "the idea that pharmacy has to be a profession executed by scientifically educated people in order to really fulfill the tasks assigned to it within the service of public welfare."[5] After

2 years with Lotz, Kremers enrolled at the Philadelphia College of Pharmacy but stayed only 1 year (1884–85). He returned to Wisconsin and enrolled in the new Department of Pharmacy at the university in Madison, where he carried both a PhG (1886) and a BS (1888). While in Madison he worked with Professor Frederick B. Power, who had been the first professor of analytical chemistry at the Philadelphia College of Pharmacy and an outstanding researcher in the area of volatile oils. In 1888 Kremers traveled to Bonn and became a graduate student of Otto Wallach, who would receive the Nobel Prize in Chemistry in 1910. After receiving his PhD in 1890, Kremers returned to Madison and took a teaching position in the Department of Pharmacy.

On July 6, 1892, Edward Kremers married Laura Haase, also from Milwaukee and of German descent. They had four children, two boys and two girls. Edwards Kremers died in Madison, Wisconsin, on July 9, 1941, at the age of 76.[6]

When this photograph of Edward Kremers was taken in 1911, he had already served as APhA Scientific Section chairman (1897–1898), AACP president (1902–1903), and APhA Council member (1905–1907).

UNIVERSITY OF WISCONSIN

The course in pharmacy at the University of Wisconsin opened in 1883, only the second department of pharmacy to be created as part of a state university. Power, a graduate pharmacist of the Philadelphia College of Pharmacy who received his PhD in Germany before returning to teach chemistry in Philadelphia, became the first director of Wisconsin's pharmacy department. In 1884 Wisconsin took a major step by requiring either a high school diploma or prior attendance at an institution of higher learning for admission.[7] In 1890 Edward Kremers was appointed instructor and placed in charge of the pharmaceutical laboratory; when Power left in 1892 Kremers succeeded him as director of the department.

In 1892 Kremers' title was Professor of Pharmaceutical and Pharmacognostical Chemistry, a change that was prescient of future changes, according to Urdang. The course at Wisconsin was immediately increased to 2 years of three full terms and the nation's first 4-year course in pharmacy was introduced as an option.[1]

Kremers carried his spirit of evangelism for public pharmaceutical education to the American Pharmaceutical Association (APhA) meeting in 1895 when he challenged the old colleges of pharmacy that depended on large student enrollments for financial stability. After excoriating the proliferation of different degrees and titles he addressed the issue of giving apprenticeship precedence over education, citing the example of the "oldest College of Pharmacy, the bulwark of the educational ideas of the past" where "the man with the experience of selling the soda water and cigars is entitled to the doctor's degree, whereas he with possibly the better education, and who spends his time more profitably at college, is dismissed with the modest degree of pharmaceutical chemist."[8] He advised the traditional colleges to give up their independence and seek affiliation with state universities. In the same address, Kremers took the position that entrance requirements for pharmacy should be the same as for all other university programs and added that the true role of university education was the preparation for what would become recognized as lifelong learning: "*University courses are to endow men and women with a great capacity for becoming efficient in their calling after they really enter into the same in the every-day battle of life.* [Italics in original.]"[8]

An undergraduate research thesis had been a Wisconsin graduation requirement when Power was the director, and Kremers continued and strengthened this requirement. Other university departments opposed the department of pharmacy granting a graduate pharmacy degree, but Kremers eventually prevailed.[1] In 1893 the first master's degree was awarded, in 1902 the first PhD in pharmaceutical chemistry, and in 1917 the first PhD in pharmaceutics under the direction of a pharmacy program in the United States. The recipient, Andrew G. DuMez, became an educational leader and reformer in his own right.[7] Kremers' students were recruited for positions in both industry and academia, and by the time of his death a large number of deans of American pharmacy schools had graduated from his program.[9]

For many years Kremers held a joint appointment in the chemistry department at the University of Wisconsin. His research focused on plant chemistry, and he had an early interest in establishing an area for the cultivation of medicinal plants as part of the school. In 1908 the first research-oriented medicinal plant garden in the United States was developed with the assistance of the university and the U.S. Department of Agriculture.[10] The next step was the development of an experimental station, and at his recommendation the state pharmacy association passed a resolution in 1912 favoring the establishment of such an effort.[11] In June the Wisconsin legislature passed a law establishing the first pharmaceutical experimental station in the United States. Funding continued for the experimental station until the appropriations were discontinued in 1933 during the Great Depression.[7] (The experimental station was revived in 2001 when the University of Wisconsin School of Pharmacy moved to its new home, Rennebohm Hall.)

Kremers served as the director of the University of Wisconsin School of Pharmacy for 43 years until he retired in 1935.

EDITOR

Edward Kremers received his PhG in 1886. In 1887 he received an Ebert Prize for two companion papers on the volatile oils of pennyroyal and citronella, which were presented at the APhA annual meeting.[12,13] He quickly came to the notice of Fredrick Hoffmann, who was the owner–publisher of *Pharmaceutische Rundschau*, a German-language monthly published in New York. Beginning in 1895 Kremers coedited the journal with Hoffmann. In 1896 Kremers purchased it, changed the title to *Pharmaceutical Review* and published it in English.[14] The venture finally came to an end in 1909, probably due in Hoffmann's mind to Kremers' lack of business acumen, but possibly influenced by advertisers' hesitancy to support the editorial positions taken by the editor. In 1898 Kremers started a second journal, *Pharmaceutical Archives*, and restricted its content to original scientific work, but it was discontinued in 1903. In 1930 he also founded *The Badger Pharmacist*, "the first American periodical devoted to pharmaceutical history." It was published irregularly until the last issue appeared in 1941.[15]

In 1900 Kremers translated Eduard Gildemeister and Friedrich Hoffmann's *Volatile Oils*. This was enlarged and issued as a three-volume work in 1913. In 1905 Kremers was one of the editors of the *National Standard Dispensatory*, a work designed to succeed the *National Dispensatory* of Stillé and Maisch. His best known work, however, was as the coauthor of Kremers' and Urdang's *History of Pharmacy: A Guide and Survey,* published in 1940.

ASSOCIATIONS

Kremers was an accomplished organizational leader. Despite his skepticism that the private colleges and university departments could work together, he was one of the founders of the American Conference of Pharmaceutical Faculties (now American Association of Colleges of Pharmacy [AACP]) and served on the first executive committee. In 1902–03 he was the organization's third president. In answer to the question of how to encourage the state boards of pharmacy in increasing educational standards, Kremers recommended that the Conference hold joint meetings with the boards. A resolution for a joint conference between the colleges and the boards of pharmacy scheduled for 1904 was passed.[16] The boards formed the National Association of Boards of Pharmacy in 1904; in 1935, after he retired from the university, Kremers was appointed to the Wisconsin board for a 5-year term.[6]

The Wisconsin Pharmaceutical Association (now Pharmacy Society of Wisconsin), formed in 1880, was influential in the establishment of the Department of Pharmacy in 1883. Edward Kremers was active in the association, which he joined in 1886, served on a number of committees, and provided open communications between the association, the university's department, and the state board.[17] In 1895 Kremers wrote that the graduates of Wisconsin had received their professional education from the state, which "expects them to return their indebtedness with compound interest, not in money, but in rendering good service to the people of the state. No small

Edward Kremers prepared an exhibit on USP history at the 1933 APhA annual meeting in Madison, Wisc. His interest in the past is reflected by the materials that he displayed.

part of this indebtedness can be paid by becoming active members in the state pharmaceutical association."[18] In 1930, Kremers was elected association president.

Edward Kremers joined APhA in 1887 while still a student. He remained an active participant his entire life. He served as the chair of the Scientific Section in 1897–98. He also served as the first Association Historian from 1902 to 1912. He was nominated for President but refused to allow his name to be placed on the ballot.[19] He was elected Honorary President in 1933–34.

HISTORIAN

In his obituary of Kremers in the *American Journal of Pharmaceutical Education*, Urdang commented on Kremers' historical orientation and his fight for humanizing technical sciences.[5] Kremers spoke on this philosophy at the 1892 APhA annual meeting: "In our utilitarian and materialistic age, too little attention is given to history even in the academic courses of our colleges and universities. The professional student should at least have a fair knowledge of the history of his profession."[20] Kremers later recalled that he began informal instruction in the history of pharmacy at Wisconsin as early as 1892 and, in 1908, taught formal courses both on the history of chemistry and the history of pharmacy.[21]

At the 1902 APhA annual meeting, Edward Kremers, John Uri Lloyd, and Albert Ethelbert Ebert proposed the establishment of a standing Committee on Historical Pharmacy, with the directive to hold an annual meeting.[22] Kremers was appointed chair of the committee and, subsequently, historian of APhA.

Kremers was an inveterate collector of all things relating to pharmacy. Under his guidance the university's international collection of historical books and journals, biographical materials, correspondence, college and manufacturer catalogs, and clippings became a major source for the history of pharmacy that he coauthored with Urdang.[23] In 1941 Kremers became one of the founders of the American Institute of the History of Pharmacy (AIHP).

RECOGNITION

Kremers was a principled man who vigorously challenged the status quo to achieve the changes in pharmacy education, which he believed were essential if pharmacy was ever to gain the recognition that it deserved. His blunt approach undoubtedly cost him the support of those who felt threatened by his uncompromising crusade for academic parity; however, many shared his vision.

During his career, Kremers received most of the honors the profession could bestow on one of its own. APhA awarded him two Ebert Prizes (1887 and 1900) for his research and writing and, in 1930, the Remington Medal. He was also elected as its Honorary President after earlier refusing to run for president. He served as the third president of AACP and the president of the Wisconsin Pharmaceutical Association. He was named the Honorary President of the National Association of the Boards of Pharmacy in recognition of his efforts in its creation and his work with the Wisconsin State Board of Pharmacy. The University of Michigan awarded him an ScD in 1913 and a number of international pharmacy groups elected him to membership. In 1941, with the creation of AIHP, he was named the first honorary president. In 1962 AIHP created the Edward Kremers Award to recognize periodically an original and scholarly publication on the history of pharmacy by an American.

LEGACY

Edward Kremers, in his 1930 presidential address to the Wisconsin Pharmaceutical Association, recounted that his education was unconventional: "If my early pharmaceutical career was the cause of non-conformity with conventional educational standards, my university education caused me to be a non-conformist with regard to the professional standards of pharmacy as they were generally held in my younger years."[19] Sonnedecker[15] recalled that Kremers' outspoken assaults on the status quo frequently put him in an adversarial position with the influential professional leadership of the day. However, his vision for improvement of pharmaceutical education and practice also won him many adherents and, eventually, widespread recognition.[15] His legacy is evident today: pharmacy is equal with other professions in demanding rigorous academic standards. Every PhD in pharmacy in the United States is a beneficiary of Kremers' pioneer efforts to develop graduate-level standards in pharmacy. His love of the history of the pharmacy is embodied, through the AIHP, in its Kremers Award and the Kremers Reference Files.

REFERENCES

1. Urdang G. Edward Kremers (1864–1941) reformer of American pharmaceutical education. *Am J Pharm Educ.* 1947;11:631–58.

2. Kremers E. Comments to report of committee on adulteration. *Proc Wis Pharm Assoc.* 1895;16:28–9.

3. Pharmacy leader decries soda trade. *New York Times.* May 6, 1930:60.

4. Goetzendorff H. *Louis Lotz (1843–1923) and the Deutsche Apotheke in Milwaukee.* Edinburgh, Scotland: 37th International Congress for the History of Pharmacy; June 22–25, 2005.

5. Urdang G. Edward Kremers. *Am J Pharm Educ.* 1941;5:402–5.

6. Edward Kremers. *National Cyclopedia of American Biography.* New York: James T. White & Co.; 1943;XXX:75–6.

7. Buckner C, Connors KA, Parascandola J, et al. *The University of Wisconsin School of Pharmacy: Its First Century.* Madison, Wis.: Office of University Publications; 1997.

8. Kremers E. The position of the American Pharmaceutical Association toward pharmaceutical education. *Proc Am Pharm Assoc.* 1895;43:447–53.

9. Ihde AJ. *Chemistry, as Viewed from Bascom's Hill: A History of the Chemistry Department at the University of Wisconsin in Madison.* Madison, Wis.: University of Wisconsin; 1990:469.

10. Kremers E. Report on the course in pharmacy at the university. *Proc Wis Pharm Assoc.* 1909;29:17–9.

11. Fifth session, Friday June 21. *Proc Wis Pharm Assoc.* 1912;32:43

12. Kremers E. Analysis of the volatile oil of hedeoma pulegioides person. Proc *Am Pharm Assoc.* 35;1887:546–61.

13. Kremers E. Chemical examination of the oil of andropogen nardus, L., or citronella oil, with a review of the different species of anropogon of interest in pharmacy. *Proc Am Pharm Assoc.* 1887;35:562–78.

14. Schütze SK. *Friedrich Hoffman (1832–1904) and the Pharmaceutische Rundschau.* Berlin: Peter Lang; 2002:119–25.

15. Sonnedecker G. Edward Kremers. In: *American National Biography*. New York: Oxford University Press; 1999;12:916–7.

16. Second session. Proceedings of the fourth and fifth annual meetings of the American Conference of Pharmaceutical Faculties. 1904:19–22.

17. Bardell EB. *Wisconsin Show Globe: The Wisconsin Pharmaceutical Association 1880–1980.* Madison, Wis: Wisconsin Pharmaceutical Association; 1983:130.

18. Heimstreet EB. Pharmacy in Wisconsin: history of the school of pharmacy of the University of Wisconsin. *Proc Wis Pharm Assoc.* 1895;15:73–7.

19. Kremers E. Presidential address. *Proc Wis Pharm Assoc.* 1930;50:28–32.

20. Kremers E. Notes on pharmaceutical education. *Proc Am Pharm Assoc.* 1892;40:309–22.

21. Kremers E. History of pharmacy and chemistry at Madison, Wisconsin. *ISIS.* 1925; 7:109–10.

22. Fourth session of the council. *Proc Am Pharm Assoc.* 1902;50:44.

23. Higby G, Stroud E. Pharmaco-historical resources in Madison, Wisconsin III. Kremers Reference Files *Pharm Hist.* 1988;30:157–62.

J. Leon Lascoff (1867–1943):
Champion of Professionalism

Obituaries of J. Leon Lascoff in the pharmacy press described him as a leading professional pharmacist. The term "professional pharmacy" had become accepted by the 1930s to describe the "type of pharmacy in which the professional services are of paramount importance while the commercial or merchandising phases are minimized or eliminated."[1] Lascoff was an influential leader, acclaimed for his role in the development of the American Pharmaceutical Association's *Pharmaceutical Recipe Book* and the formation of the American College of Apothecaries. His visibility as a representative figure of pharmacy was known to the New York public because of his pharmacy on Lexington Avenue. Robert Swain, editor-in-chief of *Drug Topics*, wrote that with his passing "there came to a close the most significant pharmaceutical career of this day and generation."[2] For all of his roles in pharmacy, one that Lascoff undoubtedly held most important was that of professional community pharmacist.

EARLY YEARS

Jacob (usually shortened to J.) Leon Lascoff, the son of Israel David and Anna (Reiser) Lascoff, was born in Vilna, then part of the Russian Empire, on August 28, 1867.[3] Vilna was the capital city of Lithuania and a center of Jewish education and culture. Lascoff completed his professional education and had 6 years of practical experience before immigrating to the United States in 1892 at age 25.[4] Within 24 hours of landing in New York he secured his first position with David Hayes, a pharmacist who owned two pharmacies and was a member of the New York State Board of Pharmacy. Lascoff later recalled that he conducted his job search while wearing a silk hat and Prince Albert coat. Hired immediately, he washed windows in this, his best attire.[5] Registered as a pharmacist in 1893, he worked for Hayes until joining the Merck & Co Professional Pharmacy in New York. He also worked for Dr. Gustave Pfingsten and for Tsheppe & Schur. In 1899 he opened his own pharmacy.[3]

J. Leon Lascoff married Clara Joachimson in New York City on October 4, 1896. The couple had one son, Frederick D. Lascoff, who was a partner in the J. Leon Lascoff & Son Apothecaries in New York. J. Leon died on May 4, 1943.[3]

COMMUNITY PHARMACIST

The most common descriptor of J. Leon Lascoff was as a "professional" pharmacist. While the term defies a short definition, Lascoff clearly knew how he wanted to practice his profession. In 1905 his pharmacy was considered one of the busiest and most interesting in New York.[6] The shop was described as a historical apothecary with all of the most modern fixtures and equipment. Two stories high, the pharmacy accommodated 18 employees in the prescription room and a manufacturing area in the basement.[7] A list of services provided noted a vast array and inventory of medicines, including "the most important of English, German, French and other European medicinal preparations."[8]

In 1936 the Lascoff pharmacy filled its one millionth prescription, an astounding total for a time when many physicians still dispensed.[9] In 1938, 75% of the pharmacy's annual gross revenue was from prescriptions; 5,000 prescriptions were filled per month compared with an estimated national average of 400 per month.[10] By 1941, a second prescription room had been added on the second floor. Lascoff was an inveterate collector of pharmacy antiques, many of which decorated the apothecary.

Lascoff provided a set of rules for establishing a good reputation since he believed that was the framework for an individual's professionalism. The rules included honest advertising, accuracy, standardization, and courteous treatment of customers.[11] He defined professional pharmacy most clearly in 1922 when he wrote about the need to be "pharmacy-minded" and to fill the role of a man of science. He added, "[Professionalism] leads through the prescription department. The professional pharmacist of today who emphasizes this side of his business, who carries the necessary side lines but does not let them carry him away from the true conception of his functions as a servant of the community can, other things being equal, build up and maintain a reputation and a business."[12]

ASSOCIATION ACTIVIST

Lascoff was deeply involved with association work, both as a citizen and as a pharmacist. He was a pharmacist representative to both the Red Cross and Salvation Army as well as a member of the New York Board of Trade and the advisory board of the New York City Board of Trade.

He joined the New York State Pharmaceutical Association in 1900. In 1911 he was one of the organizers of the New York County Pharmaceutical Society and later of the New York Veteran Druggists' Association. In 1910 he was named to the New York State Board of Pharmacy, serving continuously for more than 30 years; he was president in 1914, 1921, and 1929. His board work with practical examinations was especially noteworthy. During World

J. Leon Lascoff served as 1938–1939 APhA president, 4 years before his death. His efforts led him to be recognized as the "father" of the American College of Apothecaries.

War I he was the chairman of the New York State Pharmaceutical Association ambulance committee. Although he was neither an alumnus nor faculty member of the Columbia College of Pharmacy, he served as a trustee from 1916 until his death.[13]

Lascoff joined the American Pharmaceutical Association in 1903 and in 1913 was the chair of the Section on Practical Pharmacy and Dispensing. The section was formed as a standing committee in 1898 to address the needs of the retail pharmacist and in its first report noted "that there is yet

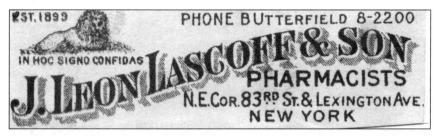

This label of J. Leon Lascoff & Son, which featured the inscription In Hoc Signo Confidas, was used in 1936 when the pharmacy had filled its one millionth prescription.

dispensing to do, that there are still preparations to be made, and hope that through our efforts some little something has come to help the dispenser, the practical pharmacist."[14] During Lascoff's chairman's address in 1913 he stated that a professional pharmacy "should be owned by registered pharmacists; should have the prescription department separate from the store; should not sell liquor; should be sanitary and well ventilated; and should have certain minimum technical equipment and reference books."[15] He also supported the creation of a certificate, signed by the president and secretary of APhA and local pharmacy and medical committees, for members who established and maintained properly equipped pharmacies.[16]

In 1936–37 Lascoff was elected first vice president of the APhA and served as its president in 1938–39. He used his presidential address to speak on the theme of professionalism and professional pharmacy. After returning to an earlier theme of "more pharmacies and fewer drug stores," he emphasized his belief that there "is a need for more pharmacies conducted by professionally minded men, conscious of their professional obligation to the public." He also urged cooperation between pharmacy and medicine "so that each would be in a better position to meet their problems and to discharge their obligations to the public." Lascoff also commented on the need for the Association to become more involved in the development of hospital pharmacy because "the hospital pharmacists will come into close contact with medicine and other medical specialists and will be in a position to interpret Pharmacy to them in a basic and fundamental way."[17]

PHARMACEUTICAL RECIPE BOOK
In 1909 Henry P. Hynson of Baltimore noted the need to develop a recipe book for the pharmacist. He explained that inclusion in both the *U.S. Pharmacopoeia* and *National Formulary* was restricted, and many formulas compounded by pharmacists were not included. The recommendation led to the formation of a committee "to investigate the advisability of the Association publishing a druggists' recipe book; to define its scope and character, and submit plans and details for consideration."[18] For the next 10 years more than 600 formulas were collected and published in *JAPhA*. In 1920, Lascoff was elected chairman of the committee. He accelerated efforts to collect and test

new formulas; by 1923 more than 1,500 recipes had been collected. After revision to confirm the suitability of each formula, the first edition of the *Pharmaceutical Recipe Book* was published in 1929 with more than 1,621 formulas in nine departments: pharmaceutical, hospital, dental, diagnostic reagents and clinical tests, veterinary, photographic, cosmetic, flavoring, and technical.

The New York Branch of the APhA held a testimonial dinner honoring Lascoff for his efforts in completing the *Pharmaceutical Recipe Book*; the guest list was a veritable who's who of American pharmacy. E.F. Kelly, general secretary of APhA, spoke about Lascoff's contribution "in stirring it to completion, and in bringing to it and keeping in view all of the time the attitude of the practicing retail pharmacist, and in determining in so far as possible that these formulae contained in it are reliable and dependable."[19]

Lascoff remained active in the development of two additional editions of the *Pharmaceutical Recipe Book*. In 1931 Chapter VIII of the Association bylaws were amended to include a separate article on the Committee of the Recipe Book with the express duty to prepare future revisions.[20] The second edition of the *Pharmaceutical Recipe Book*, published in 1936, included more than 2,000 formulas. In the third edition, published in 1943, more than 300 new formulas and a number of new sections, including the APhA Code of Ethics, were added. In 1937 Lascoff received the Remington Medal in "recognition of his services to pharmacy as chairman of the committee which compiled the original *Pharmaceutical Recipe Book*."[21]

AMERICAN COLLEGE OF APOTHECARIES

J. Leon Lascoff has been identified as the father of the American College of Apothecaries or even its grandfather.[22] The idea for an organization of professional pharmacists was first offered in 1914 by Henry Vincome Arny, the dean of the Columbia University College of Pharmacy. He suggested that those who focused their efforts on prescriptions rather than "frankly commercial retail druggists" should form the American Institute of Prescriptionists.[23] In 1938, at the beginning of his APhA presidential year, Lascoff invited a number of individuals to a breakfast session during the annual meeting to discuss forming the Conference of Professional Pharmacists. During the group's meeting in 1939, a committee was formed with Purdue Dean C. B. Jordan as chair to determine whether there would be a permanent association. At the 1940 APhA annual meeting the American College of Apothecaries (ACA) was established; Jordan, Arny, and Lascoff were among those named as honorary members. In 1943 the organization established its first award, named in honor of J. Leon Lascoff, "to recognize the most valuable contribution to professional pharmacy made by anyone."[22]

EDITOR

Lascoff's first publication came after a presentation at the APhA annual meeting in 1907. He observed that the same prescription when dispensed by different pharmacists might look different and offered several examples to make his point.[24] The theme of compounding became his editorial specialty. Beginning in 1934 he authored a column, "Back Room Problems," for *Drug Topics*. The intent was to provide answers to prescription room dilemmas furnished by community pharmacists. In the first column he answered questions on international product identification and stability, and also suggested workable formulas.[25] By 1937 he had answered more than 3,000 questions.[26]

LEGACY

In the decades that Lascoff owned his own pharmacy he worked collaboratively and practiced his belief that everything was done for the patient. In 1914 the New Jersey College of Pharmacy awarded him an honorary doctor of pharmacy degree, and in 1938, Temple University honored him with a doctor of science degree. In 1937 he became the 17th recipient of the Remington Medal. The National Association of Boards of Pharmacy named him as the

Like his father, Frederick D. Lascoff served as a member of the APhA Council (1948–1949 and 1962–1964) and was a partner of the New York J. Leon Lascoff & Son Pharmacy.

honorary president in 1940, and the ACA named their most prestigious award in his honor after he died in 1943. He gained recognition and renown for his work with both the APhA and the ACA as well as with his local and state pharmaceutical associations. His column on compounding recipes in *Drug Topics* was popular and along with the creation of the *Pharmaceutical Recipe Book* provided the pharmacist with tested formulas that could be compounded in the community pharmacy.

Lascoff's enduring legacy, however, "was the inspiration which he gave thousand of pharmacists in the practice of their profession."[27] In memorializing Lascoff, Robert Swain noted that, while his honors and distinctions were many and deserved, Lascoff was happiest in his pharmacy surrounded by its historical collections and engaged in practice, because "here he showed that pharmacy can be made a great calling when greatly pursued."[2]

REFERENCES

1. Husa WJ. Chairman's address, section on practical pharmacy and dispensing. *J Am Pharm Assoc.* 1938;27:1101–2.

2. Swain RL. A memorial: J. Leon Lascoff. *Am J Pharm Educ.* 1943;7:408.

3. Lascoff, J. Leon. *The National Cyclopaedia of American Biography.* Vol 33. New York: James T. White & Company; 1947:582–3.

4. Lascoff JL. Let us have faith. In: Griffenhagen GB, Bowles GC, Penna RP, Worthen DB, eds. *Reflections of Pharmacy by the Remington Medalists 1919–2003.* Washington, D.C.: American Pharmacists Association; 2004:96–9.

5. Lascoff JL. Testimonial dinner tendered to J. Leon Lascoff Program. New York Branch of the American Pharmaceutical Association, March 18, 1929.

6. A story that is full of morals. *Apothecary.* 1905;17:881–2.

7. The new Lascoff pharmacy—a professional wonder shop. *Drug Circ.* 1931(Oct 18–19);75:58.

8. The development of a high professional standard. J. Leon Lascoff & Son, New York City [1932?] 12 pp.

9. Clark RW. A pioneer of professional pharmacy. *The Merck Report.* 1941;50:11.

10. A tribute to J. Leon Lascoff thirty-eight years ago. *Apothecary.* 1938;50:(Mar)13.

11. Lascoff JL. The essentials of a reputable pharmacist. *Practical Druggist and Review of Reviews.* 1911(Aug);24:31.

12. Lascoff JL. The future of professional pharmacy. *The Pharmaceutical Era.* 1922;55:131–2.

13. J. Leon Lascoff. *J Am Pharm Assoc.* 1937;26:198–200.

14. Hynson HP. Report of the committee on practical pharmacy and dispensing. *Proc Am Pharm Assoc.* 1899;47:73–83.

15. Berman A. The section on practical pharmacy of the American Pharmaceutical Association. *Am J Pharm Educ.* 1953;17:351–62.

16. Lascoff JL. Chairman address: section on practical pharmacy and dispensing. *J Am Pharm Assoc.* 1913;2:1118–22.

17. Lascoff JL. President's address. *J Am Pharm Assoc.* 1939;28:766–75.

18. Committees on recipe book and on unofficial formulas of the American Pharmaceutical

Association. *The Pharmaceutical Recipe Book.* 1st ed. Washington, D.C.: American Pharmaceutical Association; 1929:v–vii.

19. Kelly EF. Testimonial dinner tendered to J. Leon Lascoff program. New York Branch of the American Pharmaceutical Association; March 18, 1929:28.

20. By-laws of the Association. *Yearbook of the American Pharmaceutical Association.* 1929;18: xxxi.

21. Quoted in: Wins pharmacy profession's highest award. *New York Times.* May 20, 1937:22.

22. Stieb EW. *American College of Apothecaries: The First Quarter Century 1940–1965.* American College of Apothecaries and the American Institute of the History of Pharmacy; 1970.

23. Arny HV. The American institute of prescriptionists. *J Am Pharm Assoc.* 1914;3:1542–7.

24. Lascoff L. Practical experience in dispensing. *Proc Am Pharm Assoc.* 1907;55:139–41.

25. Lascoff JL. Back room problems. *Drug Topics.* 1934;50(Jan 8):51.

26. Highlights in life of Dr. J.L. Lascoff. *Drug Topics.* 1937;53:(May 17):1–2.

27. Dr. J. Leon Lascoff Dies. *J Am Pharm Assoc Pract Pharm Ed.* 1943;4:142.

Ernest Little (1888-1973): Champion of the American Foundation for Pharmaceutical Education

In compiling the semicentennial history of the American Foundation for Pharmaceutical Education (AFPE), Albert B. Fisher, Jr., its president for 12 years, commemorated the contributions of Ernest Little, noting that much of its early success was due to him.[1] Indeed, the very creation of the Foundation was largely a consequence of Dean Little's work with the National Drug Trade Conference.[2] Rufus Lyman, in reporting Little's selection for the 1949 Remington Medal, wrote of his involvement "in every movement for the betterment of pharmaceutical education and practice.... No man has ever more worthily received this honor."[3]

BEGINNINGS

Ernest Little, the son of John and Martha Snook Little, was born on June 9, 1888, in Johnstown, N.Y. After graduating from high school he studied chemistry at the University of Rochester, receiving a bachelor of science degree in 1911 and master of science in 1912. From 1911 to 1914, he served as an instructor in chemistry at the university and then at Pratt Institute in Brooklyn from 1914 to 1918. He continued his graduate studies at the University of Graz in Austria before receiving a master of arts degree in 1918 and doctor of philosophy in chemistry in 1924 from Columbia University.[4]

Ernest Little married Margaret Lucy Weaver on July 1, 1913; the couple had two sons, John and Robert.[5] Ernest Little died on October 30, 1973, in St. Johnsbury, Vt.

COLLEGE OF PHARMACY

In 1918, Ernest Little accepted an appointment as an assistant professor in chemistry at Rutgers University at New Brunswick. That same year he began a part-time association with the New Jersey College of Pharmacy as professor of physics and chemistry.[6]

The New Jersey College of Pharmacy was formed in Newark as a proprietary school in 1892. While initially successful, by the first decade of the 20th century the school faced declining enrollment and accreditation difficulties with the state boards of pharmacy in both New Jersey and New York. Robert Fischelis was hired as the dean in 1921 with the mandate to secure accreditation, and he led the initial drive to affiliate the college with Rutgers University.[7] Fischelis resigned the deanship in 1925 and was succeeded by Caswell Mayo, who was not successful as a dean. The trustees of the college of pharmacy named Ernest Little acting dean in 1926, looking forward to an eventual affiliation with Rutgers.

Little's first objective was the complete consolidation of the college by the university, and in this his was a fortuitous appointment. An accomplished scientist and administrator, he was fully aware of the needs of both institutions. His initial steps to increase the quality of the curriculum and stabilize enrollment led to the 1927 university resolution accepting the college and making it an integral part of the university; at the same time the name was changed to Rutgers University, The State University of New Jersey, New Jersey College of Pharmacy.[8] Little was named dean of the college by the university trustees in 1929, with the immediate challenge of implementing the mandatory 4-year bachelor of science in pharmacy.

Ernest Little in 1926, the year that he was named acting dean of New Jersey College of Pharmacy to implement the mandatory four-year BS in pharmacy

As was the case with a number of proprietary and association schools that affiliated with state universities, administrators assumed the pharmacy programs would be financially self-sufficient. In 1938 the American Council on Pharmaceutical Education (ACPE; now the Accreditation Council on Pharmacy Education) notified all colleges of potential loss of accreditation, effective in 1944, unless at least 20% of the funding came from something other than student tuition and fees.[9] Little enlisted the support of the university administration and the New Jersey Pharmaceutical Association (NJPA) and finally gained the first state appropriation in 1941.

The war years were challenging for all pharmacy schools, and the Rutgers pharmacy school faced the challenges of declining enrollments and accelerated courses. Colleges implemented a 3-year accelerated program, but even that was not sufficient to gain draft deferment of students. Dean Little, along with the deans at Temple University and the University of Maryland, devised a super-accelerated 2-year bachelor of science program that met the minimum requirements for student contact hours but failed to gain approval of either the American Association of Colleges of Pharmacy (AACP) or the National Association of Boards of Pharmacy (NABP).[10] The strain of college and association leadership during the war years was a consideration in Little's decision to resign as dean and return to the faculty as professor of chemistry in 1946; he taught until his retirement in 1953.[4]

EDUCATIONAL STANDARDS

Ernest Little emerged early in his career as an outspoken leader for educational standards. In 1932 he served as the chair of the AACP Committee on Membership Standards during the debate on what degree should be awarded. The doctor of pharmacy degree (PharmD) had been awarded by some schools for completion of only a 3-year course of study; Little recommended the abolishment of the degree, noting that the lack of standards discredited it completely.[11] This was the same year that ACPE was organized with representatives of American Pharmaceutical (now Pharmacists) Association (APhA), AACP, NABP, and the American Council on Education with a mandate to establish criteria for accreditation of a college or school of pharmacy. In 1933 Little was elected AACP vice president and, in 1934, president. In his presidential address, Little recommended that all members read the earlier presidential addresses as the basis for ongoing discussions; he believed this would help produce a better informed membership and increase Association progress. In his effort to improve and increase educational standards, he warned against complacency brought on by past successes, for "such an attitude constitutes retrogression, and if followed for even a short time, leads only to disaster."[12] In his own candid fashion he challenged the colleges to increase the professionalism of the community pharmacist, whom he termed the cornerstone of the foundation of our profession, claiming that the leadership was the responsibility of educators. Little argued that admission criteria needed to include character, reliability, and aptitude for professional work, not just scholarship, and to meet this approach pharmacy aptitude tests needed to be developed and implemented. From 1936 to 1941 Little served as the chair of the AACP Executive Committee. In 1942, AACP appointed Little one of its representatives on the ACPE board of directors, where he served until 1948, including service as its vice president in 1946–47.

PROFESSIONAL ORGANIZATIONS

In 1933 Ernest Little served as the founding president of the Northern New Jersey Branch of APhA.[13] In 1937 he was elected vice-chairman of the APhA House of Delegates and in 1948 president of APhA.

Ernest Little was an avowed advocate of the *Pharmaceutical Survey* (1946–49), also known as the Elliott Report. In his APhA presidential address he noted that the responsibility of making the *Survey* work had to be the job of the profession, as no one else would do it. He referred to the sentiment of some that the earlier Charters Study (1924–27) may not have accomplished all that it might, but he added that it was because of pharmacy and not the study itself: "We have got to stop hoping for things and learn how to work hard for the things we desire for the future of our profession."[14]

From 1930 until 1940 Little served on the United States Pharmacopoeia Committee of Revision and as a trustee of this organization from 1940 to 1960. He headed its Committee on Usefulness in the 1950s, through which he worked to clarify the lines of responsibilities between the Board of Trustees and the Committee of Revision.[15]

AMERICAN FOUNDATION FOR PHARMACEUTICAL EDUCATION

The National Drug Trade Conference (NDTC) was formed in 1913 by five pharmacy industry and professional associations interested in legislation to control opium and narcotics: the American Drug Manufacturers Association, APhA, American Pharmaceutical Manufacturers Association, Federal Wholesale Druggists Association, and the National Association of Retail Druggists.[16] The legislation that eventually passed was the Harrison Narcotic Act in 1914. By 1935 the NDTC had expanded to include AACP, NABP, and the Proprietary Association; the National Association of Chain Drug Stores joined in 1947. From 1935 until 1940, Ernest Little served as the AACP representative to NDTC and chaired the Committee on Endowment. Charged with advising NDTC members of the financial needs of the colleges, Little's reports exposed the financial frailty of many of the colleges due to reduced funding and enrollments at a time of rising concerns about the shortages of pharmacists; he recommended the establishment of a foundation to address funding support. After a tortuous process to gain unanimous support, the NDTC approved formation of the AFPE on December 10, 1941.[17] At the incorporation meeting on June 22, 1942, Ernest Little was elected chair to serve until the first annual meeting, when he was elected the first president.[18]

Initially, the Foundation had four objectives, with the support for strong undergraduate programs the most important. As a first step two surveys were conducted to assess the needs of the colleges. Based on the data gathered about decreasing enrollment and lack of scholarship support, two scholarships of $200 were provided to each of the 64 colleges of pharmacy in 1943 and again in 1944. Each college received one $100 scholarship in 1945. Serious financial problems were reported by 17 colleges, with several reporting the possibility of closure. Grants ranging from $2,500 to $7,500 were awarded in 1944 to 13 schools having the most pressing needs. While these early grants were generous, the Foundation's total underwriting of Elliott's *Pharmaceutical Survey* was even greater. Ernest Little served as president and then director of AFPE until 1950, acting director in 1950 upon the death of Edwin Newcomb, and then on the Board of Grants until 1967.

Retiring APhA President Sylvester Dretzka (on right) installs Ernest Little as APhA President at the August 8–14, 1948, APhA Annual Meeting in San Francisco.

CHAMPION OF INCLUSION

An important aspect of AFPE was the inclusion of all parties with an interest in pharmacy education—educators, practitioners, wholesalers, and manufacturers. As might be expected, some educators had misgivings about the motives of the wholesalers and manufacturers. Rufus Lyman, editor of the *American Journal of Pharmaceutical Education* and a member of the executive board of AACP in support of Little, challenged such thinking by noting there was as much idealism in industry as in academia.[19]

In 1949 Little was chosen the Remington Medalist to recognize "his tireless efforts on behalf of pharmacy education, for his sane and intelligent attitude toward pharmacy in all its subdivisions, for his excellent handling of students who have come under his supervision...and for his great interest in the general welfare of pharmacy."[3] In his address, "The Wide Walls of Pharmacy," Little spoke of the contributions and challenges of pharmacy in all its branches—practice, education, manufacturing, and wholesaling. After noting that no part of pharmacy could be stronger than the weakest link, he concluded, "May the walls of our house of pharmacy be built wide and strong. Wide enough to include all that is best from all sectors of our diversified professions, strong enough to resist undermining influences which beset it.

From such a structure may we go forward together with a determination and a singleness of purpose which will result in accomplishments greater than ever before achieved, and which will make pharmacy's future worthy of its past."[20]

LEGACY

Despite not being educated as a pharmacist, Ernest Little was considered by others to be one. In 1945 Temple University bestowed an honorary doctor of laws on him, an event lauded by Rufus Lyman as not only honoring the man but also the progress of pharmaceutical education.[21] Little also received an honorary doctor of science from the Philadelphia College of Pharmacy and Science and a doctor of pharmacy from Rutgers. The New Jersey Pharmaceutical Association named him the first recipient of the Oscar Singer Medal for his individual achievement in the field of organized pharmaceutical activities.[22] He received the Remington Medal for his positive activism in the formation of the partnership necessary to bring the AFPE into existence. Today the programs that he helped establish through his work with all professional and trade organizations continue to support students, faculty, and colleges of pharmacy.

REFERENCES

1. Fisher AB. *A Half Century of Service to Pharmacy, 1942–1992.* Fairlawn, N.J.: American Foundation for Pharmaceutical Education [1992]:189–90.

2. Bliven C. Ernest Little. *Am J Pharm Educ.* 1974;38:125.

3. Lyman RA. Editorial. *Am J Pharm Educ.* 1949;13:552.

4. Bowers RA, Cowen DL. *The Rutgers University College of Pharmacy: A Centennial History.* New Brunswick, N.J.: Rutgers University Press; 1991:223–4.

5. Marquis AN. *Who's Who in Pennsylvania.* Chicago: A.N. Marquis Co.; 1939:524–5.

6. Anonymous. The president of the American Association of Colleges of Pharmacy, 1934–1935. *J Am Pharm Assoc.* 1934;23:651–2.

7. Worthen DB. Heroes of pharmacy: Robert Phillip Fischelis 1891–1981: pharmacy activist. *J Am Pharm Assoc.* 2006;46:294–7.

8. Bowers RA, Cowen D.L. *The Rutgers University College of Pharmacy: A Centennial History.* New Brunswick, N.J.: Rutgers University Press; 1991:53–109.

9. American Council on Pharmaceutical Education. *J Am Pharm Assoc.* 1938;27:64–5.

10. Worthen DB. *Pharmacy in World War II.* Binghamton, N.Y.: Pharmaceutical Products Press; 2004:19–28.

11. Buerki RA. In search of excellence. *Am J Pharm Educ.* 1999;63(suppl):55.

12. Little E. Address of the president of the American Association of Colleges of Pharmacy. *J Am Pharm Assoc.* 1935;24:659–73.

13. Griffenhagen GB, Higby G, Sonnedecker G, Swann J. *150 Years of Caring.* Washington, D.C.: American Pharmaceutical Association; 2002:175.

14. Little E. The president's address. *J Am Pharm Assoc, Pract Pharm Ed.* 1949;10:274–85.

15. Anderson L, Higby G. *The Spirit of Volunteerism: The United States Pharmacopoeia 1820–1995.* Rockville, Md.: United States Pharmacopoeial Convention; 1995:196–7, 348.

16. Beal JH. The proposed Pharmaceutical Federation. *Drug Circ.* 1919;63:131–5.

17. Little E. A step toward closer cooperation between industry and colleges of pharmacy. *Am J Pharm Educ.* 1942;6:111–6.

18. Fisher AB. *A Half Century of Service to Pharmacy, 1942–1992.* Fairlawn, N.J.: American Foundation for Pharmaceutical Education; 1992:1–9.

19. Lyman RA. The editor's page. *Am J Pharm Educ.* 1944;8:242–5.

20. Little E. The wide walls of pharmacy. In: Griffenhagen GB, Bowles GC, Penna RP, Worthen DB. *Reflections on Pharmacy by the Remington Medalists 1919–2003.* Washington, D.C.: American Pharmacists Association; 2004:156–9.

21. Lyman RA. The editor's page. *Am J Pharm Educ.* 1945;9:423–4.

22. Cowen DL. *The New Jersey Pharmaceutical Association, 1870–1970.* Trenton: New Jersey Pharmaceutical Association; 1970:106.

Rufus Ashley Lyman (1875-1957): A Towering Figure in the Field of Pharmaceutical Education

The *Journal of the American Pharmaceutical Association* described the 1947 Remington Medalist Rufus A. Lyman as a "towering figure in the field of pharmaceutical education" and "one of pharmacy's most loveable characters."[1] While accurate, neither statement gives a complete sense of the man who, although not a pharmacist by training, was one of the most outspoken champions of increasing standards in American pharmacy education.

BEGINNINGS

Rufus Ashley Lyman was born in Table Rock, Nebr., on April 17, 1875. His parents, William Graves and Sophie Lee (Allen) Lyman, were pioneers who moved to Nebraska in 1867, the year it was admitted to statehood. In writing about his early life, Lyman noted that he was unlikely to be successful as a farmer but had some possibilities as a country doctor. His parents insisted that he receive a proper education rather than the 6-month diploma schools that were widely available.[2] He graduated from Table Rock High School and enrolled at the University of Nebraska in Lincoln in 1892. He earned three degrees from the university, the BA in 1897, MA in 1899, and MD in 1903. Following his graduation from medical school, he was named as an instructor in physiology and pharmacology.

FOUNDING A SCHOOL

Under Nebraska law, the Board of Regents could form a school, but a new college had to be approved by the legislature. In 1908 E. Benjamin Andrews, the Chancellor of the University of Nebraska and a historian by training, decided to establish a school of pharmacy within the College of Medicine. While the dean of medicine was supportive, Lyman noted, "[A] few were violently opposed. Most faculty members were indifferent. Outside the

Rufus Lyman became Editor of the American Journal of Pharmaceutical Education *in 1937.*

University, among the practicing druggists, four were sympathetic. Most were indifferent."[3] Despite the lack of enthusiasm, the new school was created, and Lyman was named its director. He had little tolerance for the typical pharmacy curriculum of the day, maintaining that it was both devitalizing and nonstimulating. By 1913, Lyman made a 4-year high school education a prerequisite for admission to his program, when 1 year of high school was still the minimum American Conference of Pharmaceutical Faculties (ACPF) standard. He introduced more biological subjects into the curriculum and instituted what may have been the first required pharmacology course with both lectures and laboratories in a 2-year pharmacy program.[4] However, the College of Medicine's lack of support created problems. Student morale was a problem, compounded by the attitude of some pharmacists.[5] Nevertheless, the university petitioned the state legislature to elevate the school to a college in 1915, and, after approval, Lyman was named its first dean.

ASSOCIATION LEADER

The University of Nebraska joined ACPF in 1913; Lyman attended the 1914 annual meeting.[1] Lyman's level of interest and participation were evidenced by his election as president of the Conference in 1917. His agenda for educational standards and association advancement was presented in his speech at the 1917 annual meeting. He recommended that the requirement for a 4-year high school diploma become binding on all colleges of pharmacy by 1920 and the requirement of at least 1 year of college work in pharmacy be required by 1925 and 2 years by 1930. His recommendations for the Conference included the adoption of a new name, a modified committee structure that included a committee devoted to student and alumni activities, and a request for the Carnegie Foundation to do a study of "every institution purporting to teach pharmacy." He also recommended the establishment of an honorary scholarship fraternity in pharmacy. He decried the lack of involvement of many of the schools that were members of the Conference, even going as far as naming the ones who had never participated in the annual meetings. He noted, "Service is what we need most. One does not get into heaven by paying his fees. The man who buys a liberty bond does not render the same service as he who goes to the trenches in France."[6]

Status quo was not accorded a position of honored privilege in Lyman's view. He was blunt, well prepared, quick witted, and intolerant of any who stood in the way of bettering educational standards and, more importantly, pharmacy and its practitioners. The Conference did not accept all of the recommendations; the requirement of a high school diploma was delayed until 1923, and the requirement for minimum college requirements was delayed for study for at least a year.[7] The name of the Conference would not be changed to the American Association of Colleges of Pharmacy (AACP) until 1925, but the 1917 address was prescient of the vision and approach for improving pharmacy education that Lyman would use throughout his career.

EDITOR

At the 1935 annual meeting of AACP, Lyman suggested the need for a journal devoted to pharmacy education. He argued that the then-current process of publishing an annual proceedings and a small department on educational affairs in the *Journal of the American Pharmaceutical Association* was no longer adequate to meet the needs of either the organization or its members.

The association placed the development of the *Journal* and its contents squarely in Lyman's hands, and the first issue of the *American Journal of Pharmaceutical Education* (*AJPE*) was published in January 1937. In his first editorial, Lyman summarized the process leading to the inception of the *Journal* and the anticipated content. He promised that he would weigh all material to determine whether it was worth the $2.30 a page publication cost.[8] When the initial subscription numbers did not meet Lyman's expectation, he decided that he would publish the subscription list, noting that if the faculty "can't spend $2 a year in the support of a journal dealing in pharmaceutical education, I would advise them to go into some other line of work."[9] Years later Ernest Little, dean of the Rutgers College of Pharmacy and the 1935 AACP president, called the *Journal* "Lyman's Journal," recognizing the force behind the publication's success.[10]

Rufus Lyman served as the editor of *AJPE* from its founding until 1955 and as consulting editor until his death. He never wavered in his support for increasing educational standards, and he was ever willing to take on individuals and organizations that stood in the way. One example occurred in 1948 when he took up the subject of educators who averred that it was impossible to improve standards until the state boards increased licensure requirements. Lyman noted that it was the educators who used the slogan "go slow," arguing that the colleges could not increase the standards of education until the Boards increased practice standards. Lyman responded, "This was the time I first recognized the need of the funerals of a lot of deans."[11] Lyman used his editorial pen as a peacemaker as well. After the 1943 annual AACP meeting, he editorialized on the tensions between that group and the American Council on Pharmaceutical Education over the accreditation of the superaccelerated program shortening the pharmacy course to 2 years of continuous courses. He wrote of his personal dissatisfaction with those attacking the motives of the individuals serving on the accreditation body, commenting that such attacks were unjustified and inappropriate.[12] "The sign that you are doing a good job is that you are keeping the Indians stirred up," Lyman said in describing his editorial outlook to his successor, Melvin Gibson. "When you do that there is progress."[13]

Lyman believed that higher education standards would lead to better practice in the drugstore. However, as much as he loved pharmacy, he was not shy about focusing his editorial wit when practice did not meet his standards. In a 1944 editorial discussing some colleges' efforts to recruit high school students he cautioned, "The only danger in stressing the importance of pharmacy to the public is that we may make ourselves ridiculous in the public eye by claiming things that the public does not see in practice."[14] Sonnedecker noted that the editor "became legendary in American pharmaceutical education, and seemed to vindicate his opinion that 'the editorial pen of a few level headed, high thinking pharmaceutical editors can be made the most potent force in American pharmacy.'"[9]

When he received the 1947 Remington Medal from Curt Wimmer, Lyman (left) explained the difference between training and education.

In 1944 Lyman became the editor-in-chief of a new series of pharmacy texts published by J.B. Lippincott Co. The first volume of *American Pharmacy* appeared in 1945; the second volume was issued in 1947. Lyman noted in the preface that the book was to be a composite of the best pharmaceutical thought of the day, and the list of contributing authors substantiated that objective.[15] Lyman edited the first four editions of *American Pharmacy*.

STUDENT ADVOCATE

Rufus Lyman's advocacy for students was evident early in his deanship. In his 1917 ACPF presidential address he noted, "A man is not worthy of a deanship who did not keep in touch with and have a concern for his students after graduation."[6] He recommended the establishment of an honorary scholarship fraternity in pharmacy. He was also an early and ardent champion of women in pharmacy. In his role as chair of the AFPC Committee on Activities of Students and Alumni in 1921 he encouraged Zada Cooper in her formation of Kappa Epsilon. In 1955, Kappa Epsilon honored Lyman with the title of honorary founder.[16] Supporting women's role in pharmacy had an intensely personal side, as he humorously confessed in an editorial, "The Editor's Crime," which both supported women in pharmacy and commented on the organizational habit of referring recommendations to a committee rather than acting on them: "The editor is charged with criminal negligence. He is the father of three daughters, all pharmacists and [denies] that they present a problem to pharmacy. Editor admits daughters have presented problems as girls, but not as pharmacists. Editor asks that the matter be referred to President Roosevelt for girl control measure. Association refuses and refers whole matter to the Committee on the Study of Menace of Women to Pharmacy."[17]

In 1942 when students of Japanese American ancestry were removed from colleges on the West Coast, the University of Nebraska accepted many as transfer students. Pharmacy students Kazuo Kimura and Tom Miya remembered the support and mentoring that Dean Lyman provided in that time of disruption and fear.[18] Lyman showed his openness to all students, not just pharmacy students. He established the student health service at the University of Nebraska in 1919 and served as its director until 1945.[19] Years later, his son Edwin recalled that his father greeted each new university student in the registration line with a word about his home town, for as his father said, this kind word "might be the first and last that they would hear in their academic sojourn."[20]

APhA named Lyman as Honorary President in 1952, and AACP honored him in 1955.

FOUNDING A SCHOOL—AGAIN

In 1946, at the age of 72, Rufus Lyman retired from the University of Nebraska as dean emeritus. However, the University of Arizona was then forming a school of pharmacy in the College of Liberal Arts, and, in June 1947, the aging educator could not resist an invitation to move to Tucson and become the founding director. On July 1, 1949, with 2 years of experience and more than 100 students enrolled, the status of the school was elevated to that of a college; Lyman was named as founding dean for the second time in his career. In 1950 ACPE awarded a 4-Y status (the status that allowed graduates to take licensure examinations) to the school and, with the graduation of the first class in 1950, Dean Lyman once again retired.[21]

HONORS

Rufus Lyman, recognized by his peers for his lifelong advocacy of pharmacy educational standards and influential leadership, received the 1947 Remington Medal. Curt P. Wimmer, speaking for the New York Branch of the American

Pharmaceutical Association, presented him the medal, commenting, "In the councils of your colleagues, your lamp became a torch emitting red hot sparks that often burnt and seared and scorched—but always made for progress."[22] Lyman, never one to miss an opportunity to make a point, used part of his Remington speech to address the issue of the supply of pharmacists. He noted the rapidly shifting sentiment, first that there were too many graduates and, then, not enough. He went on to note the resistance of some to the formation of new schools—including his new school in Arizona. His response was to differentiate between training and education and the need for pharmacy to focus on the latter while eschewing the former. "If we *educate* instead of train, no man in this room will live to see the day when there will be an oversupply of pharmacists, for the areas of service and the avenues that lead to them will have become world-wide."[23]

In 1952, its centennial year, the American Pharmaceutical Association named Lyman its honorary president. In 1955 AACP conferred honorary membership on Dean Lyman, the highest honor the association could bestow. He was only the second recipient, the first being his long-time friend and worker in the Association, Zada Cooper.[24] In that same year the American Institute of the History of Pharmacy elected him as its honorary president.[3] In 1969 AACP established the Lyman Award for the outstanding paper published in the *American Journal of Pharmaceutical Education* during the preceding year. The University of Nebraska named the college of pharmacy building Lyman Hall.

PERSONAL LIFE

Rufus Lyman married Caroline (Carrie) Day on July 1, 1899, in Lincoln, Nebr. The couple had six children—sons Rufus and Edwin and daughters Esther, Caroline, Elizabeth, and Louise. Caroline died young; the surviving children chose health care professions as careers, both sons becoming physicians and the three remaining daughters all becoming pharmacists. Lyman died on October 12, 1957, in Lincoln, Nebr.

LEGACY

Rufus Lyman's legacy continues to influence pharmacy practice and education in the 21st century. His pioneering efforts—founding dean of two colleges of pharmacy and first editor of "Lyman's Journal," *AJPE*—endure today, influencing the education of pharmacists and providing a forum for research in pharmacy education. His efforts to support students continue through the Rho Chi and Kappa Epsilon organizations. Perhaps his most important legacy, however, was his unwavering support for increasing educational standards so that pharmacy stood on an equal footing with the other health care professions. Edward Elliott, director of the Pharmaceutical Survey and a member of the American Council on Pharmaceutical Education, wrote of Lyman's legacy: "Did I have the requisite academic authority, there would be conferred upon Rufus Lyman the degree of D.S.P.—Doctor of the Spirit of Pharmacy—in recognition of his selfless and altruistic contributions to the strength of and services to the profession he has served so long. Pharmacy will ever need men of his character and competency."[25]

REFERENCES

1. Rufus A. Lyman. Remington Medalist 1947. *J Am Pharm Assoc (Pract Pharm Ed)*. 1947;8:320–1.

2. Lyman RA. Personal notes. In: *Kremers Reference Files*. Madison, Wis.: American Institute of the History of Pharmacy; "A2" file.

3. Burt JB. Rufus Ashley Lyman, a biographical sketch. *Am J Pharm Educ*. 1956;20:1–7.

4. Parascandola J, Swann J. Development of pharmacology in American schools of pharmacy. *Pharm Hist*. 1983;26:95–115.

5. Lyman RA. Dr. Lyman comments.... *Am J Pharm Educ*. 1957;21:298–302.

6. Lyman RA. Presidential address. Proceedings of the 18th annual meeting of the American Conference of Pharmaceutical Faculties, Indianapolis, Indiana, 1917, pp. 30–70.

7. Anderson WC. Report of the committee on the president's address. Proceedings of the 18th annual meeting of the American Conference of Pharmaceutical Faculties, Indianapolis, Indiana, 1917, pp. 136–71.

8. Lyman RA. The editor's page. *Am J Pharm Educ*. 1937;1:103–6.

9. Sonnedecker G. The founding of AACP's journal. *Am J Pharm Educ*. 1986;50:491–5.

10. Little E. Lyman's journal. *Am J Pharm Educ*. 1961;25:10–1.

11. Lyman RA. The editor's page. *Am J Pharm Educ*. 1948;12:570–6.

12. Lyman R. The editor's page. *Am J Pharm Educ*. 1943;7:564–9.

13. Gibson MR. Rufus A. Lyman: journal editor. *Am J Pharm Educ*. 1975;39:3–9.

14. Lyman RA. The editor's page. *Am J Pharm Educ*. 1944;8:652.

15. Lyman RA, ed. *American Pharmacy*. Philadelphia: J.B. Lippincott Co.; 1945.

16. Henderson ML. *American Women Pharmacists: Contributions to the Profession*. Pharmaceutical Products Press: Binghamton, N.Y.; 2002: 89.

17. Lyman RA. The editor's crime. *Am J Pharm Educ*. 1937;1:209.

18. Commemorative album. University of Nebraska–Lincoln, Nisei Reunion, November 4–5, 1994.

19. Gibson MR. Memorials—Rufus Ashley Lyman. *Am J Pharm Educ*. 1958;22:100–2.

20. Tom J. Rufus Ashley Lyman: pioneer in pharmacy. *Pharm Hist*. 1972;14:90–94,111.

21. Bender GA. *The History of Arizona Pharmacy*. Arizona Pharmacy Historical Foundation; 1985:477.

22. Wimmer CP. A citation. *Am J Pharm Educ*. 1948;12:332.

23. Lyman RA. Don't confuse training with education. In: Griffenhagen G, Blockstein W, Krigstein D, eds. *The Remington Lectures: A Century in American Pharmacy*. Washington, D.C.: American Pharmaceutical Association; 1974;142–52.

24. Minutes of the annual meeting. *Am J Pharm Educ*. 1955;19:572–3.

25. Elliott EC. When? A personal measure of him who was and is. *Am J Pharm Educ*. 1956; 29:8–9.

John Michael Maisch (1831–1893):
Father of Adequate Pharmaceutical Legislation

Historian George Urdang coined the sobriquet "Father of Adequate Pharmaceutical Legislation" for John Michael Maisch.[1] Urdang later wrote that three men—William Procter, Jr., Edward Parrish, and Maisch—were among "the galaxy of men of knowledge, talent, and character who, in the second half of the 19th century, dug the channel into which the various brooks could be directed and made to form the river, The American Profession of Pharmacy."[2]

YOUTH AND IMMIGRATION

Maisch was born in Hanau, Germany, on January 30, 1831, the son of merchant Conrad Maisch and Agnese Louise Liebtreu. The young Maisch attended local schools, where he studied languages and the sciences. He gained a scholarship at the *oberrealschule* in Hanau, where he studied botany and zoology from 1844 to 1848 and learned how to use a microscope.[3] He took special classes in languages and chemistry in preparation for university studies. He was especially interested in chemical experiments, and gained experience in the chemistry of fatty acids and resins.[4]

In his late teens, Maisch joined the Turners of Hanau, a group of gymnasts and others who had embraced the goal of political reform and revolution, which included the overthrow of traditional aristocracies and the formation of a unified German democracy. Maisch was imprisoned in 1849 after being captured with other Turners at Sinsheim, near Heidelberg. He managed to escape from prison, however, and soon left for the United States. He arrived in Baltimore in September 1849, alone, penniless, and without professional training.[5] Although his formal education had been interrupted, Maisch proved himself a talented chemist. In 1853 he won two silver medals for exhibitions of chemicals that he made, one from the Maryland Institute for the Promotion of the Mechanical Arts in Baltimore and the second from the Metropolitan Mechanical Institute in Washington, D.C.[6]

Maisch presented his draft of the first model state pharmacy law at the September 1869 APhA Annual Meeting in Chicago (shown here). Two months later, he sent the proposal to create state pharmacy boards to all state governors and state legislators.

After a short stint as a factory worker, Maisch found employment in various drugstores in Baltimore, Washington, D.C., and New York City. In 1856, while working in the store of E.B. Garrigues and Robert Shoemaker & Co. in Philadelphia, Maisch attracted the attention of Edward Parrish, who in 1849 had opened his School of Practical Pharmacy at the back of his store for the instruction of medical students.[2] In 1859 Parrish invited Maisch to teach a practical pharmacy course and laboratory. Maisch stayed in this position until he left Philadelphia in 1861 to teach at the College of Pharmacy of the City of New York.[5]

NEW YORK COLLEGE OF PHARMACY

In 1861 Maisch received an invitation to take over the chair of materia medica and pharmacy at the New York College of Pharmacy. Pharmacists of the period were apprentice-trained; only a few took a series of lectures in a college of pharmacy. Maisch's course covered the preparation of medications and principles of botany while focusing on the "history, composition, properties, preparations, impurities, and adulterations of all of the officinal and the most important unofficinal drugs."[7] In his introductory address to the students, Maisch articulated his perspective on the responsibilities of those who would become pharmacists. He stated that both physicians and pharmacists owed their first responsibility to patients. He emphasized that commercial concerns were subservient to patients' needs: "He who intentionally does not fulfill his assumed duties, he who disregards the seemingly humble or unnecessary offices incidental to a pharmaceutical life, he who is constantly occupied with thoughts withdrawing his mental faculties and his manual labor from the work required of him behind the counter and in the laboratory, is unfit for the profession of pharmacy, and had better discontinue his attempts at success in it, than waste his time, or make of professional pursuits nothing but a study of how the best bargain might be made, and the most money accumulated."[8]

CIVIL WAR MANUFACTURING

During his time in New York City, Maisch worked part-time in the laboratories of Edward Robinson Squibb. At the time, Squibb manufactured medications and medicine chests for the Union Army, and Maisch learned much about large-scale manufacturing and quality control.[4] Largely due to this experience, in 1863 Squibb recommended Maisch for the position of chief chemist at the Army Medical Laboratory in Philadelphia.[9]

From 1863 through the end of the Civil War, Maisch was responsible for planning and managing the Philadelphia laboratory's administration and operations. In a postwar report, Maisch noted that the laboratory had manufactured many items at prices below current market values and, in doing so, saved the government more than $750,000. This report gives the quantities of items manufactured, their costs, and their assumed market value, thus providing a detailed list of many of the medications used during the conflict.[10] Maisch used the Philadelphia laboratory as an opportunity to teach others the manufacturing skills he had acquired. George Winston Smith noted that the Philadelphia laboratory was "an important in-training experience for young men who were able to grasp the significance of pharmacy in connection with the new industrialism that the war was helping to bring into being."[9] One of the trainees was C. Lewis Diehl, who went on to found a school of pharmacy in Louisville.

PHILADELPHIA COLLEGE OF PHARMACY

In 1860, before moving to New York, Maisch was elected a trustee of the Philadelphia College of Pharmacy (PCP). At the close of the war, he opened his own pharmacy in Philadelphia and began teaching at the college. In 1866 Maisch was selected to take the chair of pharmacy, succeeding "Father of American Pharmacy" William Procter Jr. A year later, Maisch traded this appointment with Parrish, who held the chair of materia medica. This exchange fit Maisch's interest in pharmacognosy, and the title of the chair was expanded to include materia medica and botany. It was during his 26 years in this position that Maisch gained eminence as one of America's pioneer pharmacognosists.[11] In 1870 PCP instituted a pharmaceutical and chemical laboratory under Maisch's direction. Later, Joseph Remington took on responsibility for the pharmaceutical portion of the laboratory. Maisch remained responsible for the chemical work until he resigned in 1881, when Frederick B. Power took over.

An early proponent of lifelong learning, Maisch admonished PCP's 1872 graduating class to "not neglect your studies hereafter, nor rest under the illusion that the acquisition of your new title, which you this day lawfully assume, constitutes the termination of the further attainment of knowledge; remember, on the contrary, that your admittance into the ranks of the pharmaceutical profession places you on the lower steps of the ladder to professional eminence, and that to gain the summit requires a continuation of that fruitful labor."[12] In 1879 Maisch was elected dean of the faculty of PCP; he held the position until his death in 1893.[13] He also served as the college's delegate to the United States Pharmacopoeial (USP) Convention beginning in 1870, and he served on the USP Committee of Revision for three decades.[5]

Maisch began his lifelong writing career in 1854, when he published his first paper on the adulteration of medications in the *American Journal of Pharmacy* (*AJP*). He became a consistent and prolific contributor to the journal. In 1870 he was selected to succeed Procter as *AJP* editor just as it changed from a bimonthly to a monthly publication. Maisch's research articles and editorials were common features in *AJP* until his death in 1893.[4] During his career he published more than 400 papers, mostly in *AJP* but also in the *Proceedings of the American Pharmaceutical Association* and the German publication *Repertorium für die Pharmacie*.[5] In 1879 Maisch, working with physician Alfred Stille, published the *National Dispensatory Containing the Natural History, Chemistry, Pharmacy, Actions and Uses of Medicines, Including Those Recognized in the Pharmacopoeias of the United States and Great Britain*.[14] Stille provided the clinical materials, and Maisch was responsible for the other sections of the work. The book was received enthusiastically and went through five editions. Maisch also wrote the *Manual of Organic Materia Medica*, revised Rochleder's *Proximate Analysis of Plants and Vegetable Substances*, and edited the third edition of Griffith's *Universal Formulary*.

AMERICAN PHARMACEUTICAL ASSOCIATION

Maisch joined the American Pharmaceutical Association (APhA) in 1856 and was soon appointed chairman of the Committee on the Progress of Pharmacy.[1] He served as the 1862–1863 APhA corresponding secretary and the first vice president in 1863–1864. In 1865 Maisch was appointed the first permanent secretary of the Association, a position that has changed titles over the years and is now executive vice president.

During the APhA Annual Meeting in 1867, a resolution was adopted to offer the assistance of the Association "to urge upon our legislators the importance of a judicious, but certain, determined, and as far as practicable, uniform control of the practice of pharmacy in the various states."[15] At the 1868 meeting, Maisch reported on the status of professional regulation in the various states and convinced the attendees of the need to develop model

Maisch had a rugged face, was outspoken, and possessed a retentive memory. This auto-graphed photo was taken about 1875.

legislation that states could use. At the 1869 APhA Annual Meeting in Chicago, the draft of a proposed law "To Regulate the Practice of Pharmacy and the Sale of Poisons, and to Prevent the Adulteration of Drugs and Medicines" was discussed. Although acceptance of the draft was less than complete, convention delegates did agree to have copies provided to legislators in each state. Among the most important components of the model pharmacy act were provisions in sections 5 and 6 calling for the establishment of a state pharmaceutical board and identifying board duties, respectively.[16] In 1870 Rhode Island became the first state to implement a pharmacy practice act based on the model. By the time of Maisch's death in 1893, most states had enacted pharmacy practice acts.

The model legislation was meant to help the states regulate pharmacists and pharmacy for the safety and welfare of the public. Maisch clearly understood the importance of having pharmacists in the individual states champion legislation. In 1874 he encouraged the establishment of local associations since so few states had colleges, or local associations, in place.[17] There were 14 state associations before 1878, when Maisch personally assisted in the formation of the Pennsylvania state association; pharmacists in other states soon established their own associations.[3] Thus, the passage of practice acts was influenced by the formation of state associations and by the availability of a model practice act that established pharmacy's duty to the public.[18] Maisch's contributions to the formation of state associations were evidenced by at least 15 associations, including those in New Jersey, California, and Massachusetts (all in 1871), that made him an honorary member.[6]

Just weeks before his death, Maisch was notified that he had been awarded the Hanbury Gold Medal by the Pharmaceutical Society of Great Britain in recognition of his original research into the natural history and chemistry of drugs. This marked the first time an American received the medal.

Although Maisch never completed his formal education, he received a number of honorary degrees. In 1871 the Maryland College of Pharmacy named him a graduate of pharmacy and bestowed on him the title of doctor of pharmacy. In 1888 he was named an alumnus of PCP, and the following year, the college bestowed the degree of master in pharmacy upon Maisch.[3]

Maisch possessed a remarkable memory for all things pharmaceutical.[19] He had a high sense of honor and was outspoken, even to the point of brusqueness, in condemning error. However, he always retained an open mind and was willing to change his views when facts warranted.[4] Maisch married Charlotte Justine Kuhl in 1859; they had eight children. Maisch died in Philadelphia on September 10, 1893, of a malignant growth in the throat.

LEGACY

Maisch impressed his sense of professional responsibility and idealism on the young APhA. As the organization's first permanent secretary, he implanted a vision of the pharmacist's responsibility to the public. In his early career, Maisch was largely focused on the issues of adulteration and standards, and he perceived that the best way to assure the public good was through consistent and enforceable standards. The model pharmacy practice act of 1869, its use as a basis for state practice acts, and the subsequent formation of state associations were direct consequences of Maisch's vision. In a moment of accurate prophesy, one of his obituaries noted that although Maisch was dead, "his spirit and his influence will live."[19]

REFERENCES

1. Urdang G. The fiftieth anniversary of the death of John Michael Maisch. *Am J Pharm.* 1944;116:14–24.

2. Urdang G. Edward Parrish, a forgotten pharmaceutical reformer. *Am J Pharm Educ.* 1950;4:223–32.

3. Prof. John M. Maisch, Phar.D. *Alumni Rpt Alumni Assoc Philadelphia Coll Pharm.* 1893;30: 5–9.

4. Remington JP. Prof. J.M. Maisch. *Am J Pharm.* 1894;66:1–9.

5. Cowen DL. Maisch, John Michael. In: Garraty JA, Carnes MC, eds. *American National Biography*. New York, NY: Oxford University Press; 1999:349–51.

6. Wilbert MI. John Michael Maisch, an ideal pharmacist. *Am J Pharm.* 1903;75:351–77.

7. Wimmer CP. *The College of Pharmacy of the City of New York Included in Columbia University on 1904: A History*. New York, NY: C.P. Wimmer; 1929:55.

8. Maisch JM. College of pharmacy introductory address. *Am Med Times* 1861;3:292–5.

9. Smith GW. *Medicines for the Union Army: The United States Army Laboratories During the Civil War*. Binghamton, NY: Pharmaceutical Products Press; 2001: 33, 73. Reprint.

10. Maisch JM. Statistics of the U.S. Army Laboratory at Philadelphia. *Proc APhA.* 1866;14:272–8.

11. Youngken H.W. Eminent American pharmacognosists of the nineteenth century. *J Am Pharm Assoc.* 1935;24:148–52.

12. Maisch JM. Valedictory. *Ann Rpt Philadelphia Coll Pharm.* 1872; 8:8–15.

13. England JW. *The First Century of the Philadelphia College of Pharmacy, 1821–1921* Philadelphia, Pa: Philadelphia College of Pharmacy; 1922:406.

14. Stille A, Maisch JM. *National Dispensatory Containing the Natural History, Chemistry, Pharmacy, Actions and Uses of Medicines, Including Those Recognized in the Pharmacopoeias of the United States and Great Britain*. Philadelphia, Pa: Henry C. Lea; 1879.

15. Minutes of the fifteenth Annual Meeting. *Proc Am Pharm Assoc.* 1867;15:105–6.

16. Draft of a proposed law. *Proc Am Pharm Assoc.* 1869;17:51–76.

17. Maisch JM. Pharmaceutical colleges and associations. *Am J Pharm.* 1874;46:346–7.

18. Sonnedecker G *Kremers and Urdang's History of Pharmacy*. 4th ed. Madison, Wis. American Institute of the History of Pharmacy; 1963:379.

19. John Michael Maisch. *Pharm Era.* 1893;10:243.

Edward Parrish (1822–1872): Pioneer Ethicist

In a 1950 essay, historian George Urdang characterized Edward Parrish, William Procter, Jr., and John Michael Maisch as those who "in the second half of the nineteenth century, dug the channel into which the isolated brooks could be directed and made to form the river,—'The American profession of Pharmacy.'"[1] It was Parrish who took on the role of the pioneer ethicist questioning the moral responsibilities of the pharmacist.[2]

PERSONAL LIFE

Edward Parrish was born on May 31, 1822, in Philadelphia, the seventh son of the surgeon and physician Joseph Parrish and Susanna Cox. He was brought up as a Quaker and attended the Friends' School in Philadelphia. He apprenticed with his brother Dillwyn and graduated from the Philadelphia College of Pharmacy in 1842. Sometime later, Parrish took a course in chemical analysis with Professor Booth and a medical course at the University of Pennsylvania.[3] In 1848, Edward married Margaret Hunt of Philadelphia; they had four sons and a daughter. On September 9, 1872, while serving on a government commission to Indian tribes under the supervision of the Society of Friends, Edward Parrish died of malarial fever at Fort Sill, Indian Territory (now Oklahoma).[4]

PARRISH'S SCHOOL AND TEXT

In 1843, Parrish purchased a pharmacy next to the University of Pennsylvania that resulted in close contact with medical students. This arrangement led to a successful business in outfitting country practitioners with medical supplies. It also exposed the need for physicians to have better instruction in the practical aspects of preparing medicines, especially those practicing in rural settings without the services of an apothecary. In 1849, he advertised the opening of his School of Practical Pharmacy in which physicians would be taught to "prepare the medicines of the pharmacopoeia by actual manipulation."[3] A total of 14 students were enrolled in the first course. In 1850, Edward Parrish joined his brother Dillwyn as a partner and moved the school to larger quarters where it could serve pharmacy as well as medical students. In 1857, Parrish reported that 299 medical students had completed the course during the previous 8 years. The significance of this undertaking should not be underestimated; Parrish "turned the tables on the medical profession," arguing that physicians who wanted to practice pharmacy should be taught by master pharmacists.[5]

In 1855 Parrish published the first wholly American pharmacy text, *Introduction to Practical Pharmacy*, a natural outgrowth of his teaching efforts. The full title provided a clear statement of both content and anticipated audience: *An introduction to practical pharmacy: designed as a text-book for the student, and as a guide to the physician and pharmaceutist. With many formulas and prescriptions.* Parrish's book, more representative of the practice of pharmacy in America than Procter's earlier work, went through two additional editions during Parrish's lifetime (1859 and 1864) and two editions after his death.[6]

PHILADELPHIA COLLEGE OF PHARMACY

Edward Parrish was elected a member of the Philadelphia College of Pharmacy upon graduation in 1842. He became a member of the board of trustees in March 1845 and Secretary from 1845 to 1852.[3]

It was largely due to the efforts of Parrish, Procter, and Augustine Duhamel in 1845 that the first chair in Theoretical and Practical Pharmacy was established.[7] Wanting a deeper association with the college, Parrish applied for the position of the professor of materia medica when it became vacant in 1850. He was unsuccessful because the chair had historically been held only by a physician.[8] In 1864, upon the death of the professor of materia medica, he again applied for the position and was accepted. In 1867, he exchanged chairs with John Michael Maisch, becoming the chair of pharmacy, his primary interest, and held the chair until his death in 1872.

ASSOCIATION ACTIVITIES

Although not designated as an official delegate of the Philadelphia College of Pharmacy, Edward Parrish participated in the organizational meeting of the American Pharmaceutical (now Pharmacists) Association (APhA) in October 1852. While the development of a constitution and election of officers dominated this initial meeting, Parrish offered a resolution to undertake the first national survey of the practice and practitioners of American pharmacy.[9] The survey elicited responses from at least 19 states and provided data on the number of stores and practitioners as well as local associations and laws.[10]

In 1853, Parrish was elected Recording Secretary of the Association and served as its first Vice President in 1866. At the 1866 meeting, delegates spent considerable time discussing the proper term to use for the profession and its practitioners. Delegates argued over the relative merits of the terms "apothecary," "pharmacian," "pharmaceutist," "pharmacal," and "pharmacical." Parrish's proposal to adopt the word "pharmacist" was accepted and referred

Edward Parrish was a founding member of APhA, recording secretary (1853–1854), first vice president (1866–1867), president (1868–1869), and Philadelphia community pharmacist from 1843 until his death.

to the Executive Committee. The following year, the Association voted to adopt the term "pharmacist."[11]

Parrish was elected president of the Association in 1868. In his presidential address he spoke of the Pennsylvania Medical Society's failed attempt to place all pharmacists under the scrutiny of a political officer to examine store stocks for adulterated items. Parrish unsuccessfully urged attendees to approve a draft of a proposed law that would regulate the sale of poisons and the practice of pharmacy and prevent inappropriate meddling by medical societies or state bureaucracies.[12]

ETHICIST

William Procter admired Parrish's ability to reflect and write on topics such as ethics and education.[3] The development of a code of ethics was among the first orders of business during the formation of APhA in 1852. Based on the 1848 Philadelphia College of Pharmacy Code of Ethics, APhA's version required pharmacists to swear to uphold the code as a precondition for membership. One of the articles of the Code required the "discontinuance of secret formulae and the practices arising from a quackish spirit" and to "discountenance quackery" to help control the sale of nostrums and patent medicines.[13]

In 1854, Parrish published a thought-provoking three-part essay on American pharmacy. He listed the duties of the pharmacist that were linked with public health, differentiating them from solely commercial trades. He concluded that pharmacists owed a duty to those who would follow by "imbuing them with a high appreciation of the importance and responsibility of their calling."[14] Parrish maintained that the 1852 Code of Ethics would have negative consequences by excluding those pharmacists who wanted to better their practice but were economically dependent on the sale of nonofficial medicines. He encouraged organized pharmacy to "abolish all tests of membership, and trust to the force of sound principle and the contagion of good example to spread through our ranks a higher and better standard of practice." Thus, Parrish believed that the Code represented a goal rather than the reality of practice.[14]

In 1855, the Code of Ethics was discontinued as a membership prerequisite largely as a result of Parrish's argument that the sale of patent medicine was essential to the economic survival of many pharmacists who would be barred from joining the Association.[15] This position, however, did not signal a withdrawal from Parrish's devotion to encouraging pharmacists to uphold the principles of ethical behavior. In 1857, he delivered a thoughtful address noting the need for ethical analysis, suggesting seven questions of particular note to pharmacists. He questioned the "moral right" of the pharmacist to (1) "neglect the opportunities of scientific and practical improvement within his reach," (2) keep "secret for his own advantage" discoveries or improvements that would "affect the health and consequent welfare" of the public and the practice of pharmacy, (3) neglect the "thorough education" of his apprentices, (4) take advantage of "the poor and ignorant" who have his confidence by taking their hard earnings in exchange for "costly and often worse than useless medicines, which, through the public press are plausibly and insidiously recommended to them," (5) support the "intemperate use" of stimulants and narcotic agents, (6) question the "true ethical limitations to the rules of trade" as applied to the practice of pharmacy, and (7) consider to what extent competition is "allowable in conducting the drug business."[16]

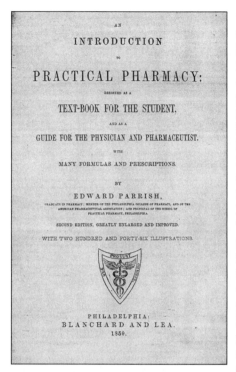

AN

INTRODUCTION

TO

PRACTICAL PHARMACY:

DESIGNED AS A

TEXT-BOOK FOR THE STUDENT,

AND AS A

GUIDE FOR THE PHYSICIAN AND PHARMACEUTIST.

WITH

MANY FORMULAS AND PRESCRIPTIONS

BY

EDWARD PARRISH,

GRADUATE IN PHARMACY; MEMBER OF THE PHILADELPHIA COLLEGE OF PHARMACY, AND OF THE
AMERICAN PHARMACEUTICAL ASSOCIATION; AND PRINCIPAL OF THE SCHOOL OF
PRACTICAL PHARMACY, PHILADELPHIA.

SECOND EDITION, GREATLY ENLARGED AND IMPROVED.

WITH TWO HUNDRED AND FORTY-SIX ILLUSTRATIONS.

PHILADELPHIA:
BLANCHARD AND LEA.
1859.

Parrish published in 1855 the first textbook on the practice of American pharmacy, which went through two expanded editions during his lifetime (1859 and 1864), and two additional editions after his death.

Both the 1848 Code of Ethics of the Philadelphia College of Pharmacy and the 1852 Code of Ethics of the Association address the differences between pharmacists and physicians and enjoin pharmacists not to prescribe. Parrish put a broader voice to such relationships between the two groups when he denounced the common representation of pharmacists as the handmaidens of physicians. He spoke against the physicians "hectoring" some pharmacists for providing some symptomatic "over the counter" relief while pointing to physicians who kept a shop where their prescriptions were prepared by their own apprentices. In conclusion, Parrish abjured the position of handmaiden for that of a sister, albeit a modest and docile one.[17]

In 1867, Parrish continued his discourse on how pharmacy should be practiced. He explained that one of the commonly recognized differences between the professional and the shopkeeper was the work of the former in the area of ideas and the latter in the shop. While Parrish believed that there was nothing wrong with professionals working in the shop, he described the ideal shop as a suite of rooms where the patient is seated with appropriate reading material while the prescription is taken to an adjoining room to be compounded. Any medicine requested without a physician's prescription "could be furnished to order, or might be the subject of consultation with a pharmacist."[18]

Parrish was an influential voice in passage of the 1872 Pennsylvania pharmacy act that initially applied only to Philadelphia. The preamble to the act stated that, for public safety, only those with a practical knowledge of the science of pharmacy could dispense on the prescription of a doctor and only after having passed the examining board. Parrish was one of the five pharmacists named to the original board.[8]

SWARTHMORE

In 1862, Parrish was one of the founding group of Swarthmore College, established to provide quality education under control of the Friends. Parrish was an enthusiastic fundraiser and was selected as the first president of the college in 1865. In addition to his presidential role, Parrish taught ethics, chemistry, and physical sciences. His liberal approach to education, including coeducation and benevolent discipline, led to clashes with conservative members of the college, and he resigned in 1871. The main building on the campus was named Parrish Hall in his honor.[19]

STUDENTS

While serving as the association's first Vice President in 1866, Parrish exhorted the association to lend its weight to establish and support the colleges, arguing that this was the way to increase the status of pharmacy in the United States. He added that the young "who are to be educated in pharmacy, will raise the American Pharmaceutical Association hereafter to be a body of far greater efficiency than it ever has been."[20] In a paper prepared before his death, Edward Parrish noted that few pharmacy educators had more experience than he and that his was with both pharmacy and medical students. Using this experience he claimed that "what is most needed in pharmacy is a higher grade of preliminary education."[21]

Parrish's involvement with students was also personal. Procter noted that he was always popular for the interest that he took in students, both individually and as a group.[3] Edward Hicks Magill, who succeeded Parrish as president of Swarthmore, echoed the same sentiments when he recorded that Parrish was "always gentlemanly, kind, and courteous in his treatment of students, and was deservedly beloved by them."[22]

LEGACY

Urdang noted that of America's three pharmacy pioneers—Procter, Maisch, and Parrish—the last's contributions were often overshadowed by the strength of the other two. Urdang concluded that "there was no one who gave to American pharmacists so many incentives and outlooks, so much to think about as Parrish."[1] He noted, however, that Parrish's suggestions when heeded could bear fruit at a later time. The seven questions that Parrish posed in his essay "Ethical Analysis" addressed the relationships of pharmacists with patients, physicians, and other pharmacists, as well as the obligations to further and to share both scientific and professional knowledge. Thus, Edward Parrish may be seen as the father of American pharmacy ethics, a kind and thoughtful leader whose insights into professional ethical issues continue to challenge America's pharmacists in the 21st century.[16]

REFERENCES

1. Urdang G. Edward Parrish, a forgotten pharmaceutical reformer. *Am J Pharm Educ.* 1950;14:223–32.

2. Buerki RA, Vottero LD. *Ethical Responsibility in Pharmacy Practice*, 2nd ed. Madison, Wis.: American Institute of the History of Pharmacy; 2002:4.

3. Procter W. Edward Parrish. *Am J Pharm.* 1873;45:225–31.

4. Du Mez AG. Edward Parrish. In: Malone D. *Dictionary of American Biography*. New York: Charles Scribner's Sons; 1934, Vol. VII:258–9.

5. Sonnedecker G. *Kremers and Urdang's History of Pharmacy*, 4th ed. Madison, Wis.: American Institute of the History of Pharmacy; 1976:229.

6. Higby G. *In Service to American Pharmacy: The Professional Life of William Procter, Jr.* Tuscaloosa, Ala.: University of Alabama Press; 1992:140–1.

7. Higby G. *In Service to American Pharmacy: The Professional Life of William Procter, Jr.* Tuscaloosa, Ala.: University of Alabama Press; 1992:27.

8. England JW. *The First Century of the Philadelphia College of Pharmacy, 1821–1921.* Philadelphia: Philadelphia College of Pharmacy and Science; 1922:151–3.

9. Proceedings of the National Pharmaceutical Convention. *Am J Pharm.* 1853;25:1–19.

10. Griffenhagen GB, Higby G, Sonnedecker G, Swann J. *150 Years of Caring.* Washington, D.C.: American Pharmaceutical Association; 2002:175.

11. Parrish E. Discourse on titles. *Proc Am Pharm Assoc.* 1866;14:77–8, 257–64.

12. Parrish E. Presidential address. *Proc Am Pharm Assoc.* 1869;17:29–35.

13. Code of Ethics of the American Pharmaceutical Association. *Proceedings of the National Pharmaceutical Convention 1852.* Philadelphia: Merihew & Sons; 1865:24–6.

14. Parrish E. American pharmacy. *Am J Pharm.* 1854;26:115–8, 211–7, 289–92.

15. Anonymous. September 13th—Morning Session. *Proc Am Pharm Assoc.* 1855;4:9–10.

16. Parrish E. Ethical analysis. *Proc Am Pharm Assoc.* 1857;6:146–50.

17. Parrish E. A plea for the handmaiden. *Proc Am Pharm Assoc.* 1863;11:271–3.

18. Parrish E. A discourse on titles. *Am J Pharm.* 1867;39:239–46.

19. Edward Parrish papers, 1859–1872. Swarthmore College Archives, RG6/D01.

20. Parrish E. Comments. *Proc Am Pharm Assoc.* 1866;14:39–40.

21. Parrish E. Preliminary education of apprentices. *Proc Am Pharm Assoc.* 1872:20:173–8.

22. Magill EH. *Sixty-Five Years in the Life of a Teacher.* Boston: Houghton, Mifflin & Company; 1907:151–2.

Albert Benjamin Prescott (1832–1905): Pharmacy Education's Revolutionary Spark

D uring the 1871 annual meeting of the American Pharmaceutical Association (APhA) debate was considerable over whether Albert B. Prescott of the University of Michigan could be seated as a delegate. At issue was whether the university's department of pharmacy met the Association's bylaws as a college of pharmacy. After deliberation, Prescott was denied a seat as a delegate although admitted as an individual member. Edward Parrish, of the Philadelphia College of Pharmacy, noted that the vote set a precedent and, further, that it would influence the future shape of pharmacy education and the role of a university in it.[1] This prescient observation was fulfilled as Prescott envisioned new standards in pharmacy education, including full-time attendance in a university-level program with substantial periods of laboratory experience.

EARLY LIFE AND EDUCATION

Albert Benjamin Prescott was born in Hastings (Oswego County), New York, on December 12, 1832, the youngest of three children of Benjamin and Experience Huntley Prescott.[2] Prescott's ancestors first settled in Massachusetts in 1640; Albert was a direct descendant of one of the military commanders at the Battle of Bunker Hill and, later in the line, the renowned historian William H. Prescott. As a youth, Albert suffered a severe knee injury that required the use of a cane for the remainder of his life. His early education was home tutoring provided by his sister. In 1853, he moved to New York City, where he became a correspondent for *The Liberator*, an antislavery newspaper, and taught school. Returning to Oswego County in 1857, he worked in the offices of Dr. Greenleaf for 3 years preparing for admission to medical school. In 1860 he enrolled in the Department of Medicine and Surgery at the University of Michigan, graduating with his MD degree in 1864. The Civil War was still raging so he entered the U.S. Volunteer Army as an assistant surgeon. He was assigned to the Foundry General Hospital in Louisville, Ky., and later to the General Hospital #16 in Jeffersonville, Ind. He also served as a member of the board of examination for appointment of surgeons in Louisville. He was discharged from service in August 1865 with the rank of brevet captain. Upon discharge he immediately returned to the University of Michigan and accepted the position of assistant professor of chemistry and lecturer of organic chemistry and metallurgy.

Silas Douglas had in 1856 developed the university's first chemistry laboratory, and by 1860 a laboratory course in pharmacy was being offered for medical students.[3] This led, in 1868, to the regents approving a course of study within the chemistry laboratory, designed for the practice of pharmacy. In 1869, after completing a course of lectures and laboratory courses in qualitative analysis and toxicology, the first class graduated with diplomas as pharmaceutical chemists. William Procter, Jr., responded to the graduation announcement with an editorial in the *American Journal of Pharmacy* questioning the reliability of an apothecary in the absence of shop, or apprenticeship, experience.[4] Prescott responded to the editorial by detailing the objective of Michigan's program: "It is our endeavor to educate scientific experts,—competent for drug assays, familiar with toxicological properties of medicines, habituated to accuracy, capable of professional truthfulness and earnest to maintain it,—not merely ready tradesmen in pharmacy…. We labor toward placing pharmacy in scientific hands; who welcomes our effort?"[5]

As professor in charge of the University of Michigan chemistry laboratory in 1876, Prescott was named director in 1884, retaining that position until his death. This illustration is from an 1887 Pharmacy College Announcement.

In December 1876, Douglas, Prescott, and other professors successfully petitioned the university's regents to establish a separate school of pharmacy. The University of Michigan thus became the first state university in the United States to incorporate a program in pharmacy as a separate school; Prescott was named the first dean.[6] The program at Michigan was revolutionary, requiring no apprenticeship for enrollment, a radical departure from custom. The course also required full-time attendance from September until June for 2 years. Prescott appears to have been the architect behind the curriculum and the founding of a separate college. In his Remington Medal address, Rufus Lyman remembers questioning whether the university approved the program based on the need for improvement of pharmaceutical education or on the high regard of Prescott. Edward Klaus, a successor dean at the University of Michigan, responded that "it was done out of regard of Prescott."[7]

In 1866 Albert Benjamin Prescott married Abigail Freeburn of Ann Arbor, Mich. They had one adopted son. Prescott died in Ann Arbor on February 25, 1905.

Pharmacy Education in the University
The APhA bylaws in 1871 stated that teachers of pharmacy, botany, and chemistry were eligible for membership and that all colleges of pharmacy and pharmaceutical organizations were entitled to five delegates.[8] However, the bylaws and constitution did not provide a definition of a college, and all previous colleges were finishing schools for apprentices that had been developed by local associations of pharmacists. The 1871 APhA Committee on Credentials recommended that the University of Michigan was not a college of pharmacy and, therefore, Prescott was not eligible to be seated as a delegate. The committee report noted that the university was "neither an organization controlled by pharmacists, nor an institution of learning which, by its rules and requirements, insures to its graduates the proper practical training, to place them on a par with the graduates of the several colleges of pharmacy represented in this Association."[9] One day later Prescott delivered his response, beginning with the charge that apprenticeship was insufficient because few apprentices could become better than their teachers, who themselves had been apprentices trained more through rote than through understanding of their work. He went on to argue that "the mental and manual discipline of laboratory science-work under the teacher, the training in care and accuracy imperative thereto, is excelled by no other discipline for the perceptive, inductive, and executive faculties, and it is discipline especially useful in the vocation of pharmacy."[10] In conclusion, he acknowledged the importance of apprenticeship and the contributions of the early colleges in American pharmacy without blunting his argument for the need of laboratory training.

Prescott's vision of university-centered pharmaceutical education continued to move ahead of the tradition-bound local association schools. Writing in 1885, he noted that Michigan required several years of a high school

Alfred Benjamin Prescott (1832–1905) taken at the time that he served as APhA president (1899–1900). This was four years after he had served as second vice president of APhA. Photo from the APhA Foundation Archives.

education as part of the entrance standard and two thirds of the admissions to the university held a high school diploma. "Three years' schooling in Latin and German, algebra through quadratic equations, botany and elementary physics, beside [sic] arithmetic through involution and evolution, and the correct writing of English" were required for those taking the university course before entering the shop. The standards for those entering the university after apprenticeship were less stringent although still higher than those normally applied by association schools.[11] The requirement for a high school diploma did not become mandatory nationally until 1923.

In May 1895, the regents of the university authorized a 4-year bachelor of science program at the University of Michigan in addition to the 2-year diploma. This approval perhaps responded to the precedent set by some of the 2-year graduates who had continued their education and received a university degree in science and literature. Prescott shared the conviction of Professor Kremers at the University of Wisconsin that pharmacy deserved to be on the same footing as other university departments of technology. The 4-year baccalaureate program was designed to broaden the education through additional courses in English, physics, and mathematics. The 2-year program was to remain for those who wished to conclude their formal education after receiving the diploma of a pharmaceutical chemist.[12]

THE CHEMIST

Most of Prescott's scientific work was in chemistry. In 1874 he authored his first book with Silas Douglas, *Qualitative Chemical Analysis*, which was a standard text for four editions over 30 years. Other classic texts in analytical chemistry followed, including *Outlines of Proximate Organic Analysis* (1875) and *Organic Chemistry: A Manual of the Descriptive and Analytical Chemistry of Certain Carbon Compounds in Common Use* (1887). As professor in charge of the Chemical Laboratory beginning in 1876, he was named the director in 1884, retaining that position until his death. His laboratory was prolific, publishing papers in the *Proceedings of the American Pharmaceutical Association* as well as the major chemical journals of the period.

Prescott was a member of the Committee of Revision for the United States Pharmacopoeia in 1880 and 1890. In 1880 he furnished the assay methods of opium and cinchona and developed the information on volumetric tests, which appeared in the revision for the first time.[13] He was also a valued advisor to the state of Michigan in issues relating to food and water safety. His work in public health was later acknowledged by Henry Vaughan, Dean of the School of Public Health at Michigan, who noted that Prescott's "work gave rise to the country's first laboratory for public health work...much of what we have in public health today came out of [his] laboratories."[14] Others called on his expertise in analytical efforts, and he is reputed to be the individual who determined "the figure of 99.44% for the purity of a common brand of soap."[15]

PROFESSIONAL ORGANIZATIONS

Albert Prescott was an active participant and leader in a number of organizations in chemistry and pharmacy. Although APhA refused to seat him as a college delegate in 1871, he joined as an individual member and was an active participant. His participation in the scientific work of the Association began with an analytical paper at the 1872 annual meeting. His participation never wavered, as later evidenced by his leadership in the Committee on Indicators (1895) and the establishment of the Special Committee on Research (1896). In 1899 the Association installed him as its president.

Prescott was denied a seat as a delegate from the University of Michigan at the 1871 APhA annual meeting (same year as this illustration of an Illinois pharmacy) because he considered laboratory training as more essential than apprenticeship.

During the 1900 APhA meeting in Richmond, Henry Hynson issued an invitation to all of the colleges of pharmacy to develop an Association of Teaching Schools of Pharmacy. An earlier attempt at such an organization had not been successful, but times had changed. Prescott was among the representatives of 21 colleges who agreed to form the American Conference of Pharmaceutical Faculties, an organization that would later become today's American Association of Colleges of Pharmacy. Prescott's leadership was recognized by his election as the first president of the nascent organization.[16]

Albert Prescott was also one of the organizers of the American Chemical Society and in 1886 was elected its president. In 1874 he was elected a member of the American Association for the Advancement of Science and in 1891 was elected its president.

HONORS

Prescott's scientific and leadership abilities were recognized both by numerous leadership positions and other honors. In 1876 he was elected a fellow of the Chemical Society of London. In 1885 he was appointed for the annual assay of the coinage of the mint by the U.S. government. In 1886 the University of Michigan bestowed a doctor of philosophy on Prescott and in 1896 added a doctor of laws. In 1892 the Philadelphia College of Pharmacy elected him to honorary membership in the college. In 1902 Northwestern University bestowed a second doctor of laws.

LEGACY

In 1871 pharmaceutical education was dominated by the local-association finishing schools for apprentices. The courses were a series of lectures that usually lasted only a few months. Those who took a second year attended virtually the same lectures for a second time. There were no laboratories since work in the shop was the laboratory for the apprentice. Consequently, the resistance of the local "colleges" to university-based education was intense. Delegates from the pharmacy association schools of the period unanimously refused to seat Albert Prescott as a delegate or consider his institution as a legitimate college for pharmacists. However, instead of abandoning pharmacy, Prescott—not a pharmacist himself—determined that to defend his vision for pharmacy based in a university education was far more important than to show offense by walking away from the group. In 1885 Prescott was elected by the APhA to serve as the second vice president. During the 1893 annual APhA meeting C. S. N. Hallberg, a pharmaceutical journalist and teacher at the Chicago College of Pharmacy, spoke of the requirements for graduation in light of the proliferation of colleges and standards for graduation. During the heated discussion that ensued, Albert Ethelbert Ebert, also from Chicago, recalled the 1871 debate and his part in denouncing the Michigan program, stating: "Time has passed, and now when I look back and see who were the men that gave instruction in that University, and the vast amount of good they have done for the American Pharmaceutical Association, I feel, as do many others, that we ought to get down on our knees and ask pardon for the adverse action that we took."[17]

Prescott was well known for his personal relationships with students.[18] In 1883 he met with a group of students who were interested in finding ways to continue their professional growth. A number of Greek fraternities already existed at the University of Michigan, providing the model for a similar opportunity for pharmacy. The minutes of the meeting noted that Prescott gave his opinion of the benefits of a pharmacy fraternity and offered the use of his office. The group formed the first professional pharmacy fraternity in America, Phi Chi; the name was changed to Phi Delta Chi in 1909. In 1915 the fraternity established the Prescott Cup to recognize scholarship at the chapter level and in 1985 established the Albert B. Prescott Leadership Lecture Award to honor a young pharmacist who was dedicated to the improvement of pharmacy as a profession.[19]

Prescott was a gifted chemist and leader. His greatest gifts, however, were the vision to put pharmacy education on the same level as other professions and the quiet determination and diplomacy that helped others bring his vision to fruition.

REFERENCES

1. *Proceed Am Pharm Assoc.* 1871;19:29–34,47.

2. In memoriam, Albert Benjamin Prescott. Ann Arbor, Mich.: Privately Printed; 1906.

3. Manasse HR. Innovation, confrontation, and perseverance...Albert B. Prescott's legacy to pharmaceutical education in America. *Pharm Hist.* 1973;15:22–8.

4. Procter W. University of Michigan School of Pharmacy. *Am J Pharm.* 1869;41:472–3.

5. Prescott AB. Letter to the editor [September 24, 1869]. *Am J Pharm.* 1870;42:85–6.

6. History of pharmacy in the University of Michigan: from the regents' proceedings. *Am J Pharm Educ.* 1948;12:388–90.

7. Lyman R. Don't confuse training with education. In: Griffenhagen GB, Bowles GC, Penna RP, Worthen DB, eds. *Reflections on Pharmacy by the Remington Medalists 1919–2003.* Washington, D.C.: American Pharmacists Association; 2004:145.

8. Constitution and bylaws of the American Pharmaceutical Association. *Proceed Am Pharm Assoc.* 1871;19:565–73.

9. Committee on credentials. *Proceed Am Pharm Assoc.* 1871;19:46–7.

10. Prescott AB. Pharmaceutical education. *Proceed Am Pharm Assoc.* 1871;19:425–9.

11. Prescott AB. The School of Pharmacy at the University of Michigan, letter of February 23, 1885. *Am J Pharm.* 1885;48:156–7.

12. Prescott AB. Degrees in pharmacy at the state university. *Pharm Era.* 1895;14:105–7.

13. Albert Benjamin Prescott. *Scien Am.* 1891;65:119.

14. Bender GA, Thom RA. *Great Moments in Pharmacy.* 2nd ed. Detroit, Mich.: Northwood Press; 1967:142.

15. Laitinen HA, Ewing GW. *A History of Analytical Chemistry.* Columbus, Ohio: American Chemical Society; 1977:67.

16. Buerki RA. In search of excellence: the first century of the American Association of the Colleges of Pharmacy. *Am J Pharm Educ.* 1999;63:17–20.

17. Hallberg CSN. The requirements for graduation in American colleges of pharmacy. *Proceed Am Pharm Assoc.* 1893;41:274–80.

18. Clarke FW. Albert Benjamin Prescott. *Science.* 1905;NS21: 601–3.

19. Grabenstein JD. *Phi Delta Chi: A Tradition of Leaders in Pharmacy.* Athens, Ga.: Phi Delta Chi Fraternity; 1995:1–5,107.

William Procter Jr. (1817–1874):
Father of American Pharmacy

J ust 6 days after William Procter's death on February 10, 1874, the students at the Chicago College of Pharmacy passed a resolution noting that his "many researches and able efforts in the cause of science and the elevation of the profession have justly entitled him to be acknowledged the 'Father of Pharmacy' in America."[1] This act was particularly significant, for the resolution did not come from Procter's home institution but, rather, from students in a distant location. Presumably, these students had never met Procter, yet they were able to recognize and honor his contributions to an emerging profession through the unique title "Father."

William Procter Jr. was raised a Quaker in Baltimore, Md.* He was born on May 3, 1817, the ninth and youngest child of Isaac Procter and Rebecca Farquahar Procter (the "Jr." was added to distinguish the young William from his uncle). William left school early and was placed in a cooper's shop, where he developed his noted dexterity with tools. In 1831, at the age of 14, he was signed on as an apprentice at the drugstore of Henry Zollickoffer in Philadelphia. He graduated from the Philadelphia College of Pharmacy in 1837.

During his professional life, Procter was a practitioner, a teacher, an editor and author, and a scientist. He opened his own prescription shop in 1844 and remained in community practice until the end of his life. He taught at the Philadelphia College of Pharmacy from 1846 until 1866, and then again from 1872 until his death in Philadelphia on February 10, 1874. He was the author/editor of the first pharmacy textbook published in America, *Practical Pharmacy: The Arrangement, Apparatus, and Manipulations of the Pharmaceutical Shop and Laboratory* (1849), and, between 1848 and 1870, the coeditor, editor, and author of some 550 articles in the first national pharmacy

---

*Gregory Higby's well-researched and well-written biography, *In Service to American Pharmacy: The Professional Life of William Procter, Jr.* (Tuscaloosa, Ala: University of Alabama Press; 1992), is the single best source for information on Procter and his times. Copies are available from the American Institute of the History of Pharmacy, 777 Highland Ave., Madison, WI 53705-2222; www.aihp.org.

Father of American Pharmacy William Procter Jr. prior to 1867, after which he allowed his whiskers and moustache to grow.

journal in the United States, the *American Journal of Pharmacy*. He was also an inveterate scientist. He did his thesis research on *Lobelia inflata*, and his distinguished research career spanned subjects of concern to the profession that ranged from ethics to percolation and purification of botanical medicines.

Yet, noteworthy and significant as these accomplishments were, they were not sufficient to earn him the title Father of American Pharmacy.

The quality that differentiated Procter and earned him the accolade was his uncompromising devotion to the progress of pharmacy in all of its facets. His innovations in the percolation process, his role in the establishment of the American Pharmaceutical Association, and his staunch support for pharmaceutical standards, as exemplified by his work on the *United States Pharmacopeia (USP)*, brought him the recognition and respect of other pharmacists.

The first colleges of pharmacy in the United States were local organizations established as associations to promote the scientific and commercial interests of the local pharmacists; education was a subordinate interest and activity. In 1851 the New York College invited other pharmacy societies to meet and address the continuing problem of importation of adulterated medicinal goods. Procter was one of the representatives from the Philadelphia College of Pharmacy. By the end of the New York sessions, the discussion had shifted to the establishment

A bronze statue of Procter, designed by William Marks Simpson, was unveiled in the rotunda of the American Institute of Pharmacy on May 5, 1941, the 124th anniversary of Procter's birth.

of a national organization. Procter, George Coggeshall of New York, and Samuel Colcord of Boston were appointed to organize a meeting to bring all of the local pharmacy groups together the following year.

Professional standards for pharmacy were minimal in the mid-1850s. Colleges were few in number and scattered. Few pharmacists had a clear vision of what the profession could become. Procter led the way in setting the agenda of the proposed organization to improve the level of practice above that of mere shopkeeper. He used his position as the editor of the *American Journal of Pharmacy* to draw attention to the future of pharmacy and the planned organizational meeting. On October 6, 1852, the representatives of the local groups assembled in Philadelphia and established the first national pharmacy organization, the American Pharmaceutical Association.

From the beginning, Procter's influence on APhA extended far beyond that of an officer who would serve his term and disappear. He was the first continuing officer of the Association, serving as the corresponding secretary twice between 1852 and 1857. The extent of his influence in the early years may be clearly seen from his involvement: in 1855 he was a member of five of the seven standing committees. He also served as APhA first vice president from 1859 to 1860 and APhA president from 1863 to 1864.

Procter was among the first pharmacists associated with the revision of the *USP*. The first edition, published in 1820, was the work of physicians ably led by Lyman Spaulding. Subsequent revisions remained in the control of physicians until 1841, when the College of Physicians of Philadelphia, which had the responsibility for that year's revision, invited the members of the Philadelphia College of Pharmacy to participate in the revision. Procter took the lead in the pharmacy group's contribution, and, after 6 months of effort, produced a 357-page report that argued for the inclusion of new items to the materia medica list, for the removal of others, and, most notably, for the addition of the percolation process to many official formulas. Procter's involvement in the *USP* would continue through the revision of 1860.[2]

William Procter Jr. exemplified the qualities of a professional hero. He established a vision of what the profession could accomplish and was able through his determination and personal ethics to encourage others to move that vision toward reality. In the concluding remarks of Procter's biography, Higby noted that Procter "championed the idea of a responsible pharmacist who had the education and self-confidence to act as a safety check between the writer and the consumer of prescriptions."[3]

REFERENCES

1. Chicago College of Pharmacy Resolution. *Am J Pharm.* 1874;46:140.

2. Anderson L, Higby G. The Wood and Bache era: The revisions of 1840, 1850, and 1860. In: *The Spirit of Volunteerism—A Legacy of Commitment and Contribution: The United States Pharmacopoeia, 1820-1995.* Rockville, Md: United States Pharmacopoeial Convention; 1995:61–93.

3. Higby G. *In Service to American Pharmacy: The Professional Life of William Procter, Jr.* Tuscaloosa, Ala: University of Alabama Press; 1992:178.

Joseph Price Remington (1847-1918): Teacher of Teachers

Every American pharmacist is familiar with the name Remington. Pharmacy students first encounter the name on the cover of the professional text *Remington: The Science and Practice of Pharmacy*. Pharmacists in every quarter look to the recipients of the Remington Honor Medal, the highest honor in American pharmacy, for professional inspiration. Less well known, however, is the individual behind the text and the prize.

Joseph Price Remington was born into a Philadelphia Quaker family on March 26, 1847. His father, Isaac Remington, was a well-known physician. His mother, Lydia Hart, was a descendant of Townsend Speakman, an apothecary in Philadelphia in the early 18th century. Joseph exhibited an early interest in science, even to the point of equipping "a chemical laboratory in which most of the apparatus was of his own devising and construction."[1] His family planned that he would enter college and take an academic degree, but this hope had to be abandoned when his father died in 1862.

One of Joseph's older sisters married Henry M. Troth, son of one of the founders of the Philadelphia College of Pharmacy. Troth guided Remington to the pharmacy of Charles Ellis, Son & Company to serve his apprenticeship during the years 1863 to 1866. This fortunate arrangement placed the young Remington under the tutelage of one of the most influential pharmacists in Philadelphia. Ellis had served his apprenticeship with Elizabeth Marshall (the first woman pharmacist in Philadelphia) and later purchased her shop. Ellis was one of the founders of the Philadelphia College of Pharmacy and served as its fourth president from 1854 to 1869.[2]

Remington's experience with Ellis was very general since the store manufactured medications on a broad scale in addition to serving its retail clientele. Ellis encouraged Remington to attend lectures at the Philadelphia College of Pharmacy during his apprenticeship. Lectures were held in the evenings, and the course normally took 2 years to complete. Remington attended the college and graduated with a PhG in 1866.

In 1867 Remington joined Edward Robinson Squibb in the latter's Brooklyn-based pharmaceutical and chemical manufacturing company. Like

Remington, Squibb was also from a Quaker upbringing, and he had served an apprenticeship as a pharmacist with Warder Morris of Philadelphia before receiving his MD degree from Jefferson Medical College.[3]

Remington's first task was to sweep the basement. However, he was soon learning how to make ether, assay cinchona bark, and manufacture products for export. Squibb also had Remington help with experiments on carbolic acid. Joseph W. England identified Squibb as "probably the most painstaking and conscientious manufacturing pharmacist of the country."[4] Squibb detested dishonesty and valued truth above all. He believed in sharing the results of his research and disdained secrecy, refusing to patent any of his research or manufacturing discoveries.

Twenty-five-year-old Joseph Remington in 1872, when he became assistant to William Procter Jr.

Remington lived with the Squibb family and remained with the firm for 3 years, until the death of his mother and his return to Philadelphia. Later, Remington spoke of this period as one of the most decisively influential of his life.[5] Remington continued to pursue his interest in pharmaceutical manufacturing and took a position in 1870 with Powers and Weightman, one of the first American manufacturers of quinine. While employed there, he also accepted an appointment as an assistant to Edward Parrish, the professor of pharmacy at the Philadelphia College of Pharmacy. After Parrish died in 1872, and William Procter Jr. returned to the position of professor of pharmacy, Procter retained the young Remington as his assistant. While little is recorded about the relationship between Remington and Procter, it is noteworthy that Remington decided to own his own pharmacy as Procter had before him. When Procter died 2 years later, Remington was elected to the position of professor of pharmacy, a position he would hold until his death 44 years later.

Remington was an early and strong advocate of laboratory instruction for pharmacy students. In 1877 he helped establish a pharmaceutical laboratory at the college, which he furnished, in part, with his own funds.[6] In 1893 he succeeded John M. Maisch as the dean of the college.

Remington was remembered as a master teacher and a friend to students by the thousands who graduated from the college during his decades of service. However, his greatest accolade might well have been the recognition that he was the teacher of teachers, for, as one eulogist wrote in 1918, "most of the successful teachers of pharmacy in America today have been pupils of his at some time in their careers."[7] Many among the alumni, including Charles LaWall, E. Fullerton Cook, Ivor Griffith, H.V. Arny, and Eugene Eberle, went on to distinguished careers in pharmacy education.

In 1872 Remington bought a retail drugstore in Philadelphia, which he retained for 13 years. This experience deepened his understanding of the profession—in particular, the need to organize pharmacists and provide them information on an ongoing basis. His drugstore would also be an important laboratory for his book *Practice of Pharmacy*, which would become the standard professional text in all American pharmacy schools.

Mature Remington in 1892, when he was elected president of APhA.

Remington embodied the role of professor in its broadest sense. In addition to the daily routine of teaching at the Philadelphia College of Pharmacy, he was an influential writer and editor. In 1879, after the death of George B. Wood, one of the founders of the *United States Dispensatory*, Remington was invited to become an associate editor, a post he retained for the rest of his life. The first edition of Remington's *Practice of Pharmacy* was published in 1885. In the textbook, Remington combined his practical retail experience with an understanding of the needs of both students and practitioners. His ambitious vision for this work is aptly summarized in the book's subtitle: *A Treatise on the Modes of Making and Dispensing Officinal, Unofficinal, and Extemporaneous Preparations, With Descriptions of the Properties, Uses and Doses. Intended as a Hand-Book for Pharmacists and Physicians and a Text-Book for Students.*[8] In 1897 he became the pharmacy editor of *Stedman's Medical Dictionary*.

Remington was an untiring leader in professional organizations. He joined the American Pharmaceutical Association (APhA) in 1867 at the beginning of his time with Squibb and served in many Association offices during his 50 years of membership. Among his most noteworthy accomplishments was creating the APhA Council. At the 1879 Annual Meeting of APhA, Remington noted that a great deal of time was expended dealing with necessary but trivial matters. He suggested establishing a Council that would work with the permanent secretary to transact the business of the Association between the Annual Meetings as well as during them. In 1887 Remington suggested the plan to organize the scientific membership of the Association into three sections—one for scientific papers, one for education and legislation, and one for commercial interests.[9] APhA frequently appointed him as its representative to the American Medical Association (AMA). This working relationship led to the creation of the Section on Materia Medica and Pharmacy (later renamed the Section of Pharmacology and Therapeutics) within AMA. Remington served as president of APhA in 1892–1893 and, in this role, presided over the meeting of the International Pharmaceutical Congress during the Chicago World's Fair in 1893. In 1878 he helped found the Pennsylvania Pharmaceutical Association, and he served as its president in 1890. He was an active participant and leader in a number of other international congresses.

Another of Remington's great professional legacies was his work and leadership on the *United States Pharmacopeia (USP)*. His first connection with the *USP* was in 1877, when he was appointed by the college to serve on the Auxiliary Committee of Revision. The excellence of his work led to his leadership role in the 1880 and 1890 *USP* revisions. In 1900 Remington was elected vice chair of the Committee of Revision. When committee chair Charles Rice died in 1901, Remington was elected to that post, which he retained until his own death.[10]

In 1874 Remington married Elizabeth Baily Collins, another Philadelphian raised in the Quaker tradition. The couple had five children: Arthur Hart, Joseph Percy, William Procter, Anna Collins, and Elizabeth Baily.[11] Remington died in Philadelphia on January 1, 1918. William became an Episcopalian priest, later bishop, and officiated at his father's funeral.

In 1918 Hugo H. Schaefer announced the New York Local Branch of APhA's plan to establish an annual award to honor a "man or woman who has done most for American Pharmacy during the preceding year or whose efforts during a number of years have culminated to a point during the preceding year where the result of these efforts would be considered as being the most important and advantageous for American pharmacy."[12] The New York branch named the medal after Joseph Price Remington, one of the leading lights of the profession, who died earlier that year. APhA assumed responsibility for the selection process and presentation of the Remington Honor Medal in 1979.

Speaking of his old professor when he received the Remington Medal in 1931, Ernest Fullerton Cook noted that "the master passion of his life … was his pride in pharmacy and his confidence in its future. He gave to its development all of his own great powers and cooperated with every sane movement of his day which promised the advancement of the art and science he loved."[13]

Joseph Price Remington left an indelible mark on his beloved profession of pharmacy. He is perhaps best remembered as a teacher of teachers. Yet, his impact as an educator went beyond the classroom and laboratory, and his voice continues to be heard by generations of pharmacists, for whom his publications are an integral part of professional formation and practice.

REFERENCES

1. Lawall CH. Professor Joseph Price Remington. *Am J Pharm.* 1918;90:65–72.

2. England JW. *The First Century of the Philadelphia College of Pharmacy.* Philadelphia, Pa: Philadelphia College of Pharmacy; 1922:355–6.

3. Blochman LG. *Doctor Squibb: The Life and Times of a Rugged Idealist.* New York, NY: Simon & Shuster; 1958:5.

4. England JW. *The First Century of the Philadelphia College of Pharmacy.* Philadelphia, Pa: Philadelphia College of Pharmacy; 1922:407.

5. Cook EF. Pharmacy, Remington, and the USP. In: Griffenhagen G et. al., eds. *The Remington Lectures: A Century in American Pharmacy.* Washington, DC: American Pharmaceutical Association; 1994:60.

6. Johnson A, Malone D. *Dictionary of American Biography.* Vol. 8. Pt. 1. New York, NY: Charles Scribner's Sons; 1958:497–8.

7. In memoriam: Joseph Price Remington, 1847-1918. *Am J Pharm.* 1918;90:82–5.

8. Remington JP. *The Practice of Pharmacy.* Philadelphia, Pa: J.B. Lippincott Company; 1885.

9. Hoffman FA. Retrospect of the development of American pharmacy and the American Pharmaceutical Association. *Proc Am Pharm Assoc.* 1902;50:100–45.

10. Anderson L, Higby G. *The Spirit of Voluntarism: A Legacy of Commitment and Contribution. The United States Pharmacopoeia, 1820-1995.* Rockville, Md: United States Pharmacoepeial Convention; 1995:198.

11. *National Cyclopedia of American Biography.* Vol. 33. New York, NY: James T. White & Company; 1947:231.

12. Schaefer HH. A pharmacy honor medal. *J Am Pharm Assoc.* 1918;7:374–5.

13. Cook, EF Pharmacy, Remington, and the *USP.* In Griffenhagen G et al., eds. *The Remington Lectures: A Century in American Pharmacy.* Washington, DC: American Pharmaceutical Association; 1974:62.

Charles Rice (1841–1901):
Creator of the Modern Scientific Pharmacopoeia and Father of the *National Formulary*

Charles Rice was one of the most enigmatic and influential pharmacists of the late nineteenth century. While extremely reticent about his personal life, he was outspoken about the need to establish standards for items that pharmacists would compound and dispense. Identified as the creator of the modern scientific pharmacopoeia, Rice established product standards for industry, prescribers, and pharmacists.[1] Remembered for his work on the revision of the *United States Pharmacopoeia* (*USP*), he was also instrumental in the creation of the *National Formulary*.

BEGINNINGS

Charles Rice was born on October 4, 1841, in Munich, Germany. His parents, originally Austrian, spelled the name "Reiss." He received his early education in Passau and Munich, Germany, and Vienna. Information about the early life and immigration of Charles Rice is both sketchy and contradictory. His early education was mostly in linguistic studies, especially the classical and Oriental languages; he apparently received no training in pharmacy or chemistry. Upon arrival in the United States, he changed the spelling of his name to correspond with that of his uncles who had immigrated in the 1830s. A biographical sketch that Rice presumably approved notes that he arrived in the United States in 1862 and soon enlisted in the Navy, serving on the *Jamestown*. He served as a surgeon's steward, or apothecary, on its round-the-world voyage.[2] Presumably, he received his training in compounding medicines while in the Navy.[3] Stories are contradictory about how Rice presented as a patient at the Bellevue Hospital (New York City's hospital established in 1736 to serve the city's poor), but he unquestionably began his lifelong connection with the institution in 1865.[4]

BELLEVUE HOSPITAL

During his recuperation Rice approached John Frey, the hospital apothecary and superintendent of the drug department, looking for employment. First assigned to glass washing, the young man soon advanced to duties with greater responsibility. In 1867 Bellevue opened one of the first outpatient departments, the Bureau of Medical and Surgical Relief for the Out of Door Poor. Charles Rice was assigned as the first apothecary. During this period Rice engaged in additional chemical studies, but no record indicates where or with whom he studied. Upon the death of Frey in 1885, Rice was appointed chemist and superintendent of the General Drug Department and later chemist of the Department of Public Charities and Corrections.[3]

Bellevue was one of the largest and most progressive city hospitals of the period, and its pharmacy operation was the largest in North America. The work of Rice's department included manufacturing pharmaceutical preparations, filling prescriptions, and testing supplies for more than 20 institutions managed by the Department of Public Charities and Corrections. Each day Rice personally tested all of the milk that was delivered to New York hospitals.[1]

COLLEGE AND ASSOCIATION WORK

In 1868 John Frey proposed Charles Rice for membership in the New York City College of Pharmacy, which was primarily an association rather than an educational institution. Rice was

Portrait photograph of Charles Rice (1841–1901) autographed on November 8, 1894. He served as APhA first vice president 1883–1884, and as one of the founders of the APhA National Formulary in 1888.

elected a trustee in 1870 and immediately became active on its board, where he labored to advance the college as a teaching institution. Although he never taught classes, he was the chair of the Library Committee and served on the examination committee.[5]

Rice joined the American Pharmaceutical Association (APhA) in 1870, and in 1872 was appointed chair of the Committee on Adulterations.[6] He served on the Council and as a first vice president of the Association in 1883–84.[7] However, he was not a regular attendee at the annual meetings since he refused to be away from his duties at Bellevue for protracted periods of time. He also served as the reporter on the *Progress of Pharmacy* in 1891–92, when C. Lewis Diehl of Louisville was ill and could not serve. Rice was in attendance at the 1877 annual APhA meeting in Toronto, Canada, when the future of the *U.S. Pharmacopoeia* was debated. In 1885 he served as the chair of the Committee on Unofficial Formulas of the American Pharmaceutical Association, which would eventually result in the development of the *National Formulary*.[8]

UNITED STATES PHARMACOPOEIA

The *USP* was first published in 1820 largely to bring uniformity to the materia medica and pharmacy preparations of the day.[9] Although the work of the first and second revisions was primarily done by physicians, Daniel B. Smith of the Philadelphia College of Pharmacy was apparently consulted.[10] After the United States Pharmacopeial Convention of 1840, the colleges of pharmacy were invited to participate in the revision process; the Philadelphia College of Pharmacy efforts were led by the 22-year-old William Procter, Jr. By 1870 physicians' interest in the *USP* had waned while that of the pharmacists was growing stronger. The future of the *USP* was debated during the 1876 APhA Annual Meeting. E. R. Squibb enumerated the problems with the *USP*, including a need for more frequent revision, increased discussion in the monographs, and correction of errors.[11]

During the 1877 APhA Annual Meeting, Friedrich Hoffmann, a New York pharmacist and editor, moved in the absence of an American Medical Association plan of action to have a committee appointed "to take into consideration the advisability and feasibility on the part of the American Pharmaceutical Association, as the national representative organization of the profession of pharmacy, to prepare a complete pharmacopoeia which may be submitted to the criticisms of the medical and pharmaceutical professions, and be proposed to the final Committee on Revision."[12] APhA formed a Committee of Revision of the Pharmacopoeia and named Rice as chair.

The Committee Report, published in 1880, provided a list of guiding principles that "marked the arrival of mature pharmaceutical science" to the United States.[9] These included the use of English rather than a combination of Latin and English, parts by weight, and the use of a single alphabetic list. Chemical formulas were to be added, as were specific gravities and atomic weights. The *USP VI* was thus a modern pharmacopoeia that moved away from manufacturing in the shop to "address the needs of professional practice, mass manufacturing, and developing regulations against drug adulteration."[9] A forerunner of modern pharmaceutical concerns was the recommendation for a table listing the "Largest Single and Daily Doses of Powerful Remedies," which would guide the pharmacist in what not to "exceed unless he has positive knowledge that the physician intended the excess."[13] The real power in the *USP* resided in the Committee of Revision, and with the 1880 revision all of the officers were pharmacists.[9] Charles Rice served as the chair of the Committee of Revision for the 1880 and 1890 *USP* revisions.

Initially Rice withdrew from the 1900 revision because of health but agreed to continue the leadership when the business duties associated with the post were removed.

NATIONAL FORMULARY

The mid-1880s was a time of rapid growth of pharmaceutical manufacturers. Many pharmacists were opposed to physicians prescribing mass-produced medicines and relegating pharmacists to "taking a number of this man's coated pills or that firm's elixir, put in box or bottle, as the case may require, and write directions upon the label."[14] There was interest in developing lists of formulas for use by physicians that would lead them to prescribe items that could be compounded by pharmacists. Simultaneously, the New York College of Pharmacy with other New York pharmacy groups developed the *New York and Brooklyn Formulary*; Charles Rice was the chair and primary mover of the committee. Rice went to the 1885 APhA Annual Meeting with the offer to turn the *Formulary* over to APhA. After prolonged debate and what appeared to be rejection, APhA agreed to accept the offer.[15] To secure the copyright to the *National Formulary* the Association incorporated in 1888. With the publication of the first edition, Rice ended his official relationship with the effort and turned all of his attention to the *USP*.

SCHOLAR/EDITOR

Charles Rice was trained in the classical and Oriental languages. Besides his native German and English, Rice spoke French, Italian, Spanish, Portuguese, Dutch, and Turkish; wrote Latin, Greek, Lithuanian, Hebrew, Arabic, Hindustani, Mahratta, Persian, and Pashto; knew some Russian, Japanese, and Chinese; and was acknowledged as a leading Sanskrit authority.[16] From 1876 until 1892 Rice was the associate editor of *New Remedies* and subsequently *American Druggist* after its merger with *Pharmaceutical Record*. Rice also worked on the pharmacy section of *Index Medicus* and the *Index Catalog of the Library of the Surgeon-General's Office* from the early 1880s until his death in 1901. In 1879 the University of the City of New York conferred on him the honorary degree of doctor of philosophy; the Philadelphia College of Pharmacy bestowed the honorary degree of master in pharmacy in 1891.

Charles Rice died in New York City on May 13, 1901. Never married, he had lived on the grounds of Bellevue Hospital from the time of his first arrival in 1865. In the memorial booklet published after his death, the leaders of pharmacy spoke of the man and provided a picture of a quiet, unassuming individual who literally worked himself into an early grave through his devotion to pharmacy and the *USP*. His humility and willingness to help others was especially noted by many of the contributors. John Uri Lloyd, a Cincinnati pharmacist and manufacturer and a friend of Rice, lamenting that he could never repay the many favors given, reported Rice's response: "You may not be able to return these favors to me, but you can return them to others."[3]

Charles Rice at his desk in the library of Bellevue Hospital in New York City, where in 1885 he was appointed as superintendent of the general drug department and later as chemist of the Department of Public Charities and Corrections.

LEGACY

One cannot consider modern compendial standards without acknowledging the vision of Charles Rice. The sixth revision of the *USP* was a marked departure from the earlier versions. One of the most important changes was building the national voice in a work that had previously been controlled by the Philadelphia medical community. The sixth revision also provided a useful tool for the pharmacists who were abandoning in-store manufacturing and becoming more focused on the responsibility for quality and standards.

Rice served a similar role in the creation of the *National Formulary*. By engaging a national perspective he was able to disseminate his goal of standardizing products that would not have been included in the *USP*. At one time the *USP* and *National Formulary* shared the distinction of being considered as national standards for the United States; both owe their prominence to the work of Charles Rice. The standards were unified in 1975 when the United States Pharmacoepeial Convention bought the *National Formulary* and the Drug Standards Laboratory from APhA. Today the *United States Pharmacopeia/National Formulary* is the official compendium of drug standards of the United States.

REFERENCES

1. Higby G. Rice, Charles. In: Garraty JA, Carnes MC, eds. *American National Biography.* Vol. 18. New York, N.Y.: Oxford University Press; 1999:404–5.

2. Dr. Charles Rice. *Am Druggist.* 1891;20:185.

3. Rice Memorial Committee. *In Memoriam: Charles Rice.* Philadelphia, Pa.: J.B. Lippincott; 1904:3.

4. Lloyd JU. Dr. Charles Rice. *J Am Pharm Assoc.* 1936;25:1143–5.

5. Wimmer CP. *The College of Pharmacy of the City of New York.* New York, N.Y.: Curt P. Wimmer; 1929:158.

6. Wolfe HG. Charles Rice (1841–1901), An immigrant in pharmacy. *Am J Pharm Ed.* 1950;14:285–305.

7. Griffenhagen G, Higby G, Sonnedecker G, Swann J. *150 Years of Caring: A Pictorial History of the American Pharmaceutical Association.* Washington, D.C.: American Pharmaceutical Association; 2002:255.

8. [Kraemer H.] Editorial: Charles Rice. *Am J Pharm.* 1901;73:303–311.

9. Anderson L, Higby GJ. *The Spirit of Voluntarism: A Legacy of Commitment and Contribution. The United States Pharmacopoeia 1820-1995.* Rockville, Md.: United States Pharmacoepeial Convention; 1995.

10. Wilbert MI. Daniel B. Smith. *Proc Am Pharm Assoc.* 1903;51:548–58.

11. Squibb ER. Resolution. *Proc Am Pharm Assoc.* 1876;24: 631–33.

12. Hoffmann F. [Pharmacopeial question.] *Proc Am Pharm Assoc.* 1877;25:532–35.

13. Death of Dr. Charles Rice. *Am Druggist Pharm Rec.* 1901;38:281,283–9.

14. Rice C. *Report of the Revision of the U.S. Pharmacopoeia Preliminary to the Convention of 1880.* New York, N.Y.: American Pharmaceutical Association; 1880:xi–xvii.

15. Bendiner S. Manufacturers of pharmaceutical preparations: a blessing and a curse. *Pharm Rec.* 1883;3:8.

16. Higby GJ. Publication of the National Formulary: a turning point for American pharmacy. In: Higby GJ, ed. *One Hundred Years of the National Formulary: A Symposium.* Madison, Wisc.: American Institute of the History of Pharmacy; 1989.

Irving Rubin (1916–1998):
Tireless Campaigner for Pharmacy

When Irv Rubin retired as the editor of *Pharmacy Times* in 1988, the chair of the Romaine Pierson Publishers board noted that Rubin had the remarkable capacity to make friends in all facets of pharmacy and that, as an editor, he unceasingly "led the fight for the public recognition of the profession he loves."[1] During his 60 years as a pharmacist, Rubin was in the vanguard of efforts to establish the Pharmacist's Oath, produce a pharmacy stamp, employ a full-time pharmacist in the U.S. Capitol, and develop a single symbol for American pharmacy.

Irving Rubin was born in New York City on April 6, 1916, to Julius and Sadie (Seidman) Rubin. He enrolled at the Brooklyn College of Pharmacy (BCP) and graduated cum laude in 1936 with a PhG. Drawn early to the role of reporter and editor, Rubin contributed his first articles on fair trade pricing while working in a community pharmacy. Encouraged by Dean Hugo Schaefer of BCP to become an editor, Rubin joined the staff of *American Druggist* in 1938.

In a personal interview with the author in March 1996, Rubin recounted his first attempt to establish a column and the hesitation of the journal to make such an investment in an unknown author. He developed a plan to convince the editors that his idea was a good one: He wrote to 60 pharmacists who were members of the committees of revision of the *United States Pharmacopoeia (USP)* and *National Formulary* and asked for comments on his idea for a column posing a number of questions that pharmacists should be able to answer. The plan worked, as the comments were uniformly positive. *American Druggist* agreed to publish the column but insisted that Rubin use a pen name. The name chosen was Xanthox Jr, which was derived from xanthoxylum, a botanical listed in the USP through the 9th edition in 1900. The first column appeared in the May 1939 issue.[2]

MILITARY CAREER
Rubin was inducted into the U.S. Army in May 1942 as a private. He was

soon assigned to Borden General Hospital in Chickaska, Okla., as the noncommissioned officer in charge of the pharmacy and the editor of the post newspaper. Subsequently selected to attend officer's candidate school, Rubin was commissioned a second lieutenant in the Medical Administrative Corps in September 1943.[3] LT Rubin was assigned as an assistant battalion surgeon in the 142nd AAA Battalion and sent overseas in time for the Battle of the Bulge. He served through three major offensives in the Ardennes, Rhineland, and Central Germany. In August 1945 Rubin received a Bronze Star Medal for meritorious pharmaceutical service in battle from December 20, 1944, to May 8, 1945, in France, Belgium, and Germany. Specifically, Rubin was recognized

for developing a mobile pharmacy whose use led to a decrease in time lost due to sickness. At the same time, he developed a public relations program for the battalion. The stories about the men he sent to hometown newspapers and radio stations raised the battalion's morale.

During his military service, Rubin also served as a roving reporter for *American Druggist*. At the end of the war, he remained in Europe for 6 months and was discharged with the rank of captain in February 1946.

EDITORIAL SERVICE

After returning home, Rubin rejoined the staff of *American Druggist* as an associate editor. He also returned to school, earning a BS in English from the Brooklyn Evening College in 1948. He remained with *American Druggist* until 1960, when he became editor of *American Professional Pharmacist*[4]

Rubin from PHARMAKON, the 1936 year-book of Long Island University's Brooklyn College of Pharmacy. (Used with the permission of Arnold & Marie Schwartz College of Pharmacy and Health Sciences.)

(*American Professional Pharmacist* changed its name to *Pharmacy Times* with the September 1969 issue).

THE PHARMACIST'S OATH

In his new position, Rubin demonstrated his passion for the profession by immediately beginning to champion new projects to draw positive public attention to pharmacy. In May 1961 he advocated that every graduating pharmacy student take the Pharmacist's Oath as part of the graduation ceremony. Since no universal oath then existed, Rubin encouraged the American Association of Colleges of Pharmacy to devise one. His rationale was the embodiment of many of his later campaigns—that the oath would "impress pharmacists-to-be, practicing pharmacists, and the public with the fact that Pharmacy merits full recognition as a health profession."[5] The suggestion hit a responsive chord, and letters came in to *American Professional Pharmacist* from many schools indicating their willingness to add an oath to their graduation ceremony and asking for help in developing one.

COMMEMORATIVE STAMP

Efforts to gain a U.S. commemorative stamp originated during the 1934 American Pharmaceutical Association (APhA) Annual Meeting, when the House of Delegates passed a resolution to establish a committee to seek a stamp honoring the dedication of the American Institute of Pharmacy, as the headquarters of APhA was called at the time. In 1939 APhA and the National Association of Retail Druggists (NARD) joined forces in urging the U.S. Postal Service to issue a stamp honoring the 120th anniversary of the *USP*. This effort was aided by Parke Davis field representatives, who distributed petitions to pharmacies in a drive to collect a half-million signatures.[6] In 1966 Rubin picked up on the stamp campaign to increase public awareness of pharmacy. The initial effort did not succeed, but by 1971 Rubin was in a full-court press to get the stamp approved and issued. He collared Elmer Bobst, the honorary board chair of Warner-Lambert, and Joseph Stetler of the Pharmaceutical Manufacturers Association with the proposal. These contacts led Rubin to Sen. Robert P. Griffin of Michigan, who agreed to submit the proposal to the Senate. In a speech on the Senate floor, Griffin spoke passionately about the issuance of a stamp: "Throughout the nation's history, the pharmacist has been an integral part of the American scene, its culture, and its folklore. As professional people, pharmacists have particularly close—and binding—ties with the people of America. Americans place their trust in pharmacists over two billion times a year."[7] Every major national health care professional and trade association, including the American Medical Association and the American Dental Association, backed the pharmacy stamp effort. On December 4, 1971, the U.S. Postal Service announced that a commemorative pharmacy stamp would be issued in 1972.[7]

PHARMACIST IN THE CAPITOL

In 1979 Rubin[8] described the campaign to gain greater recognition of the pharmacist's professional expertise in the U.S. Capitol, the military, and the Veterans Administration that had begun in 1976. One of the initiatives focused on requiring that a registered pharmacist dispense or supervise the dispensing of all prescriptions at the U.S. Capitol pharmacy. Rubin's position was that pharmacists would have better recognition if they, rather than pharmacy technicians, filled prescriptions for members of Congress. After 2 years of failure using the quiet approach, Rubin went public with *Pharmacy Times* editorials in 1978 and early 1979. In February, Sen. Jim Sasser of Tennessee "suggested" to the attending physician of the Congress of the United States that a full-time registered pharmacist be assigned to the U.S. Capitol pharmacy. On March 26, 1979, Navy LTJG Donald Denton reported for that duty.[8]

ONE SYMBOL FOR PHARMACY

The longest campaign Rubin was involved in was the drive for a single symbol for pharmacy. In a 1970 editorial in *Pharmacy Times* titled "Needed: One Symbol to Identify Pharmacy,"[9] Rubin pointed out the need for pharmacy to more visibly identify itself to the public and other health care professions. When he received the Remington Honor Medal from APhA in 1986, the title of Rubin's presentation was "One Symbol for Pharmacy";[10] the campaign was still underway. The sticking point was the lack of cooperation within pharmacy itself. Pharmacy leaders could not agree on what the symbol should be. But there was a bit of optimism in Rubin's view that the problems were in the past and associations were now working together.[10] However, it was not until 1992 that American pharmacy adopted a single symbol.

A TIRELESS CAMPAIGNER

Rubin used his bully pulpit as *Pharmacy Times* editor to advance many other initiatives during his career, even long after his "official retirement" in 1988. He advocated for the roles of pharmacists as drug information specialists and as leaders in the war against illegal drugs; he was a tireless advocate of pharmacists counseling patients on the proper use of nonprescription medications. He was a dynamic leader in the people-to-people visits of pharmacists to both Russia and China. But at all times, he continually advocated the expertise that the pharmacist could and must bring to health care. He also challenged members of the profession to deliver all that it was capable of delivering. Among his thought-provoking admonitions on this topic was, "If you were not the pharmacist, what would you expect of the pharmacist?"[11]

HONORS

Rubin received most of the honors that pharmacy bestows on its heroes. He was the Remington Medalist in 1986. He received the American College of Apothecaries J. Leon Lascoff Award in 1977 and the NARD (now National Community Pharmacists Association [NCPA]) John Dargavel Award in 1995. In 1993 Phi Lambda Sigma presented Rubin with its National Leadership Award. He also received an honorary doctor of pharmacy degree from the Massachusetts College of Pharmacy (1973), an honorary doctor of science degree from the Albany College of Pharmacy (1986), an honorary doctor of humane letters from Long Island University's Arnold & Marie Schwartz College of Pharmacy and Health Sciences (1986), and an honorary doctor of science degree from St. John's University (1989). However, what Rubin considered his most important honor was evident in the way he signed his letters and editorials: "Irving Rubin, Pharmacist."

Sen. Robert P. Griffin of Michigan (left) and Rubin discussing the petitions for the issuance of a commemorative stamp honoring pharmacy. Pharmacy Times. *July 1971:50–51. (Used with the permission of* Pharmacy Times.*)*

LEGACY

Rubin married Florence Podolsky in 1949; they had two children—Joanne and Saul. Rubin died in Great Neck, N.Y., on March 13, 1998.

A larger-than-life figure in pharmacy, Rubin spent his life telling the world what his chosen profession could do and then telling pharmacy what pharmacists must do to meet public expectations. One of the best summaries of his life was offered by Calvin Anthony of NCPA: "[Rubin] was a veritable fountain of ideas about how to better practice the profession and better serve the patient. Long before pharmacist care and disease state management were fashionable, Irv Rubin was urging his peers to take charge of the care of their patients. If pharmacy's brightest days are still before us, we owe a huge debt to Irv Rubin for tirelessly nudging us forward along the path toward a bigger, grander, more expansive role as members of the health care team."[11]

REFERENCES

1. Morando R. We salute Irv Rubin. *Pharmacy Times*. March 1988:10.

2. Xanthox Jr. Take a chance. *American Druggist*. May 1939:72, 128–30.

3. Irving Rubin rejoins *American Druggist*. *American Druggist*. March 1946:115.

4. Goldstein is A.D. pharmacy editor. *American Druggist*. November 28, 1960:16.

5. Rubin I. The Pharmacist's Oath. *American Professional Pharmacist*. May 1961:19.

6. 38-year effort behind pharmacy stamp. *J Am Pharm Assoc*. 1972;NS12:506-7, 535–40.

7. Rubin I. People and events that sparked the pharmacy stamp. *Pharmacy Times*. February 1972:38–43.

8. Rubin I. But now there's a full-time pharmacist in the U.S. Capitol pharmacy. *Pharmacy Times*. April 1979:48–53.

9. Rubin I. Needed: one symbol to identify pharmacy. *Pharmacy Times*. December 1970:17.

10. Rubin I. One symbol for U.S. pharmacies. In: Griffenhagen G, Blockstein WL, Krigstein DJ, eds. *The Remington Lectures: A Century in American Pharmacy*. Washington, DC: American Pharmaceutical Association; 1994: 321–2.

11. Irv Rubin memorial. *Pharmacy Times*. April 1998:10-2.

Edward G. Spease (1883-1957):
Father of Hospital Pharmacy Standards

In 1958, Charles O. Lee of Ohio Northern University memorialized Edward Spease, citing among his accomplishments on behalf of hospital pharmacy the development of the minimum standards for hospital pharmacies.[1] In the decennial review of the formation of the American Society of Hospital Pharmacists, Don Francke noted that the original minimum standard "served as a rallying point in the resurgence of hospital pharmacy."[2] While the sobriquet *father* is always used with some trepidation, there is no question of the significance of Spease's pioneering efforts on behalf of hospital pharmacy. Historian Glenn Sonnedecker noted that Spease, like his friend Harvey A.K. Whitney, was ahead of his time in understanding the needs of a maturing profession that was "buffeted by antithetical pressures."[3]

Beginnings
Edward Spease was born in Dresden, Ohio, on March 31, 1883, the son of George Henry Spease and Helena Cox.[4] He started his pharmacy career as an apprentice with John Hornung in Dresden before enrolling at the Ohio State University College of Pharmacy in 1903. He received a degree in pharmaceutical chemistry and was registered as a pharmacist in 1905; he received a bachelor of science in pharmacy in 1907. In 1911, Edward Spease married Alice Kelly; the couple had no children. Spease died in Akron, Ohio, on October 12, 1957.[1]

Teacher
Edward Spease started his academic career at Ohio State University College of Pharmacy in 1905 when he served as a student assistant. After graduation he remained at the university first as an instructor and then as assistant professor and secretary. He left to assume the post of professor and dean at Western Reserve University in 1916.

The Cleveland School of Pharmacy had been established by local pharmacists in 1882 and incorporated in 1886. In 1908 the school affiliated with

A 1928 photograph of Edward Spease as Dean of Western Reserve University School of Pharmacy, and President of the American Association of Colleges of Pharmacy.

Western Reserve University, maintaining its own faculty and administration until it became an operating unit of the university in 1917. In 1916 President Thwing recruited Edward Spease as dean and professor and charged him with completing the integration of the school into the university. Spease also enjoyed the support of Newton D. Baker, a university trustee who had served as Woodrow Wilson's Secretary of War.[5] Spease noted that the school "was a proprietary institution and a maker of drug clerks. ...I went to Cleveland feeling that if I could interest a medical school of the type that existed there, in the worthwhile-ness [sic] and purpose of pharmaceutical education and show them that pharmacy was an essential part of the health program, then and only then, could I be proud of being a pharmacist."[6] From the beginning, the school and university shared resources, with the pharmacy students taking elementary chemistry and liberal arts from other university units while the school's pharmacognosy department supervised the work in botany. In 1925 Spease implemented the change to the 4-year bachelor of science degree. In addition to the development of courses in hospital pharmacy, the school provided prescription service for the Student Health Department.[7]

Spease was the 1928 president of the American Association of Colleges of Pharmacy (AACP). In his presidential address he commented that the faculty is accountable to the students and the profession, asserting that the responsibility is to educate, not train, students and that this included more than just texts and classrooms—it included life. "Because you are in a professional school is no excuse for not making real men and women of your students…If you do not make a better man of him than he was when he came to you, you have failed as a teacher."[8]

Edward Spease resigned from Western Reserve University in 1940. He joined the National Association of Retail Druggists (now the National Community Pharmacists Association) as director of professional relations. He explained that his role was to "help the professional side of the business of the retail druggist, to teach him to approach and fraternize with physicians and dentists."[9] Spease remained in that position until 1944 and then as the science and prescription editor of the *N.A.R.D. Journal* until 1946 when he retired.

Hospital Pharmacy

Experience with the increasing commercialism in community pharmacy led to Spease's eventual conclusion that "if professional pharmacy was to exist, let alone grow to an ideal state, it would have to be in the hospital where the health professions were trained."[10]

Edward Spease reminisced that his interest in hospital pharmacy began as a result of a summer job, presumably while he was working in a local pharmacy during vacation. This interest was unusual, especially since so few hospitals in the pre–World War II period had in-house pharmacies or full-time pharmacists to staff them.

As early as 1921 Spease turned his attention to hospital pharmacy in both practice and education. The School of Pharmacy established a laboratory service for hospitals in the Cleveland area. Initially developed as a buying group and testing laboratory, it was also an opportunity to place the students in the senior class in the hospitals for an internship.[11]

By 1932 Spease had made significant inroads into forging a partnership between the Western Reserve College of Pharmacy and the University Hospital. He provided a summary of the relationship between his school and the university hospital pharmacy first by explaining the importance of the relationship: "Medicine today really emerges through the door of the hospital…I know of no other way to inform the pharmacists properly about how to contact physicians in an understanding manner than to have him serve a supervised internship in the hospital beside the medical interne [sic] and nurse."[12]

Spease's first partnership with the hospital was the establishment of a manufacturing laboratory in the school as a cost-saving measure for the hospital; however, equally important, it linked the school and hospital in an ongoing relationship. The school was also involved with helping area hospitals with the design of pharmacies and providing graduate pharmacists to staff them. In 1932, the college and the hospital signed a contract placing the dean as the hospital pharmacy director and adding the hospital's pharmacists to the teaching staff of the college. Every student was required to complete a rotation through the hospital in their senior year. The hospital formed a pharmacy committee comprising five physicians; the director of hospital pharmacy served as the secretary at the encouragement of Spease.[12]

In 1935 the Cleveland program was visited by Dr. Malcolm T. MacEachern, director of the American College of Surgeons (ACS), who suggested the development of a set of standards for hospital pharmacies.[13] Within months Spease and University Hospital pharmacist Robert Porter developed five principles of hospital pharmacy, which were presented at the Clinical Congress of the ACS (Table 1). In addition to the principles, the document noted that the pharmacy would carry all official preparations including those listed in *New and Nonofficial Remedies*. In the case of the latter, however, the Pharmacy Committee would choose which product to stock if there were several with "similar composition or action." The Pharmacy Committee had the responsibility to develop and update this hospital formulary; no new products would be added unless approved by the Medical Council.[14] These standards were accepted by the ACS in 1936. In 1951 ACS joined with the American College of Physicians, the American Hospital Association, the American Medical Association, and the Canadian Medical Association to form the Joint Commission on Accreditation of Hospitals.

In 1936 Spease and Porter authored a new section on hospital pharmacy in the 8th edition of *Remington's Practice of Pharmacy*. The addition of this section, including the duties of the pharmacist, the physical plant, supplies, and standards, provided an important overview of hospital pharmacy in what was arguably the most important pharmacy text of the period.[15]

In 1937, Dean Spease established "the first full-fledged combination of internship and graduate study" in hospital pharmacy at Western Reserve.[3] By 1940 enrolled in the program were 13 graduate students. The graduate students lived with the medical and nursing house staffs in dormitories, were required to attend pharmacy and therapeutics committee meetings, and worked in the manufacturing laboratory. Former students noted that this was the way that Spease "put into practice his idea that the pharmacy practitioner was an educator as well, and that this educator taught the practice of pharmacy."[16]

Table 1. Minimum Standards for a Hospital Pharmacy

Principle 1

Every hospital must have pharmaceutical service, the full time of a graduate registered pharmacist, or pharmaceutical service from an approved adjacent pharmacy.

Principle 2

A pharmacy committee shall be appointed, the members of which shall be chosen from the several divisions of the medical staff, for the purpose of determining the policy of operation of the pharmacy, addition to and deletion from the drugs used, such other matters of a pharmaceutical nature as from time to time are necessary, and supervision of purchase and issuance of drugs, chemicals, pharmaceutical preparations, biologicals and professional supplies within the hospital. This committee shall meet at regular intervals. The Pharmacist shall be a member of it and serve as its secretary, and a transcript of its proceedings shall be kept and a copy forwarded by the secretary to the proper governing body of the hospital.

Principle 3

An adequate pharmaceutical reference library must be maintained by the hospital.

Principle 4

Every hospital must use drugs, chemicals, and pharmaceutical preparations of at least United States Pharmacopoeia, National Formulary and New and Nonofficial Remedies quality in the treatment of patients.

Principle 5

The routine preparation of injectable medication and supervision of sterilization of all preparations he himself prepares, the routine manufacture of pharmaceuticals, the dispensing of drugs, chemicals and pharmaceutical preparations, the filling and labeling of all drug containers issued to nursing units from which medication is to be administered, a semimonthly inspection of all pharmaceutical supplies on nursing units, the maintenance of approved stock of antidotes in the emergency suite, the dispensing of all narcotic drugs and a perpetual inventory of them, specifications for purchase of all drugs, chemicals and pharmaceutical preparations used in the treatment of patients, specifications for purchase and storage of biologicals and all operations wherein a special knowledge of pharmacy, including a ready knowledge of weights and measures in all systems, is necessary, must be done by the pharmacist or under his immediate supervision.

Source: Reference 14.

Spease commenced his career as Assistant Professor at the Ohio State University College of Pharmacy, which was located in Chemical Hall from 1906 to 1928.

ASSOCIATION WORK

Edward Spease was one of the charter members of the Phi Chi (now Phi Delta Chi) Chapter at Ohio State in 1908 and was influential in establishing a chapter of the pharmacy fraternity at Western Reserve in 1923. He served in a number of offices including the national presidential offices from 1926 to 1935.[17]

Spease was an active member of the Ohio Pharmaceutical (now Pharmacists) Association and served for many years as the chair of the legislative committee. He has been credited as the author of the Ohio prerequisite law of 1915.[1] Ohio was among the first states to pass legislation requiring applicants wishing to take the state board examination to be graduates of a college of pharmacy.[18] Spease was one of the organizers of the Northern Ohio Branch of the American Pharmaceutical (now Pharmacists) Association (APhA). The group saw its role as a bulwark of professional pharmacy, devoted to scientific and professional questions rather than commercial issues. The branch also was interested in cooperating with the Academy of Medicine and planned to recommend members of the branch to our "physician friends as capable and trustworthy."[19]

Spease served as the chair of the Pharmaceutical Education and Legislation Committee of APhA in 1920–1921 and was elected president of AACP in 1927–

1928. He also was active with the United States Pharmacopoeial Convention, serving as its third vice president from 1930 to 1940.

LEGACY

In 1936, the Philadelphia College of Pharmacy bestowed an honorary master of science on Edward Spease for his work in hospital pharmacy. In 1950, W. Arthur Purdum, the first recipient of the Harvey A.K. Whitney Award, spoke of Edward Spease's contributions in establishing minimum standards in hospital pharmacy. In 1952, Edward Spease was the third Whitney Award recipient. He recalled the efforts to place hospital pharmacy in the forefront of professional services, adding, "the younger ones of you will find the going now far easier than we did."[10]

Despite his relatively modest academic preparation, Edward Spease made a profound impact on pharmacy education and hospital pharmacy. His leadership in establishing the Ohio requirement for graduation from a recognized college of pharmacy was a foretaste of his later efforts to improve professional standing and education. "He was a pioneer in formulary revival, in minimum standards for hospital pharmacies, in the pharmacy and therapeutics committee, and in establishing the dignity of the hospital pharmacy and the hospital pharmacist."[16] Spease's most enduring legacy was development of the first minimum standards for hospital pharmacy, as this emerged as one of the essential elements in establishing the professionalism of modern hospital pharmacy.

In 1958, historian Glenn Sonnedecker eulogized the first two honorary members of the American Society of Hospital Pharmacists, Harvey Whitney and Edward Spease, as "pioneers, who shared the excitement and the pain of breaking ground in a fertile but poorly tilled land of pharmaceutical service."[3] Edward Spease was truly a change agent; he raised hospital pharmacy's standing and dignity and his innovations changed the face of pharmacy education.[16]

REFERENCES

1. Lee CO. Edward Spease. *Am J Pharm Educ.* 1958;22:102–4 [same memorial was published in the *Am J Hosp Pharm.* 1958;15:64–5].

2. Francke DE. Evaluations and interpretations. *Bull Am Soc Hosp Pharm.* 1952;9:379–94.

3. Sonnedecker G. Harvey A.K. Whitney and Edward Spease….in memoriam. *Am J Hosp Pharm.* 1958;15:507–9.

4. Marquis AN. *Who's Who in America*, vol. 14. Chicago: A.N. Marquis Co.; 1926–1927:1786.

5. [Lyman R.] Editor's page. *Am J Pharm Educ.* 1940;4:624.

6. Spease E. The relationship of pharmacy to public health. *Am J Pharm Educ.* 1937;1:310–9.

7. Anonymous. School of pharmacy, Western Reserve University, Cleveland, Ohio. *Ohio Druggist.* 1927;4:38–40.

8. Spease E. Address of the president of the American Association of Colleges of Pharmacy. *J Am Pharm Assoc.* 1928;17:892–900.

9. Spease E. Letter. *Am J Pharm Educ.* 1940;4:631–2.

10. Spease E. Background to progress: the 1952 Whitney award lecture. *Bull Am Soc Hosp Pharm.* 1953;10:362–4.

11 Spease E. Address of the chairman of the section on education and legislation. *J Am Pharm Assoc.* 1921;10:975–80.

12. Spease E. Hospital pharmacy and the school of pharmacy. *J Am Pharm Assoc.* 1932;21:1216–8.

13. Spease E. The first minimum standard. *Bull Am Soc Hosp Pharm.* 1950;7:32.

14. Spease E, Porter RM. Minimum standards for a hospital pharmacy. *J Am Pharm Assoc.* 1936;25:65–9.

15. Cook EF, LaWall CH. *Remington's Practice of Pharmacy*, 8th ed. Philadelphia: J.B. Lippincott; 1936:iv, 1933–51.

16. Godley AP, Godley LF. Our friendship with Edward Spease. *Am J Hosp Pharm.* 1993;50:1145–50.

17. Grabenstein JD. *Phi Delta Chi: A Tradition of Leaders in Pharmacy.* Athens, Ga.: Phi Delta Chi; 1995:330–2, 455–6.

18. House Bill 376 to provide for the control of the educational requirements and registration of pharmacists. Springfield, Ohio: The State of Ohio Legislative Acts; 1915:105:329–31.

19. Spease E. Professional pharmacy: a society for its propagation in Cleveland. *Bull Acad Med Cleveland.* 1931;15:7–8.

Edward Robinson Squibb (1819–1900): Advocate of Product Standards

Writing about his former employer and mentor after his death, Joseph Remington recalled an incident when Dr. E. R. Squibb destroyed a lot of fluid extract of cinchona that did not have the correct alcoholic strength. Although it could have been mixed with another lot to attain the proper strength, Squibb explained his action as the right thing to do, even if expensive.[1] Squibb's attention to detail and insistence on standards was the hallmark of his efforts on behalf of the *United States Pharmacopoeia (USP)* and food and drug legislation. He demanded that products of his manufacture be the best possible for they were intended for the use of patients with disease. Confident of his principles and willing to battle those he perceived as thwarting standards of quality, Squibb stood alone at times but unbowed as he paraphrased Frederick Douglass, "God and one are a majority."[2]

LIFE ON ATLANTIC SEABOARD

Edward Robinson Squibb, eldest son of James Robinson Squibb and Catherine Harrison Bonsall, was born on July 4, 1819, in Wilmington, Del. The family was a charter member of the Society of Friends in America, having originally accompanied William Penn. Catherine died in 1831; Edward, his father, and surviving brother moved to Philadelphia. In 1837 he served an apprenticeship as a pharmacist with Warder Morris, a founder and trustee of the Philadelphia College of Pharmacy.[3] In 1845 he graduated from Jefferson Medical College with his doctor of medicine degree. Foremost among his professors were Franklin Bache, Professor of Chemistry. Bache was involved with the *USP* and a coauthor of the *United States Dispensatory*, the first edition of which appeared in 1833. For 2 years after graduation, Squibb served as the assistant demonstrator of anatomy, curator of the museum, and clerk of clinics at the Jefferson Medical College while establishing a medical practice.

In 1852, Edward Squibb married Caroline Lownds Cook. The couple had four children. Dr. Squibb died on October 25, 1900, in Brooklyn.

Edward Robinson Squibb was appointed assistant surgeon in the U.S. Navy on April 26, 1847, and served 4 years in South American waters and the Mediterranean. Photo courtesy of the Journal of Edward Robinson Squibb, *privately published in 1930 by Mrs. J. Munro.*

U.S. Navy

Many of Squibb's contemporaries joined the military during the Mexican War (1846–1848). As a practicing Quaker, Squibb was prohibited from taking an oath or fighting. Despite this, Squibb sought a commission as an assistant surgeon in the U.S. Navy. He served at sea for 4 years, first in South American waters and subsequently in the Mediterranean. Squibb's discontent with the quality of medicine provided on the voyages was the basis of his lifelong advocacy for standardization. In 1852 he was assigned to work with the commander of the Brooklyn Naval Hospital, Benjamin Franklin Bache, the nephew of his old teacher, Franklin Bache.[4] In addition to his duties as staff physician, Squibb was to establish a manufacturing laboratory to provide unadulterated medicines to naval vessels.[5] He personally signed the labels of the products that he manufactured or tested; his signature was recognized as a guarantee of standard labeled strength and purity throughout the Navy.[6] Remington reported that the efforts of Squibb, Bache, and others finally convinced Congress that in the case of medicine, quality was more important than the lowest price.[1]

E. R. Squibb immediately took up the problem of producing standardized ether. While the first public demonstration of the use of ether as an anesthetic in 1846 clearly indicated its potential in medicine, production methods yielded an unstandardized product and resulted in uncertain efficacy. Squibb succeeded in producing a pure standardized product using a steam process in November 1854.[7] While permissible, Squibb refused to patent this process and in 1856 published the process and plans for his apparatus in the *American Journal of Pharmacy*.[8]

In 1857, Squibb resigned his commission after the Navy rejected a request for an increase in pay. Squibb accepted a partnership with a physician, Lawrence Smith, Professor of Medical Chemistry and Toxicology at the University of Louisville, and pharmacist Thomas Jenkins in Louisville, Ky. The new business, the Louisville Chemical Works, produced a number of products, including iron oxide, potassium arsenite, cantharides, ergot, rhubarb, and subacetate of lead.[9] At the end of the year, Squibb decided to return to Brooklyn and start his own manufacturing business.

AMERICAN PHARMACEUTICAL ASSOCIATION

In 1858, Edward Robinson Squibb moved to Brooklyn to open his manufacturing laboratory. He attended the annual American Pharmaceutical (now Pharmacists) Association (APhA) meeting in Washington, D.C., and became a member. He was elected first vice president at the same meeting. Squibb served as the chair of the APhA business committee from 1863 to 1868. In 1867, the APhA Nominating Committee unanimously placed Squibb's name on the ballot unopposed for president. Citing business obligations and noting that he was not a "practical pharmaceutist," Squibb asked to be removed from the ballot and nominated John Milhau of New York in his stead.[10]

EDUCATOR AND AUTHOR

In 1869, Edward Squibb agreed to deliver a series of lectures, without pay, to the students at the College of Pharmacy of the City of New York. Bringing demonstration materials from his own laboratories, he traveled from Brooklyn to New York once a week. Squibb's inaugural lecture was memorable in his declaration that "a pharmacist is not a druggist.... The pharmacist...is an educated qualified practitioner of the art of pharmacy. He is a dealer in substances used to prevent and relieve distress...The druggist is a merchant like the grocer, the dry goods dealer, etc."[11] The following year Squibb continued at the college; he increased his lectures to two evenings a week. At the end of 1871 he discontinued his teaching because of the press of business matters but continued his interest in the college. In a student notebook from the period he was portrayed as "the master of his profession and 'the type of incarnated conscience.'"[12]

Squibb served as an important teacher and mentor to two of pharmacy's outstanding leaders of the period—Joseph P. Remington and John Michael Maisch. In 1867, upon the recommendation of William Procter, Jr., Remington joined Squibb, where he was tutored in the intricacies of large-scale manufacturing. Remington claimed that this period was "one of the greatest and most influential experiences in his life."[13] In 1861 John Michael Maisch, then teaching at the City of New York College of Pharmacy, joined Squibb and served as a chief assistant while learning how to manufacture large quantities of medicines to fill military orders. Based on this experience, Maisch was selected to become the chemist in charge of the U.S. Army Laboratory in Philadelphia in 1863.

E. R. Squibb's first publications dealt with naval issues—the medical report of the frigate *USS Cumberland* and flogging. Most of his papers were published in the *American Journal of Pharmacy* or the *Proceedings of the American Pharmaceutical Association*. Much of his writing focused on the preparation and analysis of medicines. In the process he wrote about virtually every medicine in the materia medica of the day—ranging from mercury to cinchona to chloral hydrate.[14]

In 1882, Squibb began publication of an irregular publication, *An Ephemeris of Materia Medica, Therapeutics, and Collateral Information.* The opening announcement stated that "being a mere ephemeral waif, it will be sent gratuitously to all. No subscribers are solicited nor any subscription list kept, nor are exchanges with other journals asked for....Its chief object is, in an informal way, to note down, from time to time, the results of a long experience and observation and the deductions therefrom...."[15] The first issue included articles on the pharmacopoeia, drug assay, and the status of a bill introduced to the U.S. Senate on December 20, 1881, to prevent the adulteration of foods or drugs. The publication remains a study of therapeutics of the era; Volume V contains 356 pages on materia medica, pharmacy, and therapeutics for the years 1897 and 1898. E. R. Squibb was the principal contributor to *An Ephemeris*, writing most of the 2,300 pages printed before his death. His sons were listed as coeditors of the publication and continued the effort for 2 years after their father's death.

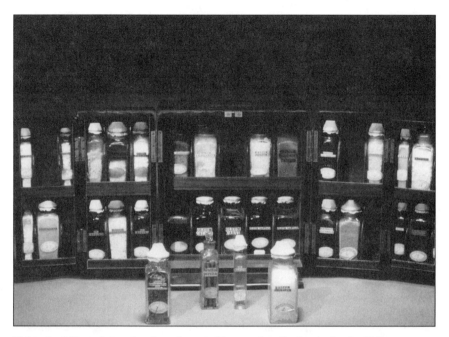

This is Squibb's medicine chest from the period he served on the Cumberland—1849–1850. Photo courtesy of the Smithsonian Institution, which holds the chest in its collections.

MANUFACTURER

While E. R. Squibb had manufacturing experience in the Navy and with the Louisville Chemical Works, it was not until 1858 that he established his own firm, "Edward R. Squibb, M.D.," in Brooklyn. Chief procurement officer of the U.S. Army Medical Corps Colonel Richard S. Satterlee, long interested in Squibb's products, committed to purchasing pharmaceuticals from the new firm. On December 5, 1858, the first order of the new firm was shipped—18 pounds of chloroform.[16] Later that month, just as success seemed imminent, a fire virtually destroyed the laboratory when a young worker dropped a bottle of ether. In an attempt to retrieve his notebooks, Squibb was badly burned on the face, body, and hand; his eyelids were destroyed and his face would bear heavy scarring for the rest of his life. Despite the destruction to body and building Squibb determined to rebuild as quickly as possible; by late fall 1859 full production had resumed. The young man who caused the fire was retained and subsequently promoted. The announcement of the return noted the availability of "a class of medical Preparations that come fully up to the standard of the National Pharmacopoeia."[17]

The new firm saw tremendous growth, partially resulting from its reputation for quality exemplified by ether, and from the Civil War. By 1863 Squibb was manufacturing a list of products representing most of the materia medica of the period and also panniers, large 88-pound packs designed to be carried to the field by mules, where surgeons' knapsacks could be refilled.

The original order in 1863 called for $40,000 of the packs, costing $111 apiece with the expectation of additional orders for 45 to 90 panniers a week.[18] Squibb opened his laboratory to a detailed inspection by the Army. Dr. Joseph Bill reported that [by 1863] Squibb had supplied one-twelfth of the medical supplies furnished to the Army and had the ability with a slight increase in apparatus and staff to furnish supplies for a million men.[19] Ether was without a doubt one of the most important contributions, for the Confederate troops as well as the Union. It was said that "Abraham Lincoln himself chose to overlook the smuggling of Squibb Ether to the South."[20]

With the war over and the business growing, Squibb turned increased attention to the issue of substandard and adulterated medicines. In 1879 he led a committee of the New York State Medical Society formed to develop legislation guaranteeing the purity of medicines and food. The proposed legislation addressed adulteration, established the *USP* as the standard, and established a state board of health to administer the law.[21] The bill was passed in both New York and New Jersey and was the basis of a federal bill introduced to the U.S. Senate in 1881 by Warner Miller of New York.[22] Squibb's efforts with the New York legislation presaged the Pure Food and Drug Act of 1906 by 26 years.

By 1883 the Squibb product catalog had grown from the original 69 items to 314 sold worldwide.[23] It also included items of his own invention such as a separating funnel and ether administration mask. In 1890 Squibb's health started to deteriorate and in 1892 he made his sons Edward H. and Charles F. partners, changing the name of the company to E. R. Squibb and Sons. The stress of day-to-day operations was removed; however, Squibb continued his work in the laboratory until his death in 1900.

United States Pharmacopoeia

E. R. Squibb's relationship with the *USP* began in 1860 when he and Caleb Green became the first to represent the New York medical community since 1830.[24] One of the most pressing issues of the Convention was the concern over weights and measures; Squibb favored the adoption of measures of weight rather than capacity, arguing that they were the more accurate.[25] Squibb became a force to be reckoned with in the deliberations of the Committee of Revision.

In 1865 Squibb articulated a growing concern with the preparation of *USP* extracts and fluidextracts, namely the cost of alcohol necessary for the percolation process. He noted that the price of alcohol had increased 10 times, and would continue to rise, making the cost higher than that of the active ingredient. After stringent testing he developed new techniques that would be practical to the pharmacists who were unable to use the apparatus of large-scale manufacturers. However, he concluded that the USP Committee of Revision must approve the changes before use since "there can be but one standard, and there can be but one kind of honesty to that standard, namely faithful obedience and truthful accuracy."[26] He would return to the issue of

When Edward R. Squibb died in 1900, many memorials were established in his honor. However, there is one without his name. While Harvey Wiley is the father of the Pure Food and Drug Act of 1906, Dr. Squibb must be the grandfather. Photo courtesy of the APhA Foundation Archives.

percolation in 1878 when he again provided full disclosure of process and apparatus without the protection of a patent. His work on percolation would later be acknowledged as one of Squibb's great services to pharmacy.[27]

The most monumental struggle of Squibb's focus on standards occurred in the *USP* revision of 1880. His dissatisfaction rested upon what he perceived as failure to accommodate advancing standards, the dependence on the *U.S. Dispensatory* to provide commentary on manufacturing processes, and the 10-year revision cycle.[28] Squibb also thought the American Medical Association (AMA) should assume responsibility for the revision. In 1876 Squibb presented his plan to both the AMA and APhA. Both associations met the proposals without enthusiasm. Squibb pressed on, bringing the issue back to the 1877 AMA meeting, where it was soon tabled without action. At the 1877 APhA meeting Squibb reported the AMA action and noted that the proposal should be dropped. Samuel Sheppard, who would later serve on the first USP Board of Trustees, called Squibb a hero of pharmacy for his "earnest efforts, during the past two or three years, to inaugurate an improvement in the revision of the *United States Pharmacopoeia*."[29] Despite the defeat, Squibb returned to serve on the Committee of Revision in 1880 and quietly supported the 1890 revision.

LEGACY

Edward Robinson Squibb was instrumental in the establishment of the Navy's first medical laboratory. His work on ether and chloroform, unpatented and open to all, delivered anesthetics to the battlefields of the Civil War and beyond. His insistence on standards and an improved *USP* built on his unique experiences as pharmacist, physician, and manufacturer.

Squibb was remembered for his personal characteristics of outspokenness and moral courage. While many may remember him only as the founder of a great pharmaceutical manufacturing house, his legacy to pharmacy was far more. Frederick Wulling, founding dean of the University of Minnesota College of Pharmacy, spoke of his relationship with Squibb, commenting on Squibb's refusal to keep his work secret in the belief that service to the sick was the primary objective.[30] Remington recalled that "probably his greatest influence in the advancement of chemical science lay in the encouragement and assistance which he gave young men, so that his services to the profession were far reaching, not only on account of the enormous volume of work which he himself accomplished, but also because he enabled others to do much."[1]

In a historical context, Squibb was ranked with the great inventors of the period, Edison, Bell, and Ford, "a shaper of American history through his influence in bringing about high standards of drug quality and purity."[31] However, his biographer summed up Squibb's passion for product standardization, arguing that while Harvey Wiley was the father, it was Squibb who was the grandfather of the Pure Food and Drug Act of 1906, which "codifies the principles for which Dr. Squibb had been fighting all his life."[32]

REFERENCES

1. Remington JP. Edward Robinson Squibb, M.D. *Am J Pharm*. 1901;73:419–31.

2. Squibb is quoted as "God and one are a majority." Douglass's original statement was "One and God make a majority."

3. England JW. *First Century of the Philadelphia College of Pharmacy*. Philadelphia: Philadelphia College of Pharmacy. 1922;216:371–2.

4. Bean JJ. Squibb, Edward Robinson. In: Garraty JA, Carnes MC, eds. *American National Biography*. New York: Oxford University Press. 1999;20:517–9.

5. Blochman LG. *Doctor Squibb: The Life and Times of a Rugged Individualist*. New York: Simon and Shuster; 1958:64.

6. Wickware FS. *The House of Squibb*. New York: E.R. Squibb & Sons; 1945:10.

7. Squibb ER. *Journal of Edward Robinson Squibb, M.D.* Privately printed. 1930;2:481–520.

8. Squibb ER. Apparatus for the preparation of ether by steam. *Am J Pharm*. 1856;28:385–91.

9. Blochman LG. *Doctor Squibb: The Life and Times of a Rugged Individualist*. New York: Simon and Shuster; 1958:108.

10. Minutes of the fifteenth annual meeting. *Proc Am Pharm Assoc*. 1867;15:34–8.

11. Wimmer CP. The College of Pharmacy of the City of New York [published by the author]. 1929:63.

12. Wimmer CP. The College of Pharmacy of the City of New York [published by the author]. 1929:69.

13. Cook EF. Pharmacy, Remington, and the USP. In: Griffenhagen GB, Bowles GC, Penna RP, Worthen DB. *Reflections on Pharmacy by the Remington Medalists 1919–2003*. Washington, D.C.: American Pharmacists Association;2004:59–65.

14. Florey K, ed. *The Collected Papers of Edward Robinson Squibb, M.D.* (1819–1900). Princeton: Squibb Corp.; 1988:xxi.

15. Squibb ER. *An Ephemeris of Materia Medica, Therapeutics, and Collateral Information*. 1882;1:1.

16. Blochman LG. *Doctor Squibb: The Life and Times of a Rugged Individualist*. New York: Simon and Shuster; 1958:116.

17. Blochman LG. *Doctor Squibb: The Life and Times of a Rugged Individualist*. New York: Simon and Shuster; 1958:129.

18. Flannery MA. *Civil War Pharmacy*. Binghamton, N.Y.: Pharmaceutical Products Press; 2004:106.

19. Smith GW. The Squibb laboratory in 1863. *J Hist Med Allied Sci*. 1958;13:382–94.

20. Wickware FS. *The House of Squibb*. New York: E.R. Squibb & Sons; 1945:12.

21. Squibb ER. Rough draft of a proposed law to prevent the adulteration of food and medicine and to create a state board of health. *Trans Med Soc NY*. 1879.

22. Blochman LG. *Doctor Squibb: The Life and Times of a Rugged Individualist*. New York: Simon and Shuster; 1958:271–3.

23. Blochman LG. *Doctor Squibb: The Life and Times of a Rugged Individualist*. New York: Simon and Shuster; 1958:283.

24. Anderson L, Higby G. *The Spirit of Volunteerism: The United States Pharmacopoeia 1820–1995*. Rockville, Md.: United States Pharmacopoeial Convention; 1995:79.

25. Squibb ER. Weights and measures of the Pharmacopoeia. *Am J Pharm*. 1860;32:26–42.

26. Squibb ER. Proposed economy of alcohol in percolation, as applied to the extracts and fluid extracts of the Pharmacopoeia. *Am J Pharm*. 1866;38:109–28.

27. Kremers E, Urdang G, revised by Sonnedecker GA. *History of Pharmacy*, 4th ed. Madison, Wis.: American Institute of the History of Pharmacy. 1976:329.

28. Kremers E, Urdang G, revised by Sonnedecker GA. *History of Pharmacy*, 4th ed. Madison, Wis.: American Institute of the History of Pharmacy. 1976:265.

29. Anderson L, Higby G. *The Spirit of Volunteerism: The United States Pharmacopoeia 1820–1995*. Rockville, Md.: U.S. Pharmacopoeial Convention; 1995:111.

30. Wulling FJ. Edward Robinson Squibb. *The Samuel W. Melendy Memorial Lectures: I–IV*. Lacrosse, Wis.: Emerson G. Wulling; 1946:29–54.

31. Florey K. Edward Robinson Squibb—the man and his company. *Pharm Hist*. 1989;19(3):2–9.

32. Blochman LG. *Doctor Squibb: The Life and Times of a Rugged Individualist*. New York: Simon and Shuster; 1958:356.

Linwood Franklin Tice (1909–1996): Champion of Students

On August 19, 1996, the Philadelphia College of Pharmacy and Science announced the death of Dean Emeritus Linwood F. Tice.[1] One of the first items to appear in a very long list of his accomplishments was an acknowledgment of his leading role in the formation of the Student Section of the American Pharmaceutical Association (APhA). In retrospect, Tice took on many professional roles during his career—teacher, administrator, researcher, editor, and outspoken association leader—but a common thread linking all of these endeavors was his interest in students and his aspirations for pharmacy.

Linwood Franklin Tice was born in Salem, N.J., on February 17, 1909, to Walter C. Tice and Bessie Waddington; he had one sibling, Anabel. When he was 12 years old, he started working in Salem in the drugstore of Dr. James L. Tuohy, a graduate of the Philadelphia College of Pharmacy (PCP) and a student of Joseph Remington. Tuohy influenced Tice both in his selection of pharmacy as a career and PCP as his school. Tice began his lifelong association with PCP when he enrolled in the college at age 17. He lived in Salem and worked for Tuohy while commuting to downtown Philadelphia to attend classes at PCP.[2] After receiving his PhG in 1929, Tice taught for a short time at the pharmacy school at Baylor University. When the school closed, he returned to PCP, earning a BS in pharmacy in 1933 and an MS in chemistry in 1935. Tice was awarded an honorary doctor of science degree from the St. Louis College of Pharmacy in 1954.

In 1938 Tice joined the faculty at PCP at the invitation of Dean Charles LaWall, and he progressed quickly through the academic ranks. He was promoted to full professor in 1940 and served as the director of the department of pharmacy for 30 years, from 1941 until 1971. He also served as an assistant dean in 1941 and was promoted to associate dean in 1956. In 1959 Tice was named the dean of pharmacy at PCP, and in 1963 he became dean of the college, serving in this post until his retirement in 1975.[3]

Tice began his research career in 1929 with the Iodine Educational Bureau, where he and LaWall developed an improved iodine tincture.[4] Tice did innovative work on various gelatins, and during World War II he was involved in the development of special gelatins as a substitute for blood plasma.[1] His contributions to the science of pharmacy and chemistry were recognized by his peers in 1940, when he was named to the Revision Committee of the *United States Pharmacopoeia*. He served on various committees in that organization for over 3 decades, including 15 years on the Board of Trustees.

In 1941 Tice became editor of the *American Journal of Pharmacy*; he remained a contributor to that journal until 1977. His editorials frequently addressed subjects that were dear to his heart, such as student recruitment and professional responsibility. He also served as the technical editor of *Pharmacy International* and its Spanish edition, *El Farmaceutico,* for 15 years. Beginning in 1948 he served as an associate editor of the 9th edition of *Remington's Practice of Pharmacy* and continued working on the publication in an editorial capacity until its 15th edition in 1975.

Linwood F. Tice as a young man, sometime before 1934. Source: Reference 11.

During World War II, Tice remained at PCP to teach and continue his research. He also served in the Coast Guard Reserve. One day each week, he served a 12-hour shift commanding a 38-foot picket boat in the Delaware Bay. The bay was a target of German submarines because of the vast amount of military shipping it accommodated. Tice's duties included transferring military ship pilots and convoying munitions-laden barges on the Delaware River. He was discharged with the rank of ensign at the end of the war.[5]

Tice was known for his candor; he admitted to a lack of diplomacy and an impatience with expediency. The announcement of his selection as recipient of the 1971 Remington Medal cited "his espousal of frequently unpopular causes, which he felt necessary for the betterment of the profession."[4] Perhaps the best-known example of this was his address as incoming president of the American Association of Colleges of Pharmacy in 1955, in which he condemned racial discrimination. He urged "that all meetings of this Association or its Districts be held only at such places and under such circumstances that all members of this Association are free to attend."[6] This recommendation was his reaction to an event that occurred during an AACP District meeting: The management of the convention hotel

Department of Pharmacy, Philadelphia College of Pharmacy, 1971. Seated (l–r): A.W. Moore, R.E. King, L.F. Tice, E. Ehrenstein, H.L. Flack. Standing (l–r): L.H. Hopkins, J.A. Linkewich, J.A. Gans, M.J. Myers, P.J. Niebergall, D.A. Hussar, W.E. Smith, E.T. Sugita, J.E. Smith, A.M. Krantz, R.L. Schnaare. Source: Reference 3.

had refused admittance to a dean of a member college because he was African American. When it was suggested that the dean should not have attempted to attend the meeting, Tice retorted, "Can any one who is worthy of the name, educator, maintain such a position, if he is honest?" A year later, in his presidential address, he chided the colleges with his belief "that some of the present weaknesses of pharmacy professionally can be laid directly at the doorstep of some of our member colleges, since all of those practitioners, whose lack of professionalism we now deplore, at one time were enrolled as students in some college of pharmacy."[7]

Tice's outspokenness was again evident in his address as APhA president-elect in 1966, when he urged his colleagues to move past their continuing ambivalence as to whether pharmacy was a profession or a business and make their choice regarding which path to follow. He stressed the professional role of pharmacy and the ultimate responsibility to the patient: "We must in our every daily act put the patient's welfare above our own self-interest and perform accordingly. Pharmacists must become patient-centered."[8]

From 1951 to 1955 Linwood Tice served on the APhA Committee on Student Branches. In 1953 there were 71 student branches with about 10,000 members. The goal of Tice's committee was to enable students to play a more active role in the Association; thus, the committee encouraged students' participation in the APhA Annual Meeting and led the way for a student representative vote in the APhA House of Delegates. During the 1953 Annual Meeting in Salt Lake City, the representatives of the Student Branches in attendance petitioned for the formation of a Student Section.[9]

*Philadelphia College of Pharmacy Dean Linwood F. Tice poses before the camera in April 1968
in the course of shooting the Continuing Education for Pharmacists series that aired on public
television in Philadelphia.*

The 1954 APhA Annual Meeting was attended by 167 students; Tice
chaired the student session. The main order of business was the formation of
the Student American Pharmaceutical Association (SAPhA), with the approval
of bylaws and the election of officers for the new organization. SAPhA was
granted a voice in the Association through its representative to the House of
Delegates.[10]

Tice married Marjorie Purnell in 1929. They had two sons, Gregory and
David. After his first wife's death, Tice married Mary-Louise Lott. Tice died in
Salem, N.J., on August 18, 1996, at the age of 87.[1]

An advocate and an agent of change for pharmacy, Tice espoused a vision
of the best that the profession could be. He eschewed the easiest or most
expedient pathways. He was outspoken in his belief that the most important
part of pharmacy was the duty to serve the public. He also spoke out against
racial discrimination at a time when such a position was unpopular with
many. His most enduring legacy, however, was his vision of improving the
profession by increasing the profile and activity of pharmacy students. The
SAPhA organization began with the fewer than 200 students in attendance
in 1954. The membership of the present-day APhA Academy of Students
of Pharmacy (APhA–ASP) numbers in the thousands. Today, students hold

their own events at the APhA Annual Meeting, have a voice in the House of Delegates equal to those of the other Academies, and hold a seat on the Board of Trustees. Tice's efforts on behalf of student participation in APhA have enriched the pharmacy profession as a whole, as other professional associations have followed APhA's lead, establishing a voice for students in their ranks as well.

REFERENCES

1. Linwood Tice, dean emeritus at Philadelphia College of Pharmacy and Science and national leader in pharmacy, dead at age 87 [press release]. Philadelphia, Pa: Philadelphia College of Pharmacy and Science; August 19, 1996.

2. Tice LF. Values based on love and respect. In: Griffenhagen GB, Blockstein WL, Krigstein DJ, eds. *The Remington Lectures: A Century in American Pharmacy*. Washington, DC: American Pharmaceutical Association; 1974; 259–61.

3. Osol A, Welch CE Jr, Kramer JE. *Sesquicentennial of Service 1821–1971 of the Philadelphia College of Pharmacy and Science*. Philadelphia, Pa: Philadelphia College of Pharmacy and Science; 1971:47.

4. Tice to receive Remington Medal [news release]. Washington, DC: American Pharmaceutical Association; August 9, 1971.

5. Curran FF, ed. *Keeping in Touch: Letters from Alumni and Students to the Philadelphia College of Pharmacy & Science During World War II*. Philadelphia, Pa: College of Pharmacy and Science Philadelphia; 1995:195.

6. Tice LF. Address of the incoming president. *Am J Pharm Educ*. 1955;19:451–9.

7. Tice LF Address of the president. *Am J Pharm Educ*. 1956;20:307–18.

8. Tice LF. Mandate from the people: professional services for public needs, *J Am Pharm Assoc*. 1966;NS6:297–8.

9. Fischelis RP. Letter to the secretaries of the APhA Student Branches. September 30, 1953.

10. Griffenhagen GB. *150 Years of Caring: A Pictorial History of the American Pharmaceutical Association*. Washington, DC: American Pharmaceutical Association; 2002:151.

11. Kamer JE, ed. First decennial supplement, 1921–1931. *First Century of the Philadelphia College of Pharmacy*. Philadelphia, Pa: Philadelphia College of pharmacy; 1934.

Henry Milton Whelpley (1861–1926): Association Worker

"Dr. Whelpley's life is better described in verbs than in adjectives," noted his friend James Hartley Beal in one of the memorials after Whelpley's death in 1926.[1] As other luminaries of the period added their memories of the deceased, most characterized him as a worker in professional associations. His service to the American Pharmaceutical (now Pharmacists) Association (APhA) was described as starting as "a high private in the rear ranks" and continuing through his role as president and long-time treasurer.[2] Beal later recalled that Whelpley's membership in an organization was marked by his activity, and his "services were of the greatest value and of lasting benefit."[3]

BEGINNINGS

Henry Milton Whelpley was born on May 24, 1861, in Harmonia, Mich., the eldest of six children of Dr. Jerome Twining and Charlotte Chase Whelpley.[4] He received his early education in Cobden, Ill., where his father moved after serving in the Civil War.[5] He moved to Otsego, Mich., to attend high school, living and reading medicine with his uncle, Milton Chase, a Civil War hospital steward and surgeon. He also worked in the drugstore of Dr. Charles Gaylord.[6] After graduation from high school he returned to Cobden to manage a pharmacy until he entered the St. Louis College of Pharmacy in 1881. He received a graduate in pharmacy degree in 1883, having attained the highest average grade in his class during 2 years of study, and moved to Mine LaMotte, Mo., to manage a drugstore. Later, he entered the Missouri Medical College, graduating with a doctor of medicine degree in 1890 and again taking first-place honors. In 1894 he graduated from the St. Louis Post-Graduate School of Medicine.[7]

In 1892 Henry Milton Whelpley married Laura Eugenia Spannagel of St. Louis; the couple had no children. Whelpley died at Argentine, Kans., on June 26, 1926.

1912 photograph of Henry Milton Whelpley during his term of service as dean of the St. Louis College of Pharmacy, and as treasurer of the American Pharmaceutical Association.

EDUCATOR

During his student years at St. Louis College of Pharmacy, Whelpley served as student assistant to Charles O. Curtman, professor of chemistry. Curtman, a German immigrant, trained in chemistry under Justus von Liebig and served in the Confederate Army during the Civil War.[8] In 1884, the college formed the Microscopical Laboratory, presumably the first of its kind in a pharmacy school in the United States, and Henry Whelpley joined the faculty as the first instructor in microscopy. The college catalogue claimed that this was the first time that "this fascinating branch of study has ever before been offered in the West.... Students cannot over estimate the importance of making use of this opportunity of acquiring proficiency in this branch of study, which is a fundamental requisite for the study of pharmacognosy."[9]

Whelpley also served as quiz master. This position, gaining popularity in many pharmacy schools, provided a daily review for materials covered in class. Whelpley described the duty of the quiz master as one standing "midway between the classes and the professors, in such a manner that he imparts to the inquiring mind knowledge that does not properly fall from the lips of a lecturer."[10] In 1887 Whelpley was named the professor of microscopy. The microscope was gaining importance as a tool for studies in materia medica and pharmacognosy, and Whelpley wrote enthusiastically of its applications to both professional and social uses.[11] In 1918 he was named the professor of practical pharmacognosy, and in 1922 the course was expanded and the title changed to professor of physiology, pharmacognosy, and materia medica. In 1909, the college celebrated the silver anniversary of Whelpley's teaching and, as happened on other memorable occasions, Joseph P. Remington supplied a poem acknowledging the honoree, which included the lines:[12]

Who trains and loves the college boys,
With all their work and all their noise;
Henry Milton Whelpley.

In 1904 Henry Whelpley was named dean of the faculty. He served in the office until his death in 1926.[13]

APhA Past Presidents James H. Beal (right) and Whelpley pose for this photo in 1908 at Niagara Falls, New York. Both also served as AACP presidents and journal editors.

After his graduation from the Missouri Medical College in 1890, Whelpley was named to the faculty, where he taught physiology and histology and served as the director of the biological laboratory.[5] The Missouri Medical College became part of the Medical Department of Washington University in 1899. Whelpley served until 1910, when the Flexner Report forced the resignation of part-time faculty from many of the medical schools. He also served as the professor of physiology and secretary of the faculty of the St. Louis Post-Graduate School of Medicine, his other alma mater.[14]

EDITOR

In 1884, after a short period managing a drugstore in Mine LaMotte, Henry Whelpley returned to St. Louis to become the pharmacy editor of the *St. Louis Druggist*, later renamed the *National Druggist*. Whelpley organized, augmented, and compiled the lectures of Charles O. Curtman for inclusion as a column in the journal. In 1886 he added additional and explanatory materials, systematized the organization to facilitate its use by students, and published it as the *Chemical Lecture Notes*.[15] By 1895, the book had gone through four editions.

In 1888 Meyer Brothers, a large wholesaler in St. Louis, made significant editorial revisions to its house publication, the *St. Louis Drug Market Reporter*, renaming it first the *Druggist* and, 6 months later, the *Meyer Brothers Druggist*. Whelpley was named editor with a charge to increase the literary importance of the publication by adding features that would advance the trade and "elevate the profession of pharmacy."[16]

Whelpley was also involved as writer and editor with a number of other pharmaceutical periodicals of that time, including *Pharmaceutical Era, Pacific Pharmacist,* and *Western Druggist*. In 1894 he published *Therapeutic Terms for Pharmacists and Physicians*. This small publication, which went through two editions, provided useful information for practitioners, including a dictionary of therapeutic terms and actions of official medicines.[17]

ASSOCIATION WORK

Starting in 1884, Henry Whelpley attended APhA meetings as a reporter for the *St. Louis Druggist*. In 1887 he became an APhA member and was immediately appointed secretary of the Committee on Pharmaceutical Education.[18] Always a willing worker, he served on a number of committees, including the Scientific Section and the Section of Pharmaceutical Education and Legislation. In 1893 he was named as acting general secretary when John Michael Maisch died.

In 1901–02 Whelpley was elected president and served during the golden anniversary of the formation of APhA. While his presidential address had many historical highlights, Whelpley focused on the future of education. In addition, he raised the issue of reciprocity, noting the problems of pharmacists who move from one state to another and the complexity of registration in the new locale. In keeping with his habit of consensus building, he recommended national acceptance of the James Hartley Beal model practice act, which

Photograph of Henry Whelpley and his wife Laura at an APhA convention shortly before his death in 1926. Both wear gold ladder chains recording conventions they attended.

could form the basis of reciprocity among the licensing authorities.[19] Whelpley served as the secretary of the APhA Council (now the Board of Trustees) from 1902 through 1908.[4]

Henry Whelpley's greatest APhA service was as treasurer, a post that he held from 1908 until 1921. Beal recounted that the financial fragility of the Association had reached the point where the future was in doubt. Whelpley implemented a program of financial management that included reduced expenditures and prompt payment of annual dues. He was also able, through his diplomacy, to convince members to pay delinquent dues. He launched a successful recruitment campaign for new members. When he retired as treasurer, the Association had a significant reserve for the first time in its history.[3]

In 1900, Henry Hynson of the Maryland College of Pharmacy invited other colleges to meet during the APhA annual meeting to discuss an association of colleges. Henry Whelpley editorialized in the *Meyer Brothers Druggist* that such a suggestion was timely. He attended the discussion meeting but was not an official delegate of the St. Louis College of Pharmacy.[20] St. Louis became a charter member of the American Conference of Pharmaceutical Faculties (now the American Association of Colleges of Pharmacy [AACP]). Whelpley was elected the president of AACP for 1905–06. His presidential address focused on the work of the association, the work already undertaken, and the work for the future. He noted that the earlier Conference of Schools of Pharmacy failed largely because of the unspoken motto of "do as I do or resign."[21] He argued the need for common sense rather than entrenched positions if AACP was to be successful, adding: "[W]e should aid each other in all things conducive to our mutual good and restrain such individual action as tends to any way injure our common cause."[21]

At the APhA annual meeting in 1903, while serving on the Council, Henry Whelpley returned to the topic of boards of pharmacy, which he had broached in his presidential address 2 years earlier. He noted the proliferation of state boards and state laws and the failure to provide for reasonable reciprocity of licenses by observing that "a man or woman who is competent to conduct a drug business in Missouri loses no pharmaceutical skill, moral character or business judgment when crossing the state line."[22] His motion to form a Conference of Board of Pharmacy members was carried, and the following year the National Association of Boards of Pharmacy (NABP) was formed, with George Rieman of New York serving as the chair.[23]

Henry Whelpley made major contributions to the United States Pharmacopoeial Convention (USP). Elected USP secretary in 1900, Whelpley won a place on the Board of Trustees in 1903, filling an opening created by the death of Indiana pharmacist George W. Sloan.[3] Reelected to the board in 1910 and again in 1920, Whelpley served from 1910 until his death in 1926 as board secretary, a pivotal position in an era when most of the USP's business was conducted through mail and telegraph. As secretary, Whelpley's principal function was to serve as a clearinghouse for correspondence among Board of Trustees members and for communications among members of the board and the Committee of Revision. During his tenure as board member and secretary, Whelpley introduced a more businesslike approach to board operations, both administratively and fiscally.[24] His calm counsel helped the

USP to survive several major problems, including a serious jurisdictional rift between the Board of Trustees and the Committee of Revision, a potentially fatal split between pharmacists and physicians over the scope and function of the *United States Pharmacopeia*, and the dramatic fiscal ups and downs associated with the revision cycle.[25] In many important respects, Whelpley defined the secretary's role for the next half century.

Whelpley was active in a number of other pharmacy and professional organizations. He served as the secretary of the Missouri Pharmaceutical Association for more than 25 years.[4] His passion outside of pharmacy was American archeology, especially pertaining to the Native Americans. He was involved with a number of museum and archeological organizations. His private collection of flint, stone, and hematite implements was one of the largest in the United States.[6]

LEGACY

Henry Milton Whelpley was an easily and frequently recognized figure in American pharmacy. His round, bald head and small, well-trimmed beard were in attendance at APhA meetings for 42 consecutive years, a record in the days preceding air travel. An inveterate photographer, he recorded the events and personalities of the period. Described as generous and kindly tolerant, he was willing and able to seek cooperation through a spirit of "fairness, good-will and good sense, and the uniform courtesy which governed his daily contact with his fellow men."[3]

Professional work clearly was an important part of Henry Whelpley's life. In 1904 his address to the graduates of the Pharmacy Department at Purdue University was titled, "Work, the Master Impulse." He averred that work was a pleasure and the sure way to happiness and success. Whelpley, referring to his historical interests, declared that individuals of importance who are public figures are likely to be workers. He counseled the graduates that if they were to be the best they should "form an unbreakable habit of doing well the work that each day brings forth."[26] He picked up the theme in his Remington address when he talked about his long-standing relationships in work and play with the association leadership.[27] His efforts on behalf of APhA, AACP, NABP, and other pharmacy associations embodied this belief.

Henry Whelpley served at the beginning of AACP and was, if not the father of NABP, instrumental in its founding. His management abilities were particularly important to the financial and organizational needs of both APhA and USP. Henry Milton Whelpley's capacity for important association work was the outstanding characteristic of his contribution to pharmacy. American pharmacy recognized him with the Remington Medal in 1925. Today his memory is honored by an academic building on the campus of the St. Louis College of Pharmacy that bears his name. The lobby of the building houses a collection of photographic plates that Whelpley took during his busy and storied life. James Hartley Beal summarized the legacy of Whelpley by noting that his work with students, as an editor, and through his beloved associations "left an estate that will increase through the years even though its source be forgotten."[3]

REFERENCES

1. Beal JH. In memory of Henry Milton Whelpley. *J Am Pharm Assoc*. 1926;15:714–20.

2. Kremers E, Lyman RA, Caspari CE. Henry Milton Whelpley. *Proc Am Assoc Coll Pharm*. 1926;27:17–8.

3. Beal JH. The life and character of Dr. Henry Milton Whelpley. *J Am Pharm Assoc*. 1927;16:60–6.

4. Eberle EG. Henry Milton Whelpley. *J Am Pharm Assoc*. 1926;15:523–5.

5. Anonymous. Pharmaceutical personalities: Henry Milton Whelpley. *Druggists Circ*. 1924;68:58.

6. Beal JH. Henry Milton Whelpley, MD, PhM. *J Am Pharm Assoc*. 1921;10:921–4.

7. Obituary: Henry Milton Whelpley. *Am J Pharm*. 1926;98:427–8.

8. Winkelmann JP. *History of the St. Louis College of Pharmacy*. St. Louis, Mo.: St. Louis College of Pharmacy; 1964:156.

9. Prospectus of the St. Louis College of Pharmacy October 1886–March 1887. St. Louis, Mo.: Hailman Brothers Printers; 1886:9.

10. Whelpley HM. How to conduct a quiz class. *Proc Am Pharm Assoc*. 1889;37:161–8.

11. Whelpley HM. Synopsis of a course in microscopy for pharmacists. *Proc Am Pharm Assoc*. 1890;38:252–7.

12. Remington JP. Henry Milton Whelpley [unpublished poem]. A2: Whelpley, Henry M.;— Kremers Reference Files, School of Pharmacy, University of Wisconsin–Madison.

13. Prospectus of the St. Louis College of Pharmacy 1904–1905. St. Louis, Mo.: St. Louis College of Pharmacy; 1904:2.

14. Winkelmann JP. *History of the St. Louis College of Pharmacy*. St. Louis, Mo.: St. Louis College of Pharmacy; 1964;143–4.

15. Whelpley HM. Chemical lecture notes: taken from Prof. C.O. Curtman's lectures at the St. Louis College of Pharmacy. St. Louis, Mo.: H.M. Whelpley; 1886.

16. Anonymous. To our readers. *The Druggist*. 1888;9:1.

17. Whelpley HM. Whelpley's therapeutic terms for pharmacists and physicians. St. Louis, Mo.: H.M. Whelpley; 1894.

18. *Proc Am Pharm Assoc*. 1887;35:iv.

19. Whelpley HM. The American Pharmaceutical Association in 1902. *Proc Am Pharm Assoc*. 1902;50:7–22.

20. Whelpley HM. The American Pharmaceutical Association's annual meeting. *Meyer Brothers Druggist*. 1900;21:162–3.

21. Whelpley HM. President's address. *Proc Seventh Ann Meet Am Conf Pharm Faculties*. 1906;7:7–33.

22. Whelpley HM. A conference of board of pharmacy members. *Proc Am Pharm Assoc*. 1903;51:487–9.

23. Green MW. *Epilogue, Prologue: From the Past Comes the Future*. Chicago: National Association of Boards of Pharmacy; 1979:3,44.

24. Anderson L, Higby G. *The Spirit of Volunteerism: The United States Pharmacopoeia 1820–1995*. Rockville, Md.: United States Pharmacopoeial Convention, Inc.; 1995:196–7, 237–41.

25. Anderson L, Penningroth K. *Good Work and True: United States Pharmacopoeial Convention Board of Trustees 1900–2000*. Rockville, Md.: United States Pharmacopeial Convention, Inc.; 2000:21–3.

26. Whelpley HM. Work, the master impulse. *Meyer Brothers Druggist*. 1904;25:126–30.

27. Whelpley HM. Traits of human nature. In: Griffenhagen GB, Bowles GC, Penna RP, Worthen DB. *Reflections on Pharmacy by the Remington Medalists 1919–2003*. Washington, D.C.: American Pharmacists Association; 2004:38–40.

Harvey A.K. Whitney (1894-1957): Pioneer in Hospital Pharmacy

We know the pioneers will have to apply themselves seriously and conscientiously to the work of building a pathway through the uncharted areas and imposing obstacles that are before us.

—Harvey A.K. Whitney, 1943[1]

Harvey Allan Whitney—hospital pharmacy pioneer, professional leader, technical innovator, and editor—was born in Adrian, Mich., on November 7, 1894, to Harry Arthur and Emma Whitney, the first of their three children. Arthur was the fire chief in Adrian, a sleepy town just north of the Ohio state line whose principal distinction was the presence of Adrian College, a private liberal arts school affiliated with the Methodist Church.

Young Whitney's exposure to pharmacy began while he was in the eighth grade in 1907, when he began working part-time in a local drugstore. After he graduated from Adrian High School in 1912, he worked for a year as a bank clerk at Adrian State Savings Bank, earning $40 per month. In 1913 he was hired as a pharmacy apprentice by Beufer & Nachtreib in Adrian and also by Rupp & Bowman, a drugstore in Toledo, Ohio. In 1916 he left Toledo for a better paying job ($110 per month) as a die design draftsman for Dodge Brothers Motors in Detroit. During World War I, he served in the Medical Corps.*

After the war, Whitney enrolled in the University of Michigan College of Pharmacy. He first surfaced as a leader in pharmacy during his student days. He was a member of the Alpha Chapter of Phi Delta Chi[2] and has been credited with suggesting that the original name for the pharmacy honor

---

*Most of this biographical information has been drawn from George L. Phillips' Whitney Lecture in 1973.[5] Phillips was one of Whitney's residents at the University of Michigan in the 1940s and later served as president of the American Society of Hospital Pharmacists.

society, Aristolochite Society, be changed to Rho Chi. He also proposed the idea for the design for the society's key and seal.[3] In 1923, at the age of 28, Whitney graduated with a PhC degree. He accepted a position as pharmacist–manager for the Kimling and Sheehan Drug Company in Jackson, Mich., and was employed there for about 2 years.

That same year, Whitney married his college sweetheart, Hildreth K. Wheeler. His son, Harvey A.K. Whitney Jr., was born in 1930. The K stands for Kim, the title character in the Rudyard Kipling novel. After naming his son, Whitney added Kim to his own name, as well.

Whitney's long and productive association with hospital pharmacy began in 1925, when he was appointed to the pharmacy staff at the University Hospital in Ann Arbor; in 1927 he was named chief pharmacist. In the same year, he established the first formal internship in hospital pharmacy. This was the forerunner of today's residency programs in hospital pharmacy. It would be another 10 years before Edward Spease established the second program, which combined the internship with graduate education, at Western Reserve University.[4]

Whitney was at the forefront of many of the changes that took place in hospital pharmacy in the first third of the 20th century. In his 1973 Whitney Award Lecture, George Phillips identified those areas in which Whitney made innovations.[5]

By the early 1930s, Whitney had established the pharmacy at the University of Michigan University Hospital as a service that far exceeded filling prescriptions and sending them to the floors. He worked with the pharmacy and therapeutics committee

Harvey A.K. Whitney was the first chairman of the American Society of Hospital Pharmacists. He introduced a number of innovative programs, including the first internship program in hospital pharmacy and an early formulary system. The highest honor in hospital pharmacy was named for him in recognition of his visionary leadership.

to develop a formulary that allowed the stocking of only one brand of a chemical entity and authorization of his judgment of which brand that would be. He published pharmacy bulletins for circulation to the professional staffs of the hospital and established the first drug information center to support these early information efforts, probably the first of these services in the United States. Whitney also pioneered the manufacture of products for use in the hospital. He prepackaged medications, fully coded and dated, into convenient sizes, a forerunner of today's' unit dose and unit-of-use packs.

He also pioneered sterile manufacturing of allergenics and surgical fluids before they were available commercially and was manufacturing a wide variety of dermatologic preparations. The formulary, drug information center, staff bulletins, prepackaging, and specialty manufacturing would become hallmarks of progressive hospital pharmacy practice.

Whitney was active in his profession at both the state and national levels. At various times, he was president of the Michigan Board of Pharmacy, president of the Michigan Branch of APhA, vice president of APhA, and member of the Revision Committee for the *National Formulary*. However, the capstone of Whitney's career was his effort to develop a national association for hospital pharmacists.

By 1935 a group of leaders in hospital pharmacy, including Spease, Whitney, and Louis Zopf, had begun actively promoting their common vision for improvement and standardization in hospital pharmacy. In 1936 their efforts bore fruit with the formation of the Sub-Section on Hospital Pharmacy within APhA's Section on Practical Pharmacy and Dispensing. Whitney was the chair of the Section and Louis Zopf was elected as the first chair of the newly formed Sub-Section.

From its first meeting in 1937, the Sub-Section's attention was focused on the unique needs of institutional practitioners. By 1939, given the growing belief among many members of the Sub-Section that a more autonomous organization was needed, debate began on elevating the group to the Section level. Many Sub-Section members, however, were raising their voices in favor of forming a national organization of hospital pharmacists. At the 1940 APhA Annual Meeting, the Sub-Section developed and presented a resolution calling for the establishment of such an organization. At the 1941 meeting of the Sub-Section, Whitney took the floor and outlined the advantages of forming a national association of hospital pharmacists affiliated with APhA. Spurred in large part by Whitney's reasoning, by the conclusion of the session the participants had laid the groundwork for a new organization, provisionally called the Conference of Hospital Pharmacy, with Whitney as its first chair. A petition for affiliate status was forwarded to APhA and accepted. When the new organization first met in 1942, it had been renamed the American Society of Hospital Pharmacists (ASHP), with Whitney as the first chair.[6]

Whitney also made a lasting contribution to hospital pharmacy literature with the establishment of the *Official Bulletin of the American Society of Hospital Pharmacists* in 1943. He and Leo W. Mossman served as the editors for this publication through 1944. Initially a mimeographed newsletter on green paper, the publication evolved into the *Bulletin of the American Society of Hospital Pharmacists* with the January/February 1945 issue, and then into the *American Journal of Hospital Pharmacy* in 1958. In 1995 it was renamed the *American Journal of Health-System Pharmacy*. The formulary that Whitney instituted at University Hospital in the early 1930s would emerge in 1959 as the *American Hospital Formulary Service*. Thus, two of the most important and continuing efforts to provide information of particular importance to hospital pharmacists were part of Whitney's vision and legacy.

In May 1944 Whitney left the University of Michigan to join the World War II effort by heading the pharmacy department at the Hanford Engineering Works in Richland, Wash. At the end of the war, he joined Ortho Products as the director of pharmaceutical research. He left this post in 1947, however, and began working in community pharmacy when, upon the death of his brother-in-law, he returned to Michigan to help his sister raise her children.

In 1950 the Michigan Society of Hospital Pharmacists (now the Southeastern Michigan Society of Health-System Pharmacists) established the Harvey A.K. Whitney Lecture Award in honor of the first chairman of ASHP. The award, which for more than a half century has been given annually, was established to honor "the hospital pharmacist who has contributed most to the progress of the profession in the previous year."[7] In 1963 ASHP assumed responsibility for the administration of the award. The Whitney Award stands as one of the preeminent honors in professional pharmacy.

Of the residents that Whitney had at the University of Michigan in 1940-41, five would go on to win the Whitney Award: Don Francke, Warren McConnell, Paul Parker, George Phillips, and John Zugich. A number of others who were interns under Whitney also went on to win this and other awards in recognition of their vision for and leadership of the profession. The closing admonition of Whitney's address to the new ASHP in 1943 continues to echo through the years: "Demonstrate your professional character and the rest will follow—prestige, respect, integrity, ability and living reward."[8]

Whitney underwent surgery for an abdominal aneurysm on December 5, 1957. He died in Ann Arbor on December 15 of postoperative complications.

REFERENCES

1. Whitney HAK. Address of the chairman. *J Am Pharm Assoc (Sci Ed)*. 1943;32:457.

2. Grabenstein JD. *Phi Delta Chi: A Tradition of Leaders in Pharmacy*. Athens, Ga: Phi Delta Chi Pharmacy Fraternity; 1965:262.

3. Bowers RA, Cowen DL. *Rho Chi Society*. 3rd ed. Madison, Wis: Rho Chi Society; 1966:7.

4. Sonnedecker G. Harvey A.K. Whitney and Edward Spease ... in memoriam. *Am J Hosp Pharm*. 1958;15:507–09.

5. Phillips GL. Uncle Harvey. *Am J Hosp Pharm*. 1973;30: 886–91.

6. Niemeyer G, Berman A, Francke D. The formative period. *Bull Am Soc Hosp Pharm*. 1952;9:279–421. [Reprinted as: Niemeyer G, Berman A, Francke D. Chapter 1. In: *Ten Years of the American Society of Hospital Pharmacists*. American Society of Hospital Pharmacists.]

7. Harvey A.K. Whitney. *J Am Pharm Assoc (Pract Pharm Ed)*. 1958;19:22.

8. Whitney HAK. Address of the chairman. *J Am Pharm Assoc (Sci Ed)*. 1943;32:458.

Index